Supervising Student Independence

"This book is a gift to academic supervisors! Like a set of beautiful matryoshka dolls.

The two Swedish authors bring to light their findings from an extensive – and impressive – empirical study on supervision at Swedish and Russian universities. These findings show, like the dolls, a united complexity of answers to the authors' starting point: How can supervision be designed to best contribute to student learning and development?

A similar question can be a starting point in everyone's academic supervision, bearing in mind one of the authors' findings that 'supervision should be seen as a social and collegial practice'. A part of this practice is to listen to our students' voices, our own and our colleagues' voices, to expectations, emotions, roles and relationships – actively, with an open mind and an open heart. Active listening is opening up a pathway to dialogic supervision! And to student independence and supervisor growth!

Unwrap your gift: see, share, and enjoy the inspiration, insights, findings, and tools in this book – in your own supervision work!"
—Randi Benedikte Brodersen, supervisor and teacher of academic writing, *University of Bergen, Norway*

"Supervision is a core activity in university teachers' work, stimulating the independence of students. This book provides tools and perspectives on this important effort in order to both favour the work and to enhance students' independence. The discussions and practical advice are well-grounded in unique and solid research, which is also presented in this highly interesting book for university teachers in all disciplines."
—Mona Blåsjö, Professor of Swedish, *Stockholm University, Sweden*

Maria Zackariasson • Jenny Magnusson

Supervising Student Independence

A Research-based Approach to Academic Supervision in Practice

Maria Zackariasson
School of Historical and
Contemporary Studies
Södertörn University
Stockholm, Sweden

Jenny Magnusson
School of Culture and Learning
Södertörn University
Stockholm, Sweden

ISBN 978-3-031-66370-3   ISBN 978-3-031-66371-0 (eBook)
https://doi.org/10.1007/978-3-031-66371-0

© The Editor(s) (if applicable) and The Author(s) 2024. This book is an open access publication.

Open Access This book is licensed under the terms of the Creative Commons Attribution-NonCommercial-NoDerivatives 4.0 International License (http://creativecommons.org/licenses/by-nc-nd/4.0/), which permits any noncommercial use, sharing, distribution and reproduction in any medium or format, as long as you give appropriate credit to the original author(s) and the source, provide a link to the Creative Commons license and indicate if you modified the licensed material. You do not have permission under this license to share adapted material derived from this book or parts of it.

The images or other third party material in this book are included in the book's Creative Commons license, unless indicated otherwise in a credit line to the material. If material is not included in the book's Creative Commons license and your intended use is not permitted by statutory regulation or exceeds the permitted use, you will need to obtain permission directly from the copyright holder.

This work is subject to copyright. All commercial rights are reserved by the author(s), whether the whole or part of the material is concerned, specifically the rights of reprinting, reuse of illustrations, recitation, broadcasting, reproduction on microfilms or in any other physical way, and transmission or information storage and retrieval, electronic adaptation, computer software, or by similar or dissimilar methodology now known or hereafter developed. Regarding these commercial rights a non-exclusive license has been granted to the publisher.

The use of general descriptive names, registered names, trademarks, service marks, etc. in this publication does not imply, even in the absence of a specific statement, that such names are exempt from the relevant protective laws and regulations and therefore free for general use.

The publisher, the authors and the editors are safe to assume that the advice and information in this book are believed to be true and accurate at the date of publication. Neither the publisher nor the authors or the editors give a warranty, expressed or implied, with respect to the material contained herein or for any errors or omissions that may have been made. The publisher remains neutral with regard to jurisdictional claims in published maps and institutional affiliations.

This Palgrave Macmillan imprint is published by the registered company Springer Nature Switzerland AG.
The registered company address is: Gewerbestrasse 11, 6330 Cham, Switzerland

If disposing of this product, please recycle the paper.

Acknowledgements

First of all, we would like to sincerely thank all supervisors and students who participated in the research project this book is based on! Thank you for giving us access to the spaces where supervision takes place and giving us a glimpse of all the interaction, meetings and discussions that emerge there and thank you for sharing your experiences, views and knowledge with us in the focus group discussions. We would also like to thank our colleagues Gregory Goldenzwaig and Jan-Olof Gullö, who were originally part of the research group and who contributed significantly to the first phases of the project.

This book is a translated, updated and revised version of a book previously published in Swedish by the authors: *Handledning i praktiken. Om studenters självständighet och akademiska litteracitet* (Supervision in practice. On student independence and academic literacies) at Studentlitteratur (Magnusson and Zackariasson 2021).

Competing Interests This study as well as the open access of this publication were funded by means from *The Foundation for Baltic and East European Studies*. Grant nr 2015/3.1.1/1423.

Ethics Approval All research participants in the empirical material used in the book have given their informed consent to participate in the study.

Contents

1 Introduction 1

2 Starting Points and Theoretical Perspectives 11

3 Academic Supervision and Student Independence 37

4 The Supervisor-Student Relationship 69

5 Emotional Dimensions of Supervision 107

6 Scaffolding Tools for Student Independence 151

7 The Supervisor as Assessor 185

8 Concluding Findings and Reflections 219

List of Materials 229

Index 233

About the Authors

Maria Zackariasson is Professor of Ethnology at Södertörn University, Stockholm, Sweden. Her research interests include various perspectives on higher education in Sweden and the Baltic Sea area, such as academic supervision and the experiences and choices of higher education students, PhD students and alumni. In addition, she has done several research projects on young people's societal involvement through e.g. social movements and religious organisations. Zackariasson is currently coordinator of practice-based research related to school at Södertörn University and teaches courses within teaching and learning in higher education.

Jenny Magnusson is Associate Professor of Swedish at Södertörn University, Stockholm, Sweden. She is currently director of research at teacher education at Södertörn University. In addition, she teaches in the teacher education programme's degree project courses but also courses on supervision within teaching and learning in higher education. Her research concerns academic writing and supervision in Sweden and the Baltic Sea region, as well as writing at different school levels and education systems.

List of Tables

Table 3.1	Examples of independence/autonomy in higher education policy documents (emphasis added)	39
Table 3.2	Independence matrix	63
Table 4.1	Table of speaking space in supervision conversations (cf Magnusson and Zackariasson 2021, 79)	92
Table 4.2	Supervisor-driven conversation (cf Magnusson and Zackariasson 2021, 82)	95
Table 4.3	Student-driven conversation (cf Magnusson and Zackariasson 2021, 85)	98

CHAPTER 1

Introduction

In order to complete their education and obtain a degree, university students in various disciplines and academic programmes around the world are generally expected to produce some form of major written academic work or thesis. Such theses or degree projects[1] are usually produced under the guidance of a supervisor, making supervision an extensive activity within higher education in many countries. This raises issues relating to teaching and learning in higher education, but also to time and funding. How do we ensure that all these people, time and money are well spent? And, given the time and financial frameworks available, how can supervision be designed to best contribute to student learning and development? This last question is the starting point for this book, in which we will discuss degree project supervision in relation to student independence and academic literacies.

Not all higher education students are required to produce an academic thesis as part of their education, as higher education systems and degree requirements vary between countries, universities and academic programmes. Nevertheless, in many parts of the world, this is a common requirement for students at bachelor's and master's level. Eurydice, the European Commission's website providing information on higher

---

[1] This type of student work may be called a bachelor's or master's thesis, an essay, a degree project, a student dissertation or an undergraduate project, depending on the national and local academic context. In this book, we mainly use the terms degree project and student thesis, as these cover different types of academic theses at both bachelor and master levels.

education systems in the European Union, shows, for instance, that degree projects generally are a compulsory element for students to obtain a bachelor's or master's degree (European Commission 2023).[2] The Bologna Declaration on Higher Education, which focuses on students obtaining academic degrees that are relatively equivalent between participating countries, also includes countries outside the European Union, such as the United Kingdom, Norway and, earlier, Russia,[3] all of which follow the same organisation of higher education with a bachelor's and master's level (European Ministers in charge of Higher Education 1999; Curaj et al. 2012). Also outside Europe, a student thesis is commonly required for a bachelor's or master's degree, which means that a considerable amount of time and resources are devoted to the supervision of these degree projects, making this a significant part of the workload for many university lecturers and professors.

Academic supervision of student theses has traditionally been associated with an individualistic learning culture, where individuals, mainly students and supervisors, are part of a primarily dyadic pedagogical relationship, characterised by relatively informal relationships and meetings, where one person teaches and another is taught (Vehviläinen and Löfström 2016). In recent years, this view has been increasingly challenged and the social and collective aspects of supervision have been more widely acknowledged. This can be understood in terms of how practical, economic and pedagogical circumstances have made it common for students to be supervised in pairs or groups for all or part of the supervision process, with implications for supervision interactions and relationships. However, it can also be seen in the light of a greater focus on the collegial structures and collective learning of the academic community, with more attention being paid to the process in relation to the end product. Troelsen

---

[2] It has been estimated that more than 100,000 degree projects are written each year in Sweden alone, according to a report by Segerstad et al. (2008), based on statistics from Statistics Sweden, which may give some indication of the numbers at the European or global level.

[3] Russia became part of the Bologna process in 2003, which meant that the Russian higher education system became similar to the higher education systems in most European countries (Pursiainen and Medvedev 2005). The country is currently not part of the Bologna process and has started to make some changes to its higher education system. However, the system of a first cycle/bachelor's degree with a compulsory degree project followed by a second cycle/master's degree was still in use in 2023 (Study in Russia 2023; Kuzminov and Yudkevich 2022).

(2021, 2) describes this as the need to open up the individual supervisory space and make visible what is happening in the supervision situation.

One way to describe these processes is in terms of academic professionalisation, which takes place through several channels: pedagogical courses on academic supervision, supervision handbooks and research on supervision, as well as collegial meetings and discussions on supervision (cf. Van Veldhuizen et al. 2021; Brodin et al. 2020; Wels et al. 2017; Epstein et al. 2007; Lee 2019). Through these channels, networks and forums are created for the exchange of expertise and experience that help to clarify what actually happens in the supervision process, as well as the factors that can influence it in different ways. This book should be seen as part of this ongoing professionalisation, with the aim of shedding light on supervision practice and contributing to its development. The ambition is that the book will serve as a starting point for individual and collegial reflection on the supervision of degree projects/theses in higher education. It has a solid research base, based on both focus group interviews and documented supervision interactions, and offers useful tools for developing supervisory skills and competences, with a theoretical starting point for discussions. Our ambition is that it will be relevant to those new to supervision at the undergraduate level, such as doctoral students or new lecturers, as well as to experienced supervisors who wish to develop their skills and practice, and to groups of supervisors/colleagues within a particular discipline or academic programme who wish to work together on the collegial development of their degree project courses and supervision practice.

The primary audience for this book is thus academic teachers/lecturers involved in supervision, and more specifically academic teachers as reflective practitioners, as the book is both research-based and aimed at professional and pedagogical reflection on the supervision of degree projects/student theses. The research project from which the examples in the book are drawn was primarily concerned with teacher education and journalism education in Sweden and Russia, but, as the research and handbooks on academic supervision indicate, the issues and challenges surrounding the supervision of degree projects are similar in many disciplines within the social sciences and humanities and in many countries.

What Is Academic Supervision?

This book starts from an empirical perspective on academic supervision, which means that the focus is on how supervision is talked about and described by supervisors, but also on what supervision interaction might look like in practice. Drawing on a multidisciplinary research project in which we have interviewed supervisors and recorded and documented supervision processes, we will highlight and discuss different perspectives on supervision and supervision practice.

What is meant by supervision—how it is defined, what activities it consists of, what it should cover and what its main purpose should be—can be understood in many different ways. At a more general level, the purpose of supervision may be defined, for example, as teaching the student to learn (Manderson 1996) or contributing to a more general development of the student's ability to work academically or scientifically (Lundström 2016, 89). However, the purpose of supervision can also be understood in a more specific sense, such as that supervision should help to socialise the individual into a particular disciplinary culture or tradition, or that the completion of the individual degree project or student thesis is the goal of supervision. Other differences in how supervision is understood and defined may concern whether it is seen as a form of teaching (Gustavsson and Eriksson 2015) or primarily as feedback or guidance (Lundström 2016), and whether it is perceived to involve only a few learning activities or a greater variety (Rienecker et al. 2019, 11).

This book focuses on the perspective and activities of supervisors and is therefore based on an inclusive and general definition of supervision, borrowed from Randi Brodersen (2009). Brodersen defines supervision as everything that supervisors do through oral and written communication in order to

1. assist the student in the process of completing academic work within a specified timeframe and in achieving an academic degree
2. promote student learning and practice of self-reflection
3. socialise the student into the disciplinary community.
   (Brodersen 2009, 181, author's translation)

Based on this definition, we have chosen to consider all dialogical activities between supervisor and student as supervision, which, based on the material we start from, includes

- oral communication in the form of supervision discussions between students and supervisors
- written communication from supervisors in the form of comments on drafts of texts either sent or used as the basis for supervision discussions
- written communication in the form of e-mails between supervisors and students.

Thus, when we talk about academic supervision in this book, we are referring to all these types of interaction between supervisors and students.

Another key feature of this book is our view of supervision as a social and collegial practice involving more actors than the individual supervisors and students. Course coordinators, programme directors, colleagues, examiners and fellow students, as well as governing documents and policies at different levels, are all important to what individual supervision practice looks like and what the interaction between supervisors and students will be like in a particular setting. In order to develop supervision practices within such local academic contexts, as well as at the individual level, there is a need for concepts and tools that can be used to share experiences and knowledge about supervision between these different actors. It is our ambition that this book will contribute to this.

Finally, we would like to return to the book's focus on supervision *practice*. Much of the existing research on academic supervision is primarily based on interviews, where a number of aspects of supervision are described by different actors in the supervision context: expectations, experiences, cultural and disciplinary differences, identity perspectives, challenges and so on (e.g. Brodin 2018; Ding and Devine 2018; Vereijken et al. 2018; Jacobsen et al. 2021; Neupane Bastola and Hu 2021; Henttonen 2023). Several studies have also proposed different types of supervision models, for example, based on identified types of supervisor styles and patterns (e.g. Scholefield and Cox 2016; Nordentoft et al. 2013; Mainhard et al. 2009; Agricola et al. 2021; Knight and Botting 2016).

There is also research that focuses on the practical level of academic supervision, for example, based on recorded supervision conversations, which often examines specific aspects of the interaction and conversations between students and supervisors, such as asking questions or giving and receiving feedback (e.g. Björkman 2015; Henricson and Nelson 2017; Magnusson and Zackariasson 2021; Thanh Ta 2021, 2023; Vehviläinen 2003, 2009, 2012; Zhang and Hyland 2022; Schneijderberg 2021).

Research based on this kind of material thus provides a further perspective on academic supervision by opening up to questions oriented towards supervision practice, such as *What do supervisors do to show commitment and support to students, and how do they do it? How do different supervisor styles emerge in the supervisory interaction?* and so on.

As this book is based on research that includes interviews with supervisors, as well as recorded supervision sessions and documented communications between supervisors and students, we are able to explore and discuss supervisors' views and experiences of supervision, as well as the actual practice—what the interaction between supervisors and students may look like. Throughout the book, we will highlight in particular two important aspects of academic supervision of student theses: student independence and academic literacies. These are discussed from five main perspectives: (1) supervisors' perceptions and understandings of student independence, (2) the relationship between supervisors and students, (3) the emotional dimension of supervision, (4) supervision tools for independence, and (5) the role of the supervisor not only as a guide and helper but also as an assessor of students' work.

REFERENCES

Agricola, Bas T., Frans J. Prins, Marieke F. van der Schaaf, and Jan van Tartwijk. 2021. Supervisor and Student Perspectives on Undergraduate Thesis Supervision in Higher Education. *Scandinavian Journal of Educational Research* 65 (5): 877–897. https://doi.org/10.1080/00313831.2020.1775115.

Björkman, Beyza. 2015. PhD supervisor-PhD Student Interactions in an English-medium Higher Education (HE) setting: Expressing Disagreement. *European Journal of Applied Linguistics* 3 (2): 205–229. https://doi.org/10.1515/eujal-2015-0011.

Brodersen, Randi Benedikte. 2009. Akademisk vejledning og skrivning - for vejledere og studerende: Mere kollektiv og dialogisk vejledning giver mere laering of flere gode opgaver. *Millimála 1*: 173–217.

Brodin, Eva. 2018. The Stifling Silence around Scholarly Creativity in Doctoral Education: Experiences of Students and Supervisors in Four Disciplines. *Higher Education* 75 (4): 655–673. https://doi.org/10.1007/s10734-017-0168-3.

Brodin, Eva, Jitka Lindén, Anders Sonesson, and Åsa Lindberg-Sand. 2020. *Doctoral Supervision in Theory and Practice.* Lund: Studentlitteratur.

Curaj, Adrian, Peter Scott, Lazăr Vlasceanu, and Lesley Wilson. 2012. *European Higher Education at the Crossroads: Between the Bologna Process and National Reforms.* Dordrecht, Heidelberg, New York, London: Springer.

Ding, Qun, and Nesta Devine. 2018. Exploring the Supervision Experiences of Chinese Overseas Phd students in New Zealand. *Knowledge Cultures* 6 (1): 62–78. https://doi.org/10.22381/KC6120186.

Epstein, Debbie, Rebecca Boden, and Jane Kenway. 2007. *Teaching and Supervision*. London: Sage.

European Commission. 2023. Eurydice. Accessed November 28, 2023. https://eurydice.eacea.ec.europa.eu/.

European Ministers in Charge of Higher Education. 1999. The Bologna Declaration of 19 June 1999: Joint Declaration of the European Ministers of Education. European Association of Institutions in Higher Education. Accessed January 09, 2017. https://www.eurashe.eu/library/bologna_1999_bologna-declaration-pdf/.

Gustavsson, Susanne, and Anita Eriksson. 2015. Blivande lärares frågor vid handledning – Gör jag en kvalitativ studie med kvantitativa inslag? *Pedagogisk forskning i Sverige* 20 (1–2): 79–99.

Henricson, Sofie, and Marie Nelson. 2017. Giving and Receiving Advice in Higher Education. Comparing Sweden-Swedish and Finland-Swedish Supervision Meetings. *Journal of Pragmatics* 109: 105–120. https://doi.org/10.1016/j.pragma.2016.12.013.

Henttonen, Ani. 2023. *Writing a Bachelor's Thesis in Nursing Education: A Tool for the Future*. Diss., Uppsala University.

Jacobsen, Michele, Sharon Friesen, and Sandra Becker. 2021. Online Supervision in a Professional Doctorate in Education: Cultivating Relational Trust Within Learning Alliances. *Innovations in Education and Teaching International* 58 (6): 635–646. https://doi.org/10.1080/14703297.2021.1991425.

Knight, Rachael-Anne, and Nicola Botting. 2016. Organising Undergraduate Research Projects: Student-led and Academic-led Models. *Journal of Applied Research in Higher Education* 8 (4): 455–468. https://doi.org/10.1108/JARHE-07-2015-0054.

Kuzminov, Yaroslav, and Maria Yudkevich. 2022. *Higher Education in Russia*. Baltimore: Johns Hopkins University Press.

Lee, Anne. 2019. *Successful Research Supervision: Advising students doing research*. 2nd ed. London: Routledge.

Lundström, Markus. 2016. Handledningens potential, examineringens låsningar – om uppsatsmomentets konflikt mellan formativ och summativ bedömning. *Utbildning & lärande* 10 (1): 88–93.

Magnusson, Jenny, and Maria Zackariasson. 2021. *Handledning i praktiken - Om studenters självständighet och akademiska litteracitet*. Lund: Studentlitteratur.

Mainhard, Tim, Roeland van der Rijst, Jan van Tartwijk, and Theo Wubbels. 2009. A model for the Supervisor–Doctoral Student Relationship *Higher Education* 58 (3): 359–373. https://doi.org/10.1007/s10734-009-9199-8.

Manderson, Desmond. 1996. Asking better Questions – Approaching the Process of Thesis Supervision. *Journal of Legal Education* 46 (3): 407–419.

Neupane Bastola, Madhu, and Guangwei Hu. 2021. Supervisory Feedback Across Disciplines: Does it meet Students' Expectations? *Assessment and Evaluation in Higher Education* 46 (3): 407–423. https://doi.org/10.1080/02602938.2020.1780562.

Nordentoft, Helle Merete, Rie Thomsen, and Gitte Wichmann-Hansen. 2013. Collective academic supervision: A model for participation and learning in higher education. *Higher Education* 65 (5): 581–593. https://doi.org/10.1007/s10734-012-9564-x.

Pursiainen, Christer, and Sergey A. Medvedev. 2005. *The Bologna Process and its Implications for Russia. The European Integration of Higher Education.* Moscow: Russian European Centre for Economic Policy.

Rienecker, Lotte, Gitte Wichmann-Hansen, and Peter Stray Jørgensen. 2019. *God vejledning af specialer, bacheloroppgaver og projekter.* Frederiksberg: Samfundslitteratur.

Schneijderberg, Christian. 2021. Supervision Practices of Doctoral Education and Training. *Studies in Higher Education (Dorchester-on-Thames)* 46 (7): 1285–1295. https://doi.org/10.1080/03075079.2019.1689384.

Scholefield, Donna, and Georgina Cox. 2016. Evaluation of a Model of Dissertation Supervision for 3rd year B.Sc. Undergraduate Nursing Students. *Nurse Education in Practice* 17: 78–85. https://doi.org/10.1016/j.nepr.2015.11.006.

Segerstad, Helene Hård af, Helen Setterud, and Göran Salerud. 2008. *Att synliggöra handledning av självständiga arbeten som stöd för studenter och handledare. Slutrapport projekt.* Linköping: Myndigheten för nätverk och samarbete inom högre utbildning.

Study in Russia. 2023. Study in Russia. Official Website about Higher Education in Russia for International Students. Accessed November 28, 2023. https://studyinrussia.ru/en/study-in-russia/info/levels-of-education/.

Thanh Ta, Binh. 2021. A Conversation Analytical Study of Story-openings in Advice-giving Episodes in Doctoral Research Supervision Meetings. *Discourse Studies* 23 (2): 213–230. https://doi.org/10.1177/1461445620966925.

———. 2023. *A Conversation Analytic Approach to Doctoral Supervision: Feedback, Advice, and Guidance.* London: Routledge.

Troelsen, Rie. 2021. Det åbne vejledningsrum. *Dansk Universitetspædagogisk Tidsskrift* 16 (31): 2.

Van Veldhuizen, Bert, Ron Oostdam, Mascha Enthoven, and Marco Snoek. 2021. Reflective Movements in the Professional Development of Teacher Educators as Supervisors of Student Research in Higher Education. *European Journal of Teacher Education* 44 (4): 452–467. https://doi.org/10.1080/02619768.2020.1777977.

Vehviläinen, Sanna. 2003. Avoiding Providing Solutions: Orienting to the Ideal of Students' Self-Directedness in Counselling Interaction. *Discourse Studies* 5 (3): 389–414. https://doi.org/10.1177/14614456030053005.

———. 2009. Student-Initiated Advice in Academic Supervision. *Research on Language and Social Interaction* 42 (2): 163–190. https://doi.org/10.1080/08351810902864560.

———. 2012. Question-prefaced Advice in Feedback Sequences of Finnish Academic Supervisions. In *Advice in Discourse*, ed. Holger Limberg and Miriam A. Locher, 31–52. Amsterdam & Philadelphia: John Benjamins Publishing.

Vehviläinen, Sanna, and Erika Löfström. 2016. 'I wish I had a Crystal Ball': Discourses and Potentials for Developing Academic Supervising. *Studies in Higher Education* 41 (3): 508–524. https://doi.org/10.1080/03075079.2014.942272.

Vereijken, Mayke W.C., Roeland M. van der Rijst, Jan H. van Driel, and Friedo W. Dekker. 2018. Novice Supervisors' Practices and Dilemmatic Space in Supervision of Student Research Projects. *Teaching in Higher Education* 23 (4): 522–542. https://doi.org/10.1080/13562517.2017.1414791.

Wels, Harry, Sioux McKenna, Jenny Clarence-Fincham, Chrissie Boughey, and J.H.M. van den Heuvel. 2017. *Strengthening Postgraduate Supervision*. Stellenbosch: SUN Press.

Zhang, Yan, and Ken Hyland. 2022. Responding to Supervisory Feedback: Mediated Positioning in Thesis Writing. *Written Communication* 39 (2): 171–199. https://doi.org/10.1177/07410883211069901.

Open Access This chapter is licensed under the terms of the Creative Commons Attribution-NonCommercial-NoDerivatives 4.0 International License (http://creativecommons.org/licenses/by-nc-nd/4.0/), which permits any noncommercial use, sharing, distribution and reproduction in any medium or format, as long as you give appropriate credit to the original author(s) and the source, provide a link to the Creative Commons license and indicate if you modified the licensed material. You do not have permission under this license to share adapted material derived from this chapter or parts of it.

The images or other third party material in this chapter are included in the chapter's Creative Commons license, unless indicated otherwise in a credit line to the material. If material is not included in the chapter's Creative Commons license and your intended use is not permitted by statutory regulation or exceeds the permitted use, you will need to obtain permission directly from the copyright holder.

CHAPTER 2

Starting Points and Theoretical Perspectives

The main theme of the book is thus the practice of academic supervision. But what constitutes this practice, and how do we access it? As discussed in Chap. 1, supervision involves a range of activities in which students and supervisors are involved in different ways. Interaction and communication between students and supervisors include supervision meetings, which may sometimes be digital, but also writing and commenting on texts, as well as questions and answers by email or telephone. In addition, the supervision process involves interaction and communication with a number of other people, such as course coordinators, seminar leaders, fellow students and colleagues. In other words, degree project supervision is a complex activity that can be understood and discussed in many ways and from different perspectives. In this chapter, we will present the theoretical perspectives and empirical material on which our discussions are based.

THEORETICAL PERSPECTIVES ON SUPERVISION

Although a first, spontaneous thought about supervision may be that it concerns primarily a relationship between the supervisor and the student, there are generally many more people involved in the supervision process. In practice, a significant proportion of degree project supervision now involves groups of students, either for specific parts of the supervision process or for the whole of the degree project period. There may be financial reasons for this, as supervision with one student and one supervisor is a comparatively expensive form of teaching, but there are also potential pedagogical advantages to bringing students together in groups, depending on how it is done (cf. Wichmann-Hansen et al. 2015; Nordentoft et al. 2013). In addition to fellow students on the course, students also come into contact with course coordinators, seminar leaders and examiners, all of whom may have opinions or influence on how the degree project work should be done. The supervisor also interacts with the course coordinators, seminar leaders and examiners within the course and sometimes holds one or more of these positions in addition to the role of supervisor. Additionally, the supervisor is part of a collective that may consist of other supervisors on the course, or colleagues who are not currently supervising degree projects, but who have experience and views on how supervision can or should be done. In multidisciplinary programmes, such collectives may be made up of scholars from different disciplines, adding to the complexity of the relationships and collaborations involved in academic supervision.

Moreover, there are a number of external conditions that influence and limit how an individual supervisor can organise and plan the supervision process. These conditions include, for example, governing documents such as curricula and syllabi, but also, as mentioned above, the financial conditions that prevail within a programme or course, which ultimately determine how much time a supervisor can spend on each degree project. There are also different local practices and power relations that are relevant to the supervision process. For example, the course coordinator may have decided on the structure of supervision for a particular course, and there may be established ways of working within a programme, course or group of supervisors that everyone is expected to follow. A further complication may be that the different local practices and expectations that exist are not necessarily explicit and visible to all supervisors, which in turn may lead to a lack of equality and transparency for students.

In other words, whatever ideals and ideas a supervisor may have cannot always be implemented within the norms, guidelines and expectations that govern and characterise a particular local academic context. It is influenced and regulated by what is desirable or possible within a certain programme or course. At the same time, the practice of individual supervisors—their attitudes, actions, interactions and relationships with students and colleagues—is key to being able to say something more about the complexity of academic supervision. For this reason, in this book, we will provide many examples from our empirical material as a basis for the discussion, reflection and analysis. Before moving on to the examples and analysis in Chap. 3 and beyond, we will briefly present our theoretical framework and describe our material in more detail.

Supervision as a Social and Collegial Practice

As mentioned earlier, we assume here that the supervision of degree projects is not only an individual but also a social and collegial practice, in the sense that the individual supervisor's practice constantly exists and develops in interaction with others. That supervision should be seen as a social practice that is developed and shaped in collective interaction has been discussed by Olga Dysthe and Akylina Samara (2006), Nordentoft et al. (2013) and Wichmann-Hansen et al. (2015), among others. They point out how such an attitude towards supervision—focusing not only on the individual supervisors and their relationship and interaction with the students, but also on the social and collegial practice—can help to improve the quality of supervision (see also Dysthe 2002; Vehviläinen and Löfström 2016). From a theoretical perspective, this could be described as the supervision context being an example of what Lave and Wenger (1991; Wenger 1998) call *communities of practice*, in that all actors who are part of this social and collective practice are aiming at the same epistemological goal—a completed student thesis of sufficiently good quality—but can contribute to it in many different ways.

The academic writing of degree projects involves a number of different actors and collectives, also from the students' perspective. Throughout the process, they may receive feedback on their ideas and texts not only from supervisors, seminar leaders or course coordinators, but also from student peers in different types of collective or group supervision meetings and seminar discussions (see e.g. Baker et al. 2014; Dysthe et al. 2006). A distinction can be made here between group supervision, where a pair or group of students writing the thesis together are supervised, and collective academic supervision (CAS), where supervisors gather a number of students writing separate theses for joint supervision meetings (see e.g. Rienecker et al. 2019, 197ff; Wichmann-Hansen et al. 2015;, Nordentoft et al. 2013, 2019).

Both group and collective supervision can be valuable in the degree project process, as students have the opportunity to interact with other students as well as supervisors. However, multi-actor supervision sessions can also be challenging for both students and supervisors, for example, if they are primarily used to a one-to-one supervisory relationship and have not been sufficiently prepared for participation and learning of different kinds (Nordentoft et al. 2013; Baker et al. 2014). In addition to the conversations and interactions that take place within the academic environment, discussions in various online groups and forums can be quite important for students' work on their theses. The fact that students can get ideas and comments on their thesis work in such contexts, both in and out of the university, is something that supervisors also need to take into account in their supervisory practice.

What, then, might it mean for the individual supervisor if supervision is seen more as a social practice and a collective and collegial matter? Potentially, such an approach may provide more opportunities for colleagues to share and learn from each other's experiences, or help to clarify previously unspoken aspects of supervision. For example, it might encourage supervisors in a particular local academic context, such as a particular programme, discipline or course, to start talking about and reflecting on things that might seem obvious or that constitute a kind of tacit knowledge that supervisors are expected to have without it always being obvious how to acquire it. This increases the opportunity to identify and articulate problems and obstacles in and around the supervision process and to develop greater consensus among supervisors on the same course or programme. This, in turn, may help to make clearer what is expected of both students within a particular course or programme and of supervisors. From this perspective, an increased focus on thesis supervision as not only an individual but also a social and collegial practice could be seen as an important part of the learning process for individual supervisors (cf. Dysthe et al. 2006).

Academic Literacies

Our understanding of the different relationships and contexts in which supervisors and students are involved during the degree project process is grounded in the socio-culturally based theoretical field of *academic literacies*. In this field—which focuses on the knowledge, competences and skills needed to cope with and meet the demands of speaking, writing and reading in the academic sphere—a starting point is that academic literacies is not just about writing itself or about working techniques that are relatively easy to learn or teach. It takes a broader perspective in that it encompasses all the activities associated with academic writing, which means that it also relates to social and institutional practices, power relations, hierarchies and identities (see e.g. Lea and Street 2000, 2006; Lillis 2001, 2003; Lillis and Scott 2007).

One of the aspects highlighted by academic literacies research is that the expectations of students or scholars within a particular academic context are shaped by different epistemological understandings, i.e. different views of what constitutes valid and relevant knowledge. This, in turn, is closely linked to views of academic writing and how one should or is expected to write in order to be accepted as relevant and valid in a particular context. That views of academic writing and what is considered good, relevant and valid writing differ between different academic contexts is thus something fundamental from an academic literacies perspective. Views vary not only between different countries or higher education institutions, but also between different disciplines, programmes and courses within the same university, and at an individual level between different university teachers or researchers. For students, this means that they have to adapt to the different approaches to academic writing—and therefore to the norms, requirements and expectations associated with it—that they encounter throughout their education.

One way of understanding this is through Mary Lea and Brian Street's notion *course switching* of (Lea and Street 2000, 37), which occurs, for example, when students move between different universities, disciplines or programmes, but also when they move between different courses within the same education. We would like to emphasise that course switching is often necessary when students move from the more basic to the more advanced parts of their education. For example, the transition that occurs when students move from academic writing in the form of written exams, take-home exams, memos and coursework to the type of academic writing required to produce a degree project. Although students benefit from the knowledge and experience of academic writing that they bring with them from previous courses and assignments, they face different demands, for example, in terms of independence, when they reach this level of their education. The skills and abilities they have developed are therefore not necessarily sufficient for the new demands placed on them.

Another aspect is that the genre in which students write their theses can vary greatly between disciplines and research fields. This has been discussed by scholars in the field of *disciplinary literacies*, who have systematically analysed genre differences and variations across different academic disciplines (see e.g. Shanahan and Shanahan 2012). Academic writing in the natural sciences may differ from writing in the humanities and social sciences in terms of scope, style and the prevalence of co-writing, but there are also significant differences within the humanities, natural sciences and social sciences that are important for student academic writing and for the supervision and assessment of student theses. This is particularly evident in multidisciplinary settings where students, supervisors and examiners may come from very different disciplinary backgrounds.

From an academic literacies perspective, then, academic writing is not regarded as a general competence or skill that students should simply acquire, but as a social practice that is negotiated and renegotiated and that varies between and within different academic contexts, cultures and genres. Still, while academic writing is in some ways discipline- and context-specific, there are also features of academic writing that are shared across disciplines and are hence the same or similar in different academic contexts. To describe this potential contradiction, the model developed by Shanahan and Shanahan (2012) can serve as a starting point, in which literacy is described at three different levels: *basic literacy*, *intermediate literacy* and *disciplinary literacy*. Basic literacy corresponds to a fundamental level of literacy where common words, decoding, et cetera, can be handled. Intermediate literacy corresponds to a more advanced level of literacy where general academic words are understood, and general strategies can be managed. Disciplinary literacy corresponds to the discipline-specific level, where variations between different contexts are understood and discipline-specific adaptations can be made on this basis. Intermediate literacy can thus be said to correspond to a general interdisciplinary academic level where there are similarities between academic language in different contexts, while disciplinary literacy corresponds to the discipline-specific level where there are differences between different disciplinary contexts. Both levels need to be taken into account in academic supervision, just as in other teaching within higher education.

The fact that diverse academic contexts are characterised by different epistemological understandings related to academic writing and literacy is important not only for students but also for supervisors, who need to adapt their own ways of working to the norms, requirements and expectations that prevail in different environments. Differences in epistemological understandings between individuals (cf. Lea and Street 2000, 38), i.e. between individual supervisors or teachers in a course, may also contribute to supervisors adopting different strategies and approaches in their work. For example, a certain epistemological understanding may lead supervisors to prefer a so-called Socratic style of supervision, which largely involves asking students open-ended questions to stimulate their thinking, whereas a different epistemological understanding of academic writing may lead supervisors to choose a more directive style of supervision, which is more concerned with guiding students along a particular path or telling them what to do next. In other words, both the norms, conceptions and expectations of academic writing in a specific local context and the supervisor's own epistemological understanding can be said to be directly relevant to individual supervisory practice.

Supervision and Relationship Building

Another central factor that is important for what individual supervision practice looks like is the relationship between supervisors and students. What the roles and relationships between students and supervisors look like, and what is expected of them, is also something that varies between different national and local academic contexts, as well as between levels of education. Time is an essential factor here, as supervisors spend much more time with doctoral students, and thus may have a closer relationship with them, than with master level students, and again more time with master level students than with bachelor level students. In some programmes, students are also offered a limited amount of supervision when writing smaller qualifying theses at an earlier stage in their education, which in turn creates very different conditions for the development of relationships between students and supervisors. Further significant aspects here include, for example, whether students write their degree projects individually, in pairs or in groups, and to what extent the supervision offered to them consists of individual meetings, group supervision or other forms of collective supervision (cf. Nordentoft et al. 2013; Wichmann-Hansen et al. 2015).

The supervisor-student relationship has been examined and discussed in research on both doctoral supervision and undergraduate supervision, in studies on, for instance, the roles of supervisors and students and how the relationship and interaction between them is experienced, where some scholars have proposed models of what supervisor-student relationships can or should look like (Agricola et al. 2021; Jacobsen et al. 2021; Mainhard et al. 2009; Van Veldhuizen et al. 2021; Wisker 2012; Ädel et al. 2023; Fisher et al. 2019; Rienecker et al. 2019). Certain studies discuss how the relationship with the supervisor, as well as with fellow students, may be directly related to the writing process and the production of an academic thesis, such as Corsini et al. (2022), who argue in their study of postgraduate education in France that the social environment to which a doctoral student belongs can be important for student productivity. Other studies, on, for instance, internationalisation of higher education and international mobility, have highlighted how national and cultural contexts can be relevant to how supervisor-student roles and relationships are viewed and experienced in terms of expectations and practices related to aspects such as student-supervisor communication, interaction and power relations (see, for example, Ding and Devine 2018; Doyle et al. 2018; Fan et al. 2018; Li 2016; Steinmetz and Mussi 2012; Wang and Li 2011).

The ethical dimensions of the supervisor-student roles and relationship are discussed, for instance, in an article by Goran Basic, based on a review of the available literature in this area. Basic concludes that ethical issues mostly arise from disappointment and unfulfilled expectations, for example, regarding the knowledge or competence of the supervisor or the doctoral student, cultural viewpoints, or roles and participation (Basic 2021). This could be understood in view of how there is an *asymmetry* built into the supervisory interaction, as in all institutional interactions (cf. Heritage 1984, 1997), where an expert (the supervisor) has more knowledge in the field and has a different role than the novice (the student). Even if the supervisor and the student have different institutional roles, the asymmetry in these roles can be reinforced or minimised in different ways in the interaction (cf. Linell and Luckmann 1991, Waring 2007). This kind of asymmetry can lead to tension and conflict, but it can also enable learning. For example, Vygotsky's notion of the zone of proximal development is based on the idea that one person knows more and can help the person who knows less to develop and learn (Vygotsky 1978). Asymmetry, in other words, is central to understanding relationship building in supervision.

As the research material on which this book is based includes both focus group interviews and recorded supervision sessions, it provides an opportunity to include and discuss several aspects of the supervisor-student relationship and how this can be relevant to actual supervision practice. The theoretical underpinning for how we do this in the following chapters starts from Olga Dysthe's (2002) now classic description of what she sees as three main types of supervisor-student relationships, characterised by *teaching, partnership* or *apprenticeship*.[1] In her definitions, a supervisory relationship characterised by teaching is primarily based on the supervisor acting or being perceived as an expert who explains to the student what to do and how to do it, while the partnership model is characterised by a more equal relationship between student and supervisor in which they work together towards a common goal, in this case the production of a degree project. In the apprenticeship model, the supervisor acts more as a role model, modelling and giving examples of how the student can proceed (Dysthe 2002).

The type of relationship between supervisor and student that predominates in a particular supervision process in turn influences the pedagogical tools used by supervisors and the demands and expectations placed on the student. Dysthe's three-part model is, of course, a generalised typology of the supervisor-student relationship. In most cases, aspects of more than one of these supervision models will be present in a particular supervisory process, not least because the relationship between supervisor and student can and generally should be different at different stages of the thesis work. In addition, the role and actions of the supervisors can be influenced by the attitudes and actions of the students, and vice versa, which in turn affects the relationship between them.

The Significance of Emotions

How the relationship between supervisor and student is built up in the supervision interaction can be discussed and analysed from many different perspectives. We will do this in part by focusing on the emotional aspects of the degree project process. That emotions are a central part of higher education, not least when it comes to academic supervision at different levels, has been discussed in a number of studies in international research (see e.g. Aitchison et al. 2012; Castello et al. 2009; Clegg 2000; Liu and Yu 2022; Wichmann-Hansen and Schmidt Nielsen 2023; Zackariasson 2018, 2020). To a considerable extent, doctoral supervision has been the focus of research into the emotional dimensions of academic writing and supervision (e.g. Aitchison and Mowbray 2013; Fisher et al. 2019; Weise

---

[1] Cf. the "students-as-partners" (SaP) initiative within teaching and learning in higher education, where everyone involved in the training will collaborate in the process of learning—when it comes to, e.g., governing documents, forms of examination, teaching methods, etc. (Healey et al. 2014).

et al. 2020; Cotterall 2013; McCormack 2009; Sambrook et al. 2008; Han and Xu 2021). For example, Jo Collins and Nicole Brown (2021) have discussed whether and how validation from supervisors can be beneficial to doctoral students' work on their dissertations, and Doloriert et al. (2012) have discussed the significance of emotions in relation to power issues within doctoral supervision.

One of the main reasons why supervision at the doctoral level has received a lot of attention is that the supervision process leading to a doctoral degree lasts several years and usually involves several emotional highs and lows along the way. However, in their book on learning and teaching in higher education, Light et al. (2009, 154ff) emphasise that there are also emotional aspects to supervising undergraduate projects. They argue that it can be an emotionally turbulent journey for both students and supervisors to start, work with and complete a student thesis. Todd et al. (2006) have also highlighted how emotional dimensions can be central components of supervising undergraduate theses, for both students and supervisors.

For supervisors, it may be difficult at times to manage various emotional aspects of the supervision interaction and relationship with the students. For instance, when things happen in a student's personal life that affect their studies and writing process, it can be difficult to know where and how to draw the line between providing mainly academic support and human or personal support. It can also be difficult for supervisors to deal with students' possible worries, fears and anxieties during the thesis work without experiencing a shift from being a supervisor to beginning to act as a psychologist or counsellor (Strandler et al. 2014). Emotional dimensions of degree project work may thus be significant for the individual supervisor's practice in several ways.

When we discuss the emotional dimensions of academic supervision practice and the supervisor-student relationship in the analysis of our material, we start from a broader emotion-theoretical framework based on Margaret Wetherell's (2012) theories of affect and *affective practices*. One fundamental aspect of this is that we do not focus on the emotions themselves, i.e. the affective processes that take place within the individual, but rather on how these are expressed in the interaction between supervisor and student, i.e. the affective practices that tend to emerge in and shape a particular supervision situation.

More specifically, we also use two concepts borrowed from Barsics et al. (2016)—*anticipatory emotions* and *anticipated emotions*, which they use in their discussion of how thoughts about the future, prospective thoughts, often evoke emotions and emotional responses in people. The first category, anticipatory emotions, is defined as the emotional reaction that occurs when you think about something that is going to happen—for example, for degree project students this could include concern about the upcoming examination and thesis defence, or joy at thinking about all the fun things that will happen when the semester is over. The second category, anticipated emotions, involves imagining how you will feel in the future—for degree project students, this might include how relieved they will be when they have passed the course, or how nervous they will be when they have their first interview for the empirical study.

These are relevant concepts to raise in relation to supervision practice, as one central aim of academic supervision is to encourage students to think and plan ahead, for example, to make it easier for them to anticipate problems they may encounter later in the process. In other words, prospective thinking is a fundamental aspect of academic supervision and the development of academic skills, which in turn can evoke emotions and emotional responses. We would like to emphasise that, again, our starting point is how such anticipated or anticipatory emotions may be expressed or referred to in supervision interaction, in other words, what role they may play in the affective practices that arise in a supervision situation (cf. Wetherell 2012). Thus, we do not claim to be able to access the affective processes that take place within a person, but only how these can be reflected and expressed in the recorded supervision conversations.

Supervision Tools

Several studies of academic supervision have examined and discussed possible strategies and tools for supervisors, such as feedback, praise, questions, advice and prompts. How such tools can be used in degree project supervision has been explored by a number of scholars in relation to different national higher education contexts. For example, Binh Thanh Ta (2021, 2023) has written about how story openings can be used as a tool when supervisors in Australia give advice to doctoral students and how they can problematise student responses in order to use them as a basis for feedback, while Neupane Bastola and Guangwei Hu (2021) have examined how supervisors give response and feedback on master's theses with a particular focus on non-Western countries, primarily Nepal. In a Nordic context, Sofie Henricson and Marie Nelson have compared how supervisors in Finland and Sweden give feedback and response to students (Henricson and Nelson 2017; Nelson et al. 2015), while Sanna Vehviläinen (2003, 2012) has written about the use of questions and the provision of solutions in supervision interaction in a Finnish context. Anita Eriksson and Susanne Gustavsson (2016) have conducted an autoethnographic analysis of the use of demands, recommendations and questions in Sweden (see also Magnusson 2020, 2021).[2]

In this book, we discuss several potential supervisory tools, such as praise, questions, recommendations and feedback, and the use of these tools by supervisors. In order to place these tools in a theoretical context and thus gain a broader perspective on the practice of individual supervisors, we start from the theoretical framework of *scaffolding*. The term scaffolding is originally borrowed from the construction sector, but has frequently been used in educational research as a metaphor for the support students may need to complete a task that they are not yet ready to undertake on their own (van de Pol et al. 2010, 271ff). In international research on school and education, the concept of scaffolding has a long history, and the understanding and use of the concept have varied, as can be seen in literature that uses the concept in relation to higher education (see, for example, Barkat 2014; Castillo-Montoya 2018; Korhonen et al. 2018; Wass et al. 2011; Collins 2021; Eklund Heinonen and Lennartson-Hokkanen 2015; Zhang and Hyland 2022).

The fact that the term is so widely used means that it sometimes tends to be watered down, so that more or less anything a teacher does to support a student could be defined as scaffolding. To avoid this, we start from the more specific definition and understanding of the concept presented by Janneke van de Pol et al. (van de Pol et al. 2010; van de Pol 2012). They emphasise that one of the main principles of a fundamental theoretical understanding of the concept of scaffolding is that it should include activity from both teachers and students, or in our case, supervisors and students. In other words, scaffolding is not about the teacher or supervisor unilaterally providing support to the student, but about a process of mutual give and take, where together you build the imaginary 'scaffold' that can provide support and help when someone takes on something new and unknown (van de Pol et al. 2010, 272).

---

[2] There are also studies that examine how students use questions in supervision discussions and how this affects the interaction and the supervisors' behaviour (e.g. Gustavsson and Eriksson 2015; Vehviläinen 2009).

Van de Pol et al. point to three key features that they argue recur in different uses of the term scaffolding, and which should therefore be seen as fundamental premises for being able to claim that scaffolding takes place. The first key feature is that the teacher has knowledge of and builds on the students' prior knowledge, which they use the term *contingency* to describe. The second key feature is that the teacher gradually withdraws as the process progresses, which they describe as *fading*. The third key feature, which they argue should be present in order for scaffolding to fully take place, can be seen as a natural consequence of the teacher's gradual withdrawal, namely that the responsibility for the task is gradually transferred to the student, which they use the term *transfer of responsibility* to describe (van de Pol 2012, 31ff; van de Pol et al. 2010, 274ff).

Van de Pol et al. also make a distinction between what they call *scaffolding means*—which are the tools the teacher/supervisor uses to support the learner in different ways—and *scaffolding intentions*, which are what the teacher/supervisor wants to achieve with the support. Possible scaffolding means/tools in a supervision context would be, for example, giving feedback on the student's performance, giving hints that can help the student to move forward, giving instructions that explain what the student should do next, being a role model or giving examples of how the student could proceed (modelling), and asking questions that make the student think and explain, i.e. questions that require an active cognitive and linguistic response (van de Pol 2012, 36; van de Pol et al. 2010, 277).

Scaffolding intentions mentioned by van de Pol et al. that may be relevant in a supervision context include getting students interested in the task at hand, helping students cope with the demands of the task, managing students' prior knowledge, contributing to frustration control, reducing freedom by taking over tasks that students are not yet ready for, and keeping learning focused on the goal (van de Pol 2012, 36; van de Pol et al. 2010, 278). We would argue that student independence can also be seen as such a scaffolding intention in the supervision context, based on the fact that it is a fundamental skill or competence that supervisors, through their actions in the supervision interaction, seek to contribute to the students achieving.

The supervision context may in many respects be regarded as an excellent arena for scaffolding, as the relationship between supervisors and students is generally built up over a longer period of time than the teacher-student relationship in many other types of courses, and involves close interaction between a few individuals. Thus, the supervision situation provides favourable conditions for both students and supervisors to be active in the scaffolding process, and for the supervisor to base supervision on an awareness of the student's existing knowledge and skills. The degree project process also offers good conditions for the gradual withdrawal of the supervisor, as increasing responsibility for producing a degree project that meets quality standards is taken on by the student. At the same time, it is far from obvious that all supervision interactions work in such a way that one can speak of scaffolding in this more specific definition, which we will return to in the analysis in later chapters.

How to Study Supervision Practice?

As the supervision of degree projects is a complex and multifaceted pedagogical activity involving a variety of actors and actions, several types of empirical material are needed to study it. In the multidisciplinary research project on understandings of student independence in higher education in Sweden and Russia, on which our discussions and conclusions in this book are based, we have therefore included interviews, documented supervision interactions and governing documents of various kinds. The intention was to obtain a broad range of material that could provide many different entry points for understanding and discussing academic supervision of degree projects, which was our primary focus. We wanted to include the experiences and reflections of supervisors, gain insight into what the interaction between individual supervisors and students might look like, and also relate this to the guidelines and regulations at different levels that are central to what supervision practice might look like in various national and local contexts. Below we present the material that forms the empirical foundation for our discussions and analyses in the rest of the book.

Discussions About Supervision

To capture how degree project supervisors themselves describe their practice and the diverse issues and problems associated with it, the project researchers conducted a series of focus group interviews with supervisors in journalism education and teacher education at two Swedish universities and four Russian universities.[3] Focus group interviews were chosen as they are usually a good tool for gaining knowledge about how people reason and relate to different phenomena, in this case degree project supervision (Ahrne and Svensson 2015; Krzyzanowskii 2008; Morgan and Krueger 1993). The focus group interviews conducted within teacher education included supervisors from different disciplines. They often had experience of supervising student theses both within their own discipline and within teacher education programmes. Some of the focus group participants had been supervising degree projects for a long time and were very experienced, while for others it was a relatively new experience.

As the research project focused on independence in higher education, this was a starting point for the focus group discussions. However, in the course of the discussions, the participating supervisors also touched on many other aspects of the supervision of degree projects. A number of issues and problems that supervisors felt they had to contend with in their supervision recurred in the discussions. These included the question of the students' respective supervisors' responsibility for the quality and completion of the degree project, and the perceived problems of achieving coherence between different actors within the course, such as supervisors, course coordinators, seminar leaders and examiners. By initiating collegial discussions about different aspects of thesis supervision in this way, we gained insight into the dilemmas and challenges that supervisors themselves experienced in their work, as well as similarities and differences in how supervisors from different disciplines and higher education institutions in two different countries may think and reason about supervision practice. By this, the focus groups provided important background and context for the rest of the material we collected.

The focus group interviews also clearly showed that there were a number of different views and understandings of what student independence might mean in a degree project context and what it entailed in relation to

---

[3] A total of 12 focus group interviews were conducted within the research project, involving a total of 58 supervisors from 2 universities in Sweden and 4 universities in Russia. Each focus group interview lasted one hour. The focus group interviews were conducted in Russian and Swedish, by native-speaking project members, and all examples given in this book have been transcribed and translated into English by the authors (Swedish) and research assistants (Russian). All participants in the focus group interviews gave their informed consent to participate in the study and have been pseudonymised in the text. The ethical guidelines for research in the social sciences and humanities in Sweden were followed during the project.

academic writing and thesis supervision, which we will return to and discuss further in Chap. 3. At the same time as there were many ways in which supervisors described their understanding of student independence, there were also many commonalities, regardless of programme, university or country. For example, although there were some differences in how the supervisors in the focus groups in Russia and Sweden reasoned about academic supervision and student independence, for example in how and when they raised the issue of plagiarism, the participating supervisors tended to talk about these issues and their experiences in quite similar ways. According to the focus group interviews in our project, supervisors at different universities and in both countries thus in many ways appeared to face fairly similar challenges in the supervision process, even though the conditions for and structures of supervision and degree project courses varied (Zackariasson and Magnusson 2020; Magnusson and Zackariasson 2018).

Supervision Interaction

To gain an insight into the actual supervision interaction, and not just the supervisors' descriptions and reflections on their practice, we asked a number of supervisors to record the conversations that took place during their supervision sessions with students.[4] As a significant part of academic supervision consists of answering students' questions or giving feedback on drafts via email, we asked the participating supervisors to also forward the email conversations they had with the students. In addition, we asked them to send the drafts they had discussed with the students, if possible with the supervisor's comments.[5] As many of the supervision discussions

---

[4] The material for this book includes 37 supervision sessions in total, recorded by 9 supervisors at 2 universities in Sweden. Some of the recorded supervision sessions were group or collective supervision involving two or several students, which means that significantly more students than supervisors appear in the recorded material. The supervision meetings were conducted in Swedish, and all examples given in this book have been transcribed and translated into English by the authors. All students and supervisors who participated in the recorded supervision sessions gave their consent to participate in the study and have been pseudonymised in the text.

[5] A total of 41 text drafts from 8 supervision processes and email conversations from 9 supervision processes are included in the research project material. A small part of the material comes from a pilot project, which was carried out before the start of the main project (supervisor G). The degree project courses from which these texts originate typically lasted 10 weeks (15 ECTS) and resulted in student theses of around 30–40 pages.

revolved around the students' drafts, access to this material could deepen the understanding of the recordings and provide an opportunity to see if and how the students acknowledged and worked with the supervisors' comments and advice.

Our ambition was to document the entire supervision process in each case, from the students' first meeting with the supervisor to the last supervision session, when an almost-finished final manuscript was available for discussion. In practice, however, this proved to be difficult to achieve, for example, because the participating supervisors forgot to record conversations, or because the degree project ran into problems and the student no longer wanted the supervision to be recorded. Thus, the documented supervision interaction consists partly of complete supervision processes and partly of partial supervision processes.

As the research project was interdisciplinary and included researchers from different disciplines and research traditions, the material was interpreted and analysed in several ways and from multiple perspectives. Sometimes the linguistic details were important for the analysis, sometimes it was what was said rather than how it was said, and in some cases it was a combination of the two. When the focus was on the linguistic interaction between supervisors and students, we used both quantitative and qualitative methods in the analysis. Quantitative analysis of the supervision sessions allowed us to see, for example, how much speaking space was used by supervisors and students in the supervision conversations, while qualitative methods allowed us to analyse the conversational exchange between supervisors and students at a micro level.

All in all, the recorded supervision sessions are a rich material that provides opportunities for several types of analysis. However, it has certain limitations. For example, because the material consists of audio rather than video recordings, we do not have access to the facial expressions and movement patterns of either students or supervisors, even if things like tone of voice, sighs and laughter are included in the audio recordings. The main reason why we still chose to make audio recordings is that it allowed the supervisors to easily manage the recordings themselves. This meant that we, as researchers, or other outsiders, did not have to attend the supervision meetings, which we considered to be positive and necessary, as supervision situations can be emotionally charged events and stressful for students.

Governing Documents

In addition to focus group interviews and documented supervision interactions, the project drew on texts and documents that in different ways govern and regulate supervision and the context in which it takes place. At the most general level, governing documents such as Higher Education Acts and Higher Education Ordinances are of course central (e.g. Swedish Council for Higher Education 1993). The objectives and general structures set out there form the foundation for how syllabi and curricula are written for specific programmes and courses and thus, in the long run, have effects for the practice of individual supervisors.

In order to gain insight into this level—the governing documents for specific degree project courses—we have collected and analysed a large number of curricula for degree project courses at undergraduate level in the humanities and social sciences from universities in Sweden and, to some extent, Russia. To see how the curricula could be put into practice, we also looked at grading criteria and assessment matrices from a smaller selection of degree project courses in Sweden, including those taught by supervisors who participated in the study. The overall analysis of these documents showed that there were considerable similarities in the way the assessment criteria were formulated in different disciplines and at different higher education institutions, although of course there were also certain differences in the formulations and in what was included and emphasised. Recurring fundamental aspects included, for example, that the purpose and questions of the degree projects should be clearly formulated and answered, and that there should be a theoretical grounding and an account of previous research in the field.

As mentioned above, curricula and programme syllabi, as well as grading criteria, assessment matrices and student manuals, are of substantial importance for individual supervision practice and what it will look like. On a day-to-day basis, it is to a large extent such local governing documents that regulate what is expected of and possible for supervisors within a specific course or in a certain local academic context. The purpose of including this kind of material in our study is thus to be able to place what happens in the meeting between individual supervisors and students in a larger context and to show how individual supervision practice is always related to guidelines, laws and regulations at many levels.

* * *

The different themes we have introduced in this chapter—supervision as a social and collegial practice, relationship building as part of supervision practice, and possible pedagogical tools in supervisory interaction—are of course directly related and interdependent. In the following chapters, we explore these different aspects and perspectives of supervision and discuss them in relation to examples from our empirical material. We begin by looking more closely at student independence, how it is an essential part of the degree project process and academic supervision, and how the supervisors who participated in the focus group interviews understood and related to the idea and ideals of student independence in their supervision practice.

References

Ädel, Annelie, Julie Skogs, Charlotte Lindgren, and Monika Stridfeldt. 2023. The Supervisor and Student in Bachelor Thesis Supervision: A Broad Repertoire of Sometimes Conflicting Roles. *European Journal of Higher Education* 1–21. https://doi.org/10.1080/21568235.2022.2162560.

Agricola, Bas T., Frans J. Prins, Marieke F. van der Schaaf, and Jan van Tartwijk. 2021. Supervisor and Student Perspectives on Undergraduate Thesis Supervision in Higher Education. *Scandinavian Journal of Educational Research* 65 (5): 877–897. https://doi.org/10.1080/00313831.2020.1775115.

Ahrne, Göran, and Peter Svensson. 2015. *Handbok i kvalitativa metoder*. Stockholm: Liber.

Aitchison, Claire, and Susan Mowbray. 2013. Doctoral Women: Managing Emotions, Managing Doctoral Studies. *Teaching in Higher Education* 18 (8): 859–870. https://doi.org/10.1080/13562517.2013.827642.

Aitchison, Claire, Janice Catterall, Pauline Ross, and Shelley Burgin. 2012. 'Tough Love and Tears': Learning Doctoral Writing in the Sciences. *Higher Education Research and Development* 31 (4): 435–447. https://doi.org/10.1080/07294360.2011.559195.

Baker, Mary-Jane, Elizabeth Cluett, Lorraine Ireland, Sheila Reading, and Susan Rourke. 2014. Supervising Undergraduate Research: A Collective Approach Utilising Groupwork and Peer Support. *Nurse Education Today* 34 (4): 637–642. https://doi.org/10.1016/j.nedt.2013.05.006.

Barkat, Janet C G. 2014. *Handing over the Baton: An Intervention Study Looking at Improving Students' Motivational Attitudes Towards Taking Greater Ownership of their Learning at KS4*. London: University of London. Diss.

Barsics, Catherine, Martial Van der Linden, and Arnaud D'Argembeau. 2016. Frequency, Characteristics, and Perceived Functions of Emotional Future

Thinking in Daily Life. *The Quarterly Journal of Experimental Psychology* 69 (2): 217–233. https://doi.org/10.1080/17470218.2015.1051560.

Basic, Goran. 2021. Ethical Issues in Doctoral Supervision: An Analysis of Inherent Conflicts and Roles in Supervision Practice. *Future Students' Perspectives on Higher Education* 3 (2): 17–48. https://doi.org/10.5281/zenodo.7492713.

Castello, Montserrat, Anna Inesta, and Carles Monereo. 2009. Towards Self-Regulated Academic Writing: An Exploratory Study with Graduate Students in a Situated Learning Environment. *Electronic Journal of Research in Educational Psychology* 7 (3): 1107–1130. https://doi.org/10.1016/j.system.2020.102312.

Castillo-Montoya, Milagros. 2018. Rigor Revisited: Scaffolding College Student Learning by Incorporating Their Lived Experiences. *New Directions for Higher Education* 2018 (181): 37–46. https://doi.org/10.1002/he.20269.

Clegg, Sue. 2000. Knowing Through Reflective Practice in Higher Education. *Educational Action Research* 8 (3): 451–469. https://doi.org/10.1080/09650790000200128.

Collins, Jo. 2021. Validation in Doctoral Education: Exploring PhD Students' Perceptions of Belonging to Scaffold Doctoral Identity Work. *International Journal of Doctoral Studies* 16: 715–735. https://doi.org/10.28945/4876.

Collins, Jo, and Nicole Brown. 2021. Where's the Validation? Role of Emotion Work and Validation for Doctoral Students. *Higher Education Research and Development* 40 (7): 1389–1402. https://doi.org/10.1080/07294360.2020.1833315.

Corsini, Alberto, Michele Pezzoni, and Fabiana Visentin. 2022. What Makes a Productive Ph.D. student? *Research Policy* 51 (10): 104561. https://doi.org/10.1016/j.respol.2022.104561.

Cotterall, Sara. 2013. More than Just a Brain: Emotions and the Doctoral Experience. *Higher Education Research and Development* 32 (2): 174–187. https://doi.org/10.1080/07294360.2012.680017.

Ding, Qun, and Nesta Devine. 2018. Exploring the Supervision Experiences of Chinese Overseas Phd students in New Zealand. *Knowledge Cultures* 6 (1): 62–78. https://doi.org/10.22381/KC6120186.

Doloriert, Clair, Sally Sambrook, and Jim Stewart. 2012. Power and Emotion in Doctoral Supervision: Implications for HRD. *European Journal of Training and Development* 36 (7): 732–750. https://doi.org/10.1108/03090591211255566.

Doyle, Stephanie, Catherine Manathunga, Gerard Prinsen, Rachel Tallon, and Sue Cornforth. 2018. African International Doctoral Students in New Zealand: Englishes, Doctoral Writing and Intercultural Supervision. *Higher Education Research & Development* 37 (1): 1–14. https://doi.org/10.1080/07294360.2017.1339182.

Dysthe, Olga. 2002. Professors as Mediators of Academic Text Cultures: An Interview Study with Advisors and Masters Degree Students in Three Disciplines in a Norwegian University. *Written Communication* 19 (4): 493–544. https://doi.org/10.1177/074108802238010.

Dysthe, Olga, and Akylina Samara. 2006. *Forskningsveiledning på master- og doktorgradsnivå*. Oslo: Abstrakt forlag.

Dysthe, Olga, Akylina Samara, and Kariane Westrheim. 2006. Multivoiced Supervision of Master's Students: A Case Study of Alternative Supervision Practises in Higher Education. *Studies in Higher Education* 31 (3): 299–318. https://doi.org/10.1080/03075070600680562.

Eklund Heinonen, Maria, and Ingrid Lennartson-Hokkanen. 2015. Scaffolding Strategies: Enhancing L2 Students' Participation in Discussions about Academic Texts. *Journal of Academic Writing* 5 (1): 42–51.

Eriksson, Anita, and Susanne Gustavsson. 2016. Krav, uppmaningar och frågor - en autoetnografisk reflektion över handledning av självständiga arbeten. *Utbildning och Lärande* 10 (1): 70–87.

Fan, Luo, Monowar Mahmood, and Md. Aftab Uddin. 2018. Supportive Chinese Supervisor, Innovative International Students: A Social Exchange Theory Perspective. *Asia Pacific Education Review.* 20: 101–115. https://doi.org/10.1007/s12564-018-9572-3.

Fisher, Aaron J., Rodolfo Mendoza-Denton, Colette Patt, Ira Young, Andrew Eppig, Robin L. Garrell, Douglas C. Rees, Tenea W. Nelson, and Mark A. Richards. 2019. Structure and Belonging: Pathways to Success for Underrepresented Minority and Women PhD Students in STEM fields. *PloS one* 14 (1): e0209279–e0209279. https://doi.org/10.1371/journal.pone.0209279.

Gustavsson, Susanne, and Anita Eriksson. 2015. Blivande lärares frågor vid handledning – Gör jag en kvalitativ studie med kvantitativa inslag? *Pedagogisk forskning i Sverige* 20 (1–2): 79–99.

Han, Ye, and Yueting Xu. 2021. Unpacking the Emotional Dimension of Doctoral Supervision: Supervisors' Emotions and Emotion Regulation Strategies. *Frontiers in Psychology* 12: 651859–651859. https://doi.org/10.3389/fpsyg.2021.651859.

Healey, Mick, Abbi Flint, and Kathy Harrington. 2014. *Engagement Through Partnership. Students as Partners in Learning and Teaching in Higher Education*. York: HE Academy.

Henricson, Sofie, and Marie Nelson. 2017. Giving and Receiving Advice in Higher Education. Comparing Sweden-Swedish and Finland-Swedish Supervision Meetings. *Journal of Pragmatics* 109: 105–120. https://doi.org/10.1016/j.pragma.2016.12.013.

Heritage, John. 1984, 1997. Garfinkel and Ethnomethodology. In *Conversation Analysis and Institutional Talk: Analyzing Data. In Qualitative Research*, ed. D. Silverman. London: Sage.

Jacobsen, Michele, Sharon Friesen, and Sandra Becker. 2021. Online Supervision in a Professional Doctorate in Education: Cultivating Relational Trust Within

Learning Alliances. *Innovations in Education and Teaching International* 58 (6): 635–646. https://doi.org/10.1080/14703297.2021.1991425.

Korhonen, A.-M., S. Ruhalahti, and M. Veermans. 2018. The Online Learning Process and Scaffolding in Student Teachers' Personal Learning Environments. *Education and Information Technologies* 24 (1): 755–779. https://doi.org/10.1007/s10639-018-9793-4.

Krzyzanowskii, Michal. 2008. Analyzing Focus Group Discussions. In *Qualitative Discourse Analysis in the Social Sciences*, ed. R. Wodak and Michal Krzyzanowski, 162–181. Basingstoke: Palgrave Macmillan.

Lave, Jean, and Etienne Wenger. 1991. *Situated Learning: Legitimate Peripheral Participation, Learning in Doing*. Cambridge: Cambridge University Press.

Lea, Mary R., and Brian V. Street. 2000. Student Writing and Staff feedback in Higher Education: An academic Literacies Approach. In *Student Writing in Higher Education. New contexts*, ed. Mary R. Lea and Barry Stierer, 32–46. Buckingham: Open University Press.

———. 2006. The "Academic Literacies" Model: Theory and Applications. *Theory Into Practice* 45 (4): 368–377. https://doi.org/10.1207/s15430421tip4504_11.

Li, Mingsheng. 2016. Developing Skills and Disposition for Lifelong Learning: Acculturative Issues Surrounding Supervising International Doctoral Students in New Zealand Universities. *Journal of International Students* 6 (3): 740–761.

Light, Greg, Roy Cox, and Susanna Calkins. 2009. *Learning and Teaching in Higher Education: The Reflective Professional*. 2nd ed. London: Sage.

Lillis, Theresa. 2001. *Student Writing: Access, Regulation, Desire*. London: Routledge.

———. 2003. Student Writing as 'Academic Literacies': Drawing on Bakhtin to Move from Critique to Design. *Language and Education* 17 (3): 192–207. https://doi.org/10.1080/09500780308666848.

Lillis, Theresa, and Mary Scott. 2007. Defining Academic Literacies Research: Issues of Epistemology, Ideology and Strategy. *Journal of Applied Linguistics* 4 (1): 5–32. https://doi.org/10.1558/japl.v4i1.5.

Linell, Per, and Thomas Luckmann. 1991. Asymmetries in Dialogue: Some Conceptual Preliminaries. In *Asymmetries in dialogue*, ed. Ivana Marková and Klaus Foppa, 1–20. Savage, MD: Barnes & Nobles.

Liu, Chunhong, and Shulin Yu. 2022. Exploring Master's Students' Emotions and Emotion-regulation in Supervisory Feedback Situations: A Vignette-based Study. *Assessment and Evaluation in Higher Education* 47 (7): 1101–1115. https://doi.org/10.1080/02602938.2021.2005770.

Magnusson, Jenny. 2020. "Jättebra, men" - Handledares beröm i handledningssamtal. *Språk och interaktion* 5 (3): 45–68.

———. 2021. Handledarens frågor: Att möjliggöra självständighet i ett handledningssamtal. *Högre utbildning* 11 (1): 56–75: 10.23865/hu.v11.2296.

Magnusson, Jenny, and Maria Zackariasson. 2018. Student Independence in Undergraduate Projects. Different Understandings in Different Academic Contexts. *Journal of Further and Higher Education* 43 (10): 1404–1419. https://doi.org/10.1080/0309877X.2018.1490949.

Mainhard, Tim, Roeland van der Rijst, Jan van Tartwijk, and Theo Wubbels. 2009. A model for the Supervisor–Doctoral Student Relationship. *Higher Education* 58 (3): 359–373. https://doi.org/10.1007/s10734-009-9199-8.

McCormack, Coralie. 2009. Postgraduate Research Students' Experience: It's all about Balancing Living. In *The Routledge International Handbook of Higher Education*, ed. Malcolm Tight, Ka Ho Mok, Jeroen Huisman, and Christopher Morphew, 181–193. New York & London: Routledge.

Morgan, David L., and Richard A. Krueger. 1993. When to Use Focus Groups and Why. In *Successful Focus Groups: Advancing the State of the Art*, ed. David L. Morgan, 3–19. London & Thousand Oaks: Sage.

Nelson, Marie, Sofie Henricson, Catrin Norrby, Camilla Wide, Jan Krister Lindström, and Jenny Nilsson. 2015. Att dela språk men inte samtalsmönster; Återkoppling i sverigesvenska och finlandssvenska handledningssamtal. *Folkmålsstudier: Meddelanden från Föreningen för Nordisk Filologi* 53: 141–166.

Neupane Bastola, Madhu, and Guangwei Hu. 2021. Supervisory Feedback Across Disciplines: Does it meet Students' Expectations? *Assessment and Evaluation in Higher Education* 46 (3): 407–423. https://doi.org/10.1080/02602938.2020.1780562.

Nordentoft, Helle Merete, Rie Thomsen, and Gitte Wichmann-Hansen. 2013. Collective Academic Supervision: A Model for Participation and Learning in Higher Education. *Higher Education* 65 (5): 581–593. https://doi.org/10.1007/s10734-012-9564-x.

Nordentoft, Helle Merete, Helle Hvass, Kristina Mariager-Anderson, Søren Smedegaard Bengtsen, Anne Smedegaard, and Sarah Damgaard Warrer. 2019. *Kollektiv akademisk vejledning. Fra forskning til praksis*. Aarhus: Aarhus Universitetsforlag.

van de Pol, Janneke. E. (2012). *Scaffolding in teacher-student interaction: exploring, measuring, promoting and evaluating scaffolding*. [Thesis, fully internal, Universiteit van Amsterdam]. https://dare.uva.nl/search?identifier=640b82ba-c27b-42d3-b9f8-fe08b1e0081f.

van de Pol, Janneke, Monique Volman, and Jos Beishuizen. 2012. Promoting Teacher Scaffolding in Small-group Work: A contingency Perspective. *Teaching and Teacher Education* 28 (2): 193–205. https://doi.org/10.1016/j.tate.2011.09.009.

van de Pol, Janneke, Monique Volman, and Jos. Beishuizen. 2010. Scaffolding in Teacher–Student Interaction: A Decade of Research. *Educational Psychology Review* 22: 271–296. https://doi.org/10.1007/s10648-010-9127-6.

Riencker, Lotte, Gitte Wichmann-Hansen, and Peter Stray Jørgensen. 2019. *God vejledning af specialer, bacheloroppgaver og projekter*. Frederiksberg: Samfundslitteratur.

Sambrook, Sally, Jim Stewart, and Clair Roberts. 2008. Doctoral Supervision... a View from Above, Below and the Middle! *Journal of Further and Higher Education* 32 (1): 71–84. https://doi.org/10.1080/03098770701781473.

Shanahan, Timothy, and Cynthia Shanahan. 2012. What Is Disciplinary Literacy and Why Does It Matter? *Topics in Language Disorders* 32 (1): 7–18. https://doi.org/10.1097/TLD.0b013e318244557a.

Steinmetz, Christine, and Eveline Mussi. 2012. "Settling In": Postgraduate Research Student Experiences; An International Perspective. Australian Association for Research in Education.

Strandler, Ola, Thomas Johansson, Gina Wisker, and Silwa Claesson. 2014. Supervisor or Counsellor? - Emotional Boundary Work in Supervision. *International Journal for Researcher Development* 5 (2): 70. https://doi.org/10.1108/IJRD-03-2014-0002.

Swedish Council for Higher Education. 1993. The Higher Education Ordinance, Svensk Författningssamling 1993:100. Ministry of Education and Research. Accessed November 29, 2023. https://www.uhr.se/en/start/laws-and-regulations/Laws-and-regulations/The-Higher-Education-Ordinance/.

Thanh Ta, Binh. 2021. A Conversation Analytical Study of Story-openings in Advice-giving Episodes in Doctoral Research Supervision Meetings. *Discourse Studies* 23 (2): 213–230. https://doi.org/10.1177/1461445620966925.

———. 2023. *A Conversation Analytic Approach to Doctoral Supervision: Feedback, Advice, and Guidance*. London: Routledge.

Todd, Malcolm J., Karen Smith, and Phil Bannister. 2006. Supervising a Social Science Undergraduate Dissertation: Staff Experiences and Perceptions. *Teaching in Higher Education* 11 (2): 161–173. https://doi.org/10.1080/13562510500527693.

Vehviläinen, Sanna. 2003. Avoiding Providing Solutions: Orienting to the Ideal of Students' Self-Directedness in Counselling Interaction. *Discourse Studies* 5 (3): 389–414. https://doi.org/10.1177/14614456030053005.

———. 2009. Student-Initiated Advice in Academic Supervision. *Research on Language and Social Interaction* 42 (2): 163–190. https://doi.org/10.1080/08351810902864560.

———. 2012. Question-prefaced Advice in Feedback Sequences of Finnish Academic Supervisions. In *Advice in Discourse*, ed. Holger Limberg and Miriam A. Locher, 31–52. Amsterdam & Philadelphia: John Benjamins Publishing.

Vehviläinen, Sanna, and Erika Löfström. 2016. 'I wish I had a Crystal Ball': Discourses and Potentials for Developing Academic Supervising. *Studies in Higher Education* 41 (3): 508–524. https://doi.org/10.1080/03075079.2014.942272.

Veldhuizen, Van, Ron Oostdam Bert, Mascha Enthoven, and Marco Snoek. 2021. Reflective Movements in the Professional Development of Teacher Educators as Supervisors of Student Research in Higher Education. *European Journal of Teacher Education* 44 (4): 452–467. https://doi.org/10.1080/02619768.2020.1777977.

Vygotsky, Lev S. 1978. *Mind In Society: The Development of Higher Psychological Processes*. Cambridge: Harvard University Press.

Wang, Ting, and Linda Y. Li. 2011. 'Tell me What to Do' vs. 'Guide me Through it': Feedback Experiences of International Doctoral Students. *Active Learning in Higher Education* 12 (2): 101–112. https://doi.org/10.1177/1469787411402438.

Waring, Hansun Zhang. 2007. Complex Advice Acceptance as a Resource for Managing Asymmetries. *Text and Talk* 27 (1): 107–137. https://doi.org/10.1515/TEXT.2007.005.

Wass, Rob, Tony Harland, and Alison Mercer. 2011. Scaffolding Critical Thinking in the Zone of Proximal Development. *Higher Education Research & Development* 30 (3): 317–328. https://doi.org/10.1080/07294360.2010.489237.

Weise, Crista, Mariela Aguayo-González, and Montserrat Castelló. 2020. Significant Events and the Role of Emotion along Doctoral Researcher Personal Trajectories. *Educational Research (Windsor)* 62 (3): 304–323. https://doi.org/10.1080/00131881.2020.1794924.

Wenger, Etienne. 1998. *Communities of Practice: Learning, Meaning, and Identity, Learning in Doing*. Cambridge: Cambridge University Press.

Wetherell, Margaret. 2012. *Affect and Emotion: A New Social Science Understanding*. London: Sage.

Wichmann-Hansen, Gitte, and Karl-Johan Schmidt Nielsen. 2023. Can Hands-on Supervision Get out of Hand? The Correlation between Directive Supervision and Doctoral Student Independence in a Danish Study Context. *Scandinavian Journal of Educational Research* (ahead-of-print): 1–16. https://doi.org/10.1080/00313831.2023.2204113.

Wichmann-Hansen, Gitte, Rie Thomsen, and Helle Merete Nordentoft. 2015. Challenges in Collective Academic Supervision: Supervisors' Experiences from a Master Programme in Guidance and Counseling. *Higher Education* 70 (1): 19–33. https://doi.org/10.1007/s10734-014-9821-2.

Wisker, Gina. 2012. *The Good Supervisor: Supervising Postgraduate and Undergraduate Research for Doctoral Theses and Dissertations*. Basingstoke: Palgrave Macmillan.

Zackariasson, Maria. 2018. 'I Feel Really Good Now!' – Emotions and Independence in Undergraduate Supervision. *Learning and Teaching: The International Journal of Higher Education in the Social Sciences* 11 (3): 1–24. https://doi.org/10.3167/latiss.2018.110303.

———. 2020. Kun kaikki ei menekään niin kuin piti: Syylisyyden tunne ja häpeä tutkielmaohjauksessa [When Things Don't Turn out the Way Expected. Guilt and Shame in Academic Supervision]. In *Afektit ja tunteet kulttuurin tutkimuksessa [Affects and Emotions in Cultural Research]*, ed. Jenni Rinne, Anna Kajander, and Riina Haanpää, 275–309. Helsingfors: Ethnos.

Zackariasson, Maria, and Jenny Magnusson. 2020. Academic Literacies and International Mobility. The Organization and Supervision of Degree Projects in Sweden and Russia. *Cogent Education* 7 (1): 1–12. 1855770. https://doi.org/10.1080/2331186X.2020.1855770.

Zhang, Yan, and Ken Hyland. 2022. Responding to Supervisory Feedback: Mediated Positioning in Thesis Writing. *Written Communication* 39 (2): 171–199. https://doi.org/10.1177/07410883211069901.

Open Access This chapter is licensed under the terms of the Creative Commons Attribution-NonCommercial-NoDerivatives 4.0 International License (http://creativecommons.org/licenses/by-nc-nd/4.0/), which permits any noncommercial use, sharing, distribution and reproduction in any medium or format, as long as you give appropriate credit to the original author(s) and the source, provide a link to the Creative Commons license and indicate if you modified the licensed material. You do not have permission under this license to share adapted material derived from this chapter or parts of it.

The images or other third party material in this chapter are included in the chapter's Creative Commons license, unless indicated otherwise in a credit line to the material. If material is not included in the chapter's Creative Commons license and your intended use is not permitted by statutory regulation or exceeds the permitted use, you will need to obtain permission directly from the copyright holder.

CHAPTER 3

Academic Supervision and Student Independence

One of the most central concepts in higher education is independence. It is a concept that appears in governing documents at various levels of higher education in many countries, and which tends to be particularly relevant in the context of the writing of academic theses and, by extension, within supervision and supervisory practice. At the same time, it is a concept with many connotations that can be understood and used in many different ways. In this chapter, we will first present some examples of how independence is made relevant in higher education policy documents from different countries and then examine and discuss how student independence can be viewed and understood in the context of supervision.

THE CONCEPT OF INDEPENDENCE IN HIGHER EDUCATION

There are a number of key concepts in higher education that are highly relevant to learning outcomes and what students are expected to achieve throughout their education, and consequently to the organisation and planning of teaching and supervision. As Tim Moore has argued, a closer examination of how such concepts are used and understood in the context of higher education is of great importance, as this plays a crucial role in how higher education is shaped or created at its different levels (cf. Moore 2011, 262). Critical thinking, agency and assessment are some of the central concepts within higher education that have been discussed and reflected upon from different angles and perspectives (see e.g. Almulla

2023; Davies 2011; Davies and Barnett 2015; Rico et al. 2023; Wass et al. 2011; Bartholomew and Jones 2022; Dufva and Aro 2015; Duff 2012; Lee 2019). Independence,[1] which is our focus here, is another, which has been discussed, for example, in relation to independent learning (Cukurova et al. 2017; Lau 2017; Meyer et al. 2008; Stoten 2014) and learner autonomy (Brew and Saunders 2020; Aprianti and Winarto 2023), as well as in relation to academic supervision at undergraduate, graduate or postgraduate level (Reitsma 2023; Zackariasson 2019; Magnusson and Zackariasson 2018; Wollast et al. 2023; Wichmann-Hansen and Schmidt Nielsen 2023; Brodin 2020).

That independence is a key concept in higher education in large parts of the world is evident when looking at policy and legislative documents on higher education in different countries. Student independence or autonomy is frequently stated as a requirement for obtaining academic degrees, both at bachelor and at master level, in governing documents such as Higher Education Acts, Higher Education Ordinances or National Qualifications Frameworks in several countries. For example, the Swedish Higher Education Ordinance states that in order to qualify for a bachelor's degree, students must, among other things,

- demonstrate the ability to identify, formulate and solve problems *autonomously* and to complete tasks within predetermined time frames
- demonstrate the skills required to work *autonomously* in the main field of study.

(Swedish Council for Higher Education 1993, emphasis added)

In Table 3.1, we have listed some further examples of how student independence or autonomy may be referred to in national-level policy

---

[1] The terms used to denote independence or autonomy, and the relationships between them, vary from language to language. For example, the Swedish word "självständighet" can be translated as either independence or autonomy, depending on the context. As in the Swedish Higher Education Ordinance, where the word "självständigt", which is used throughout the Swedish text, is translated in the English version as either independent/ly or autonomous/ly (Swedish Council for Higher Education 1993). In research on supervision and learning, both terms are used, e.g. in relation to independent learning and learner autonomy (see e.g. Cukurova et al. 2017; Lau 2017; Meyer et al. 2008; Stoten 2014; Brew and Saunders 2020; Aprianti and Winarto 2023). In this book we will primarily use the term independence.

Table 3.1 Examples of independence/autonomy in higher education policy documents (emphasis added)

Country	Example	Source
Australia	Graduates of a bachelor degree will have: … • cognitive and creative skills to exercise critical thinking and judgement in identifying and solving problems *with intellectual independence* • communication skills to present a clear, *coherent and independent exposition*	Australian Qualifications Framework, Australian Qualifications Framework Council (2013, 16).
Austria	7. 'Bachelor's papers' mean *independently prepared* papers forming part of bachelor's programmes which must be written or fulfilled artistically in connection with courses. 8. 'Diploma and master's theses' mean academic theses forming part of diploma and master's programmes which serve to demonstrate students' ability to achieve adequate standards of content and methodology when *independently addressing* scientific topics.	Federal Act on the Organisation of Universities and their Studies, Federal Ministry of Education, Science and Research (2002, §51).
Canada	All bachelor's programs are designed to provide graduates with knowledge and skills that enable them to develop the capacity for *independent intellectual work*. That capacity may be demonstrated by the preparation, under supervision, of one or more essays, a terminal research paper, thesis, project, exhibition, or other research-based or performance-based exercise that demonstrates methodological competence and capacity for *independent and ethical intellectual/creative work* and, where relevant, the exercise of professional responsibility in a field of practice.	Ministerial Statement on Quality Assurance of Degree Education in Canada, Council of Ministers of Education Canada (2007, 2).

(*continued*)

Table 3.1 (continued)

Country	Example	Source
Denmark	2. The objective of the bachelor's programmes is to: .... (2) provide the student with the necessary academic knowledge and theoretical and methodological qualifications and competencies *to independently identify, formulate and solve* complex issues within the relevant components of the subject area(s) of the programme	Ministerial Order on Bachelor and Master's (Candidatus) Programmes at Universities (the University Programme Order), Ministry of Higher Education and Science (2013, 1).
Estonia	(1) In bachelor's studies and studies in professional higher education, the student deepens their general educational knowledge, acquires the basic knowledge and skills of the field as well as knowledge, skills and attitudes required for employment, *independent work* and master's studies. ... (4) *Independent work* means acquiring knowledge necessary for *achieving learning outcomes independently*, according to tasks given by a member of the teaching staff.	Higher Education Act, Ministry of Education and Research (2019, §5). ****************** Standard of Higher Education, Ministry of Education and Research (2008, §5).
Norway	Level 7: Master (2nd cycle) The candidate … • can analyse existing theories, methods and interpretations in the field and *work independently* on practical and theoretical problems • can use relevant methods for research and scholarly and/or artistic development work *in an independent manner* • can carry out an *independent*, limited research or development project under supervision and in accordance with applicable norms for research ethics	Qualifications Framework for lifelong learning, NOKUT Norwegian Agency for Quality Assurance in Education (2023).

(*continued*)

Table 3.1 (continued)

Country	Example	Source
Spain	Article 6. Bachelor Level. 2. The characteristics of qualifications at this level are defined by the following descriptors presented in terms of learning outcomes: … f) Be able to identify their own training needs in their field of study and work or professional environment and to organise their own learning with a *high degree of autonomy* in all types of contexts (structured or not).	Código de Universidades, Agencia Estatal Boletín Oficial del Estado (2023, author's translation).

documents on higher education in a number of countries in different parts of the world.[2]

As can be seen from these examples, there are different aspects of independence that can be expected of students at the bachelor or master level, related to, for example, problem identification or solution, critical thinking, judgement, intellectual work, student research and their own learning process. In some cases, these expectations are linked to the task of completing a degree project, while in other cases this is not specified. Students are generally expected to further develop their independence or ability to work independently as they move from bachelor's to later levels of their education, as in Spain, where students at master's level are expected to have "*developed sufficient autonomy* to participate in research projects and scientific or technological collaborations within their thematic field, in interdisciplinary contexts and, where appropriate, with a high degree of knowledge transfer" (Agencia Estatal Boletín Oficial del Estado 2023, 326, author's translation, emphasis added). It could also be as in Denmark, where one of the objectives of the master's programme (candidatus) is to "develop and expand the student's academic knowledge and skills and strengthen his or her theoretical and methodological qualifications and

---

[2] We have not undertaken a systematic worldwide review of national higher education policy documents. Table 3.1 should therefore be taken as examples of how student independence or autonomy may be mentioned in such documents, rather than as a complete or comprehensive list of how or where this is done.

competences, as well as *increasing the student's independence* relative to the bachelor degree level" (Ministry of Higher Education and Science 2013, §4, emphasis added).

Student Independence in Local Governing Documents

How such nationally defined higher education goals of student independence and the ability to work independently are to be operationalised and achieved in practice is then further specified in policy documents and guidelines for academic programmes and courses. Independence may, for instance, be stated as a learning outcome for an academic programme, as in the following example from a syllabus for a teacher education programme in Sweden, where there are objectives related to independence, one of which refers to a work process and the other to the ability to reflect:

> Demonstrate an in-depth ability to *critically and independently use*, systematise and reflect on one's own and others' experiences and relevant research findings in order to contribute to the development of professional activities and the development of knowledge in the professional field.
> Demonstrate the ability to plan, implement, evaluate and develop teaching and pedagogical activities in general, *independently and with others*, in order to stimulate the learning and development of each pupil in the best possible way,
> Programme syllabus for Primary School Teacher Education with Intercultural Profile for Grades 4–6, Södertörn University, 2022, authors' translation, emphasis added.

Similarly, the concept of independence is regularly included in the intended learning outcomes formulated in course syllabi, not least in syllabi for courses that include the writing of degree projects.[3] Independence appears in different ways in syllabi and may be linked to objects (independent analysis), processes (independent investigation and evaluation) or other comparable concepts (demands for independence, complexity and reflection), and so on. For example, independence can be described as a process in which the student, after completing the course, should be able to

---

[3] A review of 50 different syllabi for degree project courses from different universities in Sweden, which we conducted in 2016, showed, for example, that the concept of independence appeared a total of 292 times in the syllabi analysed. This means that independence appeared on average almost six times in each syllabus.

independently apply several perspectives or methods, or to evaluate and identify different phenomena, as in the following examples from Swedish universities:

After the course, the student is expected to

- Be able to *independently identify, formulate and solve* a scientific problem relevant to the subject.
- Demonstrate the ability to *make independent judgements* regarding relevant scientific, social and ethical aspects.[4]
Examples from the syllabus Degree project/Bachelor thesis, University College Stockholm, 2022, authors' translation, emphasis added

To pass this module, the student must be able to

- *Independently formulate* one or more relevant sociological/social psychological research questions within the subject area of the thesis.
- *Independently design and motivate* a research design in relation to the formulated research questions
- *Independently carry out* advanced analysis of collected material according to established methods.
- *Independently apply* relevant sociological/social psychological theories to the collected material.
Examples from syllabus Sociology C, Degree project, Umeå University, 2022, authors' translation, emphasis added

As these examples illustrate, in the syllabi we examined, the concept of independence was often linked to the degree project process or to specific parts of the text to be produced, such as the identification of a research problem, the formulation of aim and research questions, the design of the empirical investigation/study, the selection and use of theories and methods, and so on. The significance of student independence in the writing process can be emphasised by linking the concept to processes such as the formulation of research questions, the application of theories and the

---

[4] Ethical aspects of the degree project work are commonly mentioned in syllabi and study guides from different programmes and disciplines, as for instance here.

conduct of analysis, etc. However, independence may also be linked to other activities within degree project courses, such as the defence of degree projects[5] or seminar discussions. In summary, the use of the concept of independence in curricula suggests that there is a great deal of variation, with independence being linked to both process and product and to both academic writing and other activities.

The perspectives and formulations concerning student independence that are evident in programme and course syllabi are then developed into more detailed instructions and information given to students, for example, in study guides and course descriptions, as well as in grading criteria. Although these are not necessarily legally binding documents within higher education, as the syllabus may be in many countries, such policy documents are central to how courses are designed and delivered in practice. Indeed, they may be even more important than the actual syllabus for students' understanding of the course and what is expected of them, as they often provide more detailed information and instructions on what to do and how to do it. In these types of documents, we can see similar patterns as in syllabi, for instance that the formulations around independence can refer to both the text and the process, as in the following example from a Swedish university:

> During the course, the student will develop in-depth knowledge of reproductive health and, based on knowledge of scientific methodology, *independently carry out* a degree project.
>
> The degree project is an *independent project*, which means that the student should be well prepared during the supervision sessions.
>
> Study Guide, Degree Project, Midwifery Programme, Uppsala University, 2023, authors' translation, emphasis added

The complexity of the concept of student independence can also be reflected in the grading criteria, for instance, in that it can be described and considered both as a separate dimension to be graded and as an aspect

---

[5] The procedures for examining degree projects vary between universities and academic programmes, but in many countries, such as Sweden and Russia, students are generally expected to undertake some form of defence of their thesis, where a discussant, who may be a fellow student, a lecturer or sometimes an external party, comments on the text and discusses it with the author in some form of seminar (cf. Zackariasson and Magnusson 2020; Kuzminov and Yudkevich 2022).

that helps to differentiate between grades, as in this example from another Swedish university:

> Pass
> that the student, in the thesis and in supervision, *shows independence* in how the work is structured, in the choices made, and in how different source materials and what emerges in supervision are related to the research problem.
> Pass with distinction
> that the student consistently demonstrates, in the thesis and in supervision, the ability to take *a critical and independent approach* to literature, method, material and their own analysis.
> Study Guide, Primary School Teacher Education, Södertörn University, 2023, authors' translation, emphasis added.

Both the above examples indicate that it is not only the finished text that is ultimately assessed in terms of independence, but also how students deal with the supervision situation, with regard to, for instance, preparation and the ability to take on board and develop the supervisor's comments and advice. Study guides may also include explanatory comments to students on how independence should be understood in the specific context of the degree project. As in the following two examples from study guides at different Swedish universities, where the first one explains what is referred to as a quality dimension, of which the 'independence dimension' is a part:

> The Independence Dimension: The further you progress in your education, the greater the demands placed on the second overall dimension of quality, the ability to demonstrate an independent approach to literature, method, material and one's own analysis. It is about the ability to formulate an original scientific problem or research question that will generate new knowledge. It is also about the ability to critically examine literature and sources, to relate different authors, traditions and approaches to each other, and to reflect on one's own work; choice of material or data, approaches to collection and analysis, empirical and theoretical results. This manifests itself in the ability to distance oneself from one's own study and to place one's work within a tradition. In this context, new questions can be discovered and new hypotheses formulated. It is often this dimension, especially at the higher levels of education, that makes the difference between grades of "pass" and "pass with distinction".

Instructions for degree project writers in Media and Communication Studies, Södertörn University, 2022, authors' translation

In this explanation, the independence dimension is broken down into a number of activities related to independence: demonstrating approaches, formulating problems, reviewing literature, and reflecting on and distancing oneself from one's own work.

In the second example, there is first a description of the process of writing a thesis and then an explanation of how independence should be understood in this particular context.

> You will work very independently, individually and/or in pairs. In the context of the degree project, you will be confronted with complex problems to which you are expected to find independent solutions. Independence here means, firstly, that you have an independent approach to your problem area and, secondly, that you are responsible for and plan your own work process.
> *Course guide, Preschool Teacher Education, Degree project in the specialisation subject, Malmö University, 2019.*

Here it is the students' approach to the problem area that is linked to independence, as well as the students' responsibility for planning the work. It is worth noting that the expected independence of the student is here explicitly extended to include not only students working individually, but also students working in pairs, which can be seen in relation to how the supervision of degree projects often includes aspects of group supervision (cf. Rienecker et al. 2019, 181ff).

All these examples from higher education governing documents at national, university and programme/course level thus illustrate that, while the concept of independence is frequently encountered in relation to degree projects at bachelor's and master's level, the way in which it is understood, described and explained encompasses a variety of dimensions and aspects. Another aspect of this is that the way in which a particular concept is related to other concepts can tell us something about how that concept is understood and what function it may have. For example, in the curricula we examined, the ideal of student independence was often linked to ideals of responsibility or critical thinking. Sometimes these concepts were used interchangeably, and sometimes there was a more hierarchical relationship between the concepts. According to Wittgenstein (1958), this is neither unusual nor unexpected. He introduced the idea of family resemblances, arguing that it is not possible or even desirable to find unambiguous definitions of key concepts as language does not work that way. All concepts, he argued, have a variety of meanings and nuances of meaning based on how the concepts are used in different contexts. What he calls family resemblance is connected to how different concepts are related to each other in many different ways in an intricate network. This fits well with the relationships between concepts such as independence, critical thinking and responsibility, where the concepts have clear similarities and overlaps, but where there are also differences.

For example, the concept of independence can be said to include critical thinking as one of several criteria, but at the same time it appears as one of several criteria for critical thinking. Thus, in addition to vagueness and flexibility, the concepts also exhibit a kind of doubleness (see Fig. 3.1).

Despite the fact that the concept of independence is frequently used and is of great importance in higher education and, more specifically, within a degree project and supervision setting, it is thus not obvious what independence means in the different contexts in which students, supervisors and, not least, examiners find themselves. Even if this is natural when it comes to how language works, in an educational context where the concept of independence is associated with skills that are to be taught and, not least, assessed on the basis of governing documents and grading criteria, there is still a need to make such differences, complexities and variations visible and explicit and, if possible, to build consensus on how it should be understood in each specific academic context.

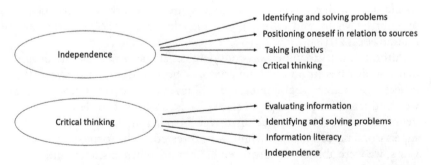

Fig. 3.1 Possible interconnections between independence and critical thinking

Supervisors' Perceptions of Independence

There are at least two dimensions to how independence can be understood in relation to supervision practice. One dimension starts with the students and the fact that they are expected to act independently in the process of completing a degree project. This dimension may involve processes of thinking and reflection as well as the practical work of the degree project, such as searching for literature, conducting an empirical study, writing, and so forth, with the essential characteristic that it is the student who is expected to be the actor. Another dimension starts with the supervisors, as they are the ones who enable and facilitate independence, for example, by opening up for it in the supervision interaction, through scaffolding work or by providing space for student independence in other ways. Both dimensions were discussed in the focus group interviews that we conducted as part of our research project.

The starting point for the focus group discussions was that supervisors were asked to describe freely how they perceived and defined independence in relation to degree project writing and academic supervision. In the discussions, it became clear that independence is one of the multifaceted key concepts in higher education that can be understood and perceived in a variety of ways. There was significant variation in how supervisors described their perceptions of student independence in the supervision context, for example, in terms of how it was expected to manifest itself in different parts of the degree project process, how it might be encouraged, what was considered a minimum level of independence and what was considered more or less advanced independence, and so on. There were also differences in how supervisors described how they related to and dealt with requirements for independence, which were formulated in course syllabi and other governing documents (Magnusson and Zackariasson 2018).

Although the variability was considerable, at the same time there were many similarities in how the supervisors—both within and between the different academic programmes, universities and the two countries where we conducted focus group interviews—talked about and described student independence and their own role in relation to it. Based on the supervisors' perceptions or definitions expressed in the focus group interviews, we were able to identify seven basic approaches to student independence in the material:

1. Taking initiatives
2. Demonstrating originality, creativity and enthusiasm

3. Relating to sources and context
4. Arguing, motivating and making choices
5. Taking responsibility
6. Demonstrating critical thinking and reflection
7. Ability to generalise and synthesise

These basic understandings of what independence might mean in the degree project context can, in turn, have implications for supervision practice and the interaction between supervisor and student. We will explore in more detail below how supervisors talked about this in the focus group material.

Initiative, Originality and Creativity

One of the ways in which student independence was described in the focus group interviews was that it involved students taking initiatives, meaning that in order to be perceived as independent in their work, students were expected to come up with suggestions and ideas for their work and to be active without always being told what to do by the supervisor. As part of this, supervisors described that it was important for students to be well prepared for supervision meetings, for example by having carefully considered the choice of topics, methods and relevant literature, and for students to contribute to initiating the themes and issues to be discussed in supervision meetings. This can be observed in the following excerpt, where a supervisor at a Swedish university described an example of how a former student had demonstrated independence in this respect:

> The student had an idea when coming to the first meeting. An idea that he had come up with himself. What he wanted to do. In other words, he had formulated the research idea independently. He also had suggestions for books that he could use, but which he wanted to check with me. The supervision was characterised by the fact that he always came prepared with a step that he had taken. One step ahead of me, so to speak, and then just wanted to have it confirmed. "Is this OK? What do you think?" and so on. I thought that was a wonderful case of independence in the way he worked.
> *Focus Group Interview 1*[6]

---

[6] All the material in the project has been transcribed in full, but for the sake of readability the extracts used in the book have been adapted to the written language and slightly edited, for example, by removing repetitions and stuttering. Laughter, sighs and other non-verbal expressions are indicated by brackets (laughs), where something has been added or changed

A similar understanding of student independence in the context of the degree project was also expressed in the Russian focus group material, as in this example:

> I want a person to start a discussion. I want them to say: "I'm going to do this and that, but is it right? I want to do this and that, and what would you recommend me?" /.../ Then I can say that if you [a student] do things this way, the result will be like this, because, let's say, you don't know the limitations, you will come across this or that, so think of something else. Roughly speaking, it is a dialogue when a person says they want it this way and I say, "OK, if you want to do this, fine. But if you want to do it differently, that is fine too".
> *Focus Group Interview 10*

As these examples illustrate, taking the initiative and being well prepared are aspects of independence that were primarily expected to be demonstrated in the supervision interaction. But it was also at times linked to the students' education in general or to their future professional role, as in this example from a Swedish university, where taking initiatives is also associated with curiosity:

> I think it's basically about curiosity and wanting to take initiatives on your own. It doesn't matter whether it's practical work in journalism or in the research part. It's about an attitude, but also an ability to first absorb theoretical and methodological knowledge and things like that. But with the help of those, to take initiatives on your own. Not to regurgitate what is written in books, but to use it and, above all, to create something new and to show that you want to do so. That you are looking for new knowledge and not just repeating what someone else has done.
> *Focus Group Interview 3*

If the students demonstrate independence by taking initiatives and being well prepared for each meeting, the supervisors' practice will largely consist of confirming and giving feedback on the students' ideas,

---

due to pseudonymisation by square brackets [place], pauses in speech by three dots ... and where a condensation has been made by excluding text by /.../. We have occasionally commented in a footnote where idiomatic expressions have been lost in translation.

rather than the supervisors suggesting possible approaches and the students responding to these. When students show independence in this way, it can be a good starting point for scaffolding work where both students and supervisors are active in the process (cf. van de Pol 2012; van de Pol et al. 2010). However, supervisors in our material described student curiosity and initiative as aspects that may be difficult for supervisors to influence or encourage. There is a risk that supervision may actually contribute to stifling student interest and curiosity, if the supervisor has to curb overly exuberant ideas or point out that what the student wants to do is not feasible within the existing framework of the degree project.

Closely related to initiative and curiosity is the notion that independence in a degree project context is about originality, creativity and enthusiasm, as indicated in the previous example. When focus group participants described student independence in terms of originality, they emphasised, among other things, the importance of doing something different from what many others have already done:

> And then, I think, simply... the ability to handle the genre in a casual way. The ability to make analyses and relate to which theory you used. How you approach it. What you can do. If you do some kind of study that is a bit original or you do one of these millions of studies of five educators who have an opinion on something. Or if you actually go in and do a completely different study.
> *Focus Group Interview 4*

Although the interviewed supervisors talked about originality, there was no explicit expectation that the students would achieve something completely new that no one had done before. Still, in order to be perceived as independent, students were expected to develop something of their own in one way or another, or to make some contribution to existing knowledge. This, in turn, is connected to the perception that independence is associated with creativity and students having a strong interest in and commitment to their work.

> The independence I'm looking for... You said it wasn't about creativity in a strong sense, but I think it is, sort of, about creativity in a weaker sense. That is, the students should be active and really create what they do in this degree project. They should be active in formulating questions that nobody has

done for them and that this is a creative process. It is also connected to the fact that they have to make choices, decisions during the process and this is also what they have to defend during the thesis defence. It also means that if students are independent in that sense, they can be proud of what they have done. Nobody else has done this. Nobody else would have done it in the same way.
Focus Group Interview 2

In many respects, this dimension of independence, that it involves students being creative in one way or another, was considered to be expressed in the supervision interaction, for instance in the articulation of a topic or research questions for the degree project. In this example, from a focus group interview at a Russian university, it was also connected to the academic programme and the future profession of the degree project students:

> I think that for students who are very independent, responsible and motivated, it is very important to try to articulate a topic themselves, as D said. Why? Because we are a creative department after all, we have mostly creative people here, and every creative person needs that freedom. Let them articulate it, even if it will be awkwardly done, they will understand it later, after your explanation. But this moment of trust, this chance that is given, is very important for our profession and our field, I think.
> *Focus Group Interview 5*

As perceptions of student independence associated with creativity and originality were linked to specific parts of the degree project process, such as choosing the topic for the degree project or formulating the research questions, these aspects of independence could also become visible in the finished work. As shown in the previous sections, aspects of originality or creativity may also be included in governing documents for degree project courses, and are sometimes mentioned in grading criteria and intended learning outcomes. Thus, originality and creativity may become something that supervisors need to address in a more specific and explicit way in their supervision practice, for example by commenting on students' thesis ideas or first drafts in terms of whether these are sufficiently original to meet the assessment criteria.

Making Decisions, Relating to Others and Taking Responsibility

Another common way of understanding student independence that emerged from the focus group interviews concerned students' ability to relate to other sources of scholarship, theoretical concepts or research traditions and to position their own study or parts of their study in relation to these. This is an aspect of independence that, according to the supervisors interviewed, could be demonstrated in the supervision interaction, in the finished text and in the defence of the degree project. The ability to engage more deeply with other scholars' research or theories was sometimes described as a relatively advanced level of independence which could not be expected of all students, as in this example from a Swedish university:

> Preferably if you have a study or a theory or something that you can be independent in relation to. For example: "I think Rosenblatt is wrong about this because…" And sort of really position yourself independently, starting from… that is, having something that they position themselves against. I think that's very independent at an advanced level. That's something we can rarely expect in these "Degree Project 1"… "Help, now I'm going to write my first degree project! What should the title page look like?" We can't really expect that from them. Maybe we should be happy if they've just written the text themselves and not copied someone else's. But when it comes to this greater independence… That you then really position yourself against something and take a stand.
> *Focus Group Interview 1*

In this example, relating one's study to something is partly described as positioning oneself by being critical of other scholars or previous research. There were, however, many instances in our material where supervisors were rather talking about this aspect of student independence in relation to the ability to see similarities or agreement with other studies. In order to be perceived as independent, students were furthermore expected to be able to relate not only to theories or previous research but also to academic norms and traditions, as well as to supervisors and their advice, in other words to the academic context they found themselves in. The importance of the supervisors in the degree project process was often emphasised, for example, by the interviewed supervisors stressing that independence in the context of a degree project does not mean that the students do the work completely on their own:

> /.../ you shouldn't just do something on your own without connecting to anything. Instead, you have to show that you can connect to traditions and norms and the supervisor's perspectives and that this is what independence is. Not that you, like, write a text alone.
> *Focus Group Interview 1*

When supervisors talked about the importance of relating or connecting to sources, literature, context and supervisors' perspectives, it could be about agreeing or disagreeing, but also about identifying similarities and differences across different perspectives and addressing these, or developing the advice given. It was neither necessary nor expected to agree with or follow all of the supervisor's advice. Rather, it was described as a matter of understanding why one should do one thing or another:

> I often /.../ say to the student. It's really you who are going to write this degree project, not me. So you have to decide for yourself if you think this is the most appropriate way to do it. That's what I usually say. Because I don't think that independence is opposed to following rules, but I think the important thing is that... If you are independent, you have to know why you are following these rules. You have to relate to them. So that's what's central and I think I work a lot with that in my supervision.
> *Focus Group Interview 2*

This attitude is closely linked to another fundamental and recurring perception of what student independence might entail in the degree project context—the ability of students to make their own choices and to be able to motivate and argue for them. Several supervisors in our material emphasised the importance of students taking responsibility for the choices they make in the course of their degree project work, whether or not these are the result of the supervisor's advice and recommendations:

> I don't think independence can be about being free from supervisors or genre or anything like that. That is not possible. Rather, it is in a sense that you take an active part in the choices that you make. That you have understood why you are making the choices that you are making, regardless of whether the origin is that it came out of your own head, that it is creative, or that it came out of dialogue with the supervisor or something. That you are actually able to... That you understand why you make the choices that you want to make. And that I'm the one who made the choices, no matter where they came from.
> *Focus Group Interview 4*

According to the supervisors in the focus group interviews, the significance of students understanding and standing by the choices they make in the course of their degree project work is related to their being able to feel more satisfied with their own performance. But it may also be related to the role and practice of the supervisor. If both the supervisors and the students agree that the students must ultimately be able to stand up for the choices they have made along the way, the supervisors have greater freedom to make suggestions and recommendations on which the students can then take a position and develop. It is also linked to how the role of the supervisors is related to that of the examiners. Although independence through the ability to motivate and argue for one's choices can be expressed both in the supervision interaction and in the finished thesis text, several of the supervisors highlighted the degree project defence as an occasion when this becomes particularly important:

> A minimum requirement I have set for my students is that they should be able to justify everything they do. Even if I would have told them 'Do this', they will at the final seminar, if they are asked: "Why do you write this way? Why did you choose this theoretical approach?", they should be able to make a good case. If they can do that, I think they have at least achieved a minimum level of independence.
> *Focus Group Interview 1*

The fact that students are expected to stand up for their choices and be able to justify them is, in turn, intricately linked to another fundamental understanding of what student independence might mean in the context of degree project writing—taking responsibility. In the focus groups, it emerged that the responsibility students were expected to take for their degree project work could refer to practical matters, such as following the guidelines for reference systems, following the templates for degree projects, or meeting deadlines. The desired responsibility also concerned more general aspects, such as the quality and originality of the degree project and being accountable for all choices made along the way. As in this example from a focus group interview at a Russian university:

> We should make it clear from the beginning that this is the students' job, their responsibility and their willingness to work hard. I act as a partner, as a facilitator, as a guiding support. I also think that independence has a lot to do with a sense of responsibility, when a person is accountable for what they do. I think that is the way it should be.
> *Focus Group Interview 8*

Taking responsibility for the degree project work by being accountable for the quality and all the choices made was subsequently a dimension of student independence that the interviewed supervisors associated to a high degree with the defence of the thesis. The desired and expected responsibility could also be associated with the ethical aspects of the degree project work, in the sense that students are expected and required to write their degree projects themselves, without plagiarism or undue help, and that they are responsible for ensuring that this is the case:

> I would add another thing. I tell my students, those I supervise, right from the start that the responsibility for the quality of what they write in general, and the originality of the text in terms of copyright compliance in particular, lies entirely with them. /.../ And that's their responsibility for independent work. The primary responsibility.
> *Focus Group Interview 6*

This understanding of student independence in the degree project context is thus related to how the interviewed supervisors talked about the significance of originality as a dimension of student independence, where they underlined that one aspect of originality is not copying or plagiarising other people's work. These last quotes suggest that the expectation of responsibility is something that is communicated to students in a relatively direct and explicit way, either from the supervisor's side or through course handbooks and degree project guides. However, while this may be the ambition of individual supervisors or within a particular programme or degree project course, this does not mean that it is always obvious to students what they are expected to take responsibility for and to what extent, or what advice and recommendations from the supervisor are actually non-negotiable if students are to pass their work.

Critical Thinking, Reflection and Generalisation

In the examples discussed above, supervisors talked about both minimum levels of independence and more advanced forms that they did not expect all students to achieve during the degree project course. We will discuss two other such more advanced aspects of student independence: the ability to think critically and reflect, and the ability to generalise and synthesise on the basis of one's own study.

In the analysis of course syllabi and governing documents at the beginning of the chapter, we discussed how independence and critical thinking were often perceived to be interrelated in the degree project context. In the focus group interviews, student independence was associated with critical thinking at two different levels: 1) with activities such as argumentation, analysis, expressing one's own opinion, problem solving and so on, and 2) with the attitude that students display towards these activities, for example being expected to approach such activities with a critical eye. Independence as critical thinking is close to the view of independence as relating to sources, theories and previous research and positioning one's own study in relation to these. But the notion of independence as critical thinking involves something more than, for instance, comparing different sources or perspectives, as shown in this example from a focus group interview at a Swedish university:

> I usually talk about breadth. That if you are independent, you can manage to be both broad and narrow. That is, if you are given the assignment that you should be able to compare different perspectives. You should not just focus on one source, but on several that you should be able to compare, but you should also be able to be critical in relation to this.
> *Focus Group Interview 3*

Independent students were thus expected to be able to read academic texts and to approach sources and theories with a critical eye, but they were also expected to be able to look critically at their own work and reflect on their process, as the following focus group interview examples indicate:

> Because I think that this thing with independence, as I have interpreted it, is about them training themselves to think critically about their own choices. Different methods that can be used and materials... Like the problem they are going to investigate. For me it has like... this that they should train themselves in their independence, it's very much about them learning to reflect critically.
> *Focus Group Interview 4*

At first you tell them one thing and they bring you something of their own and it gets a bit messy. And then comes the growing up and independent realisation that in some points they were wrong, some other points need to be changed, because they happened beforehand, and other things are effects

of these causes. And then the student reflects on these things, changes them and walks around proudly because he has done it himself. /.../ I like this manifestation of independence because it's like watching your own child grow up, watching them start to talk, walk, and so on.
Focus Group Interview 9

This aspect of independence, the ability to think critically and reflect, is a competence that could be expressed during the degree project process, in the finished text and in the defence of the degree project. That this, according to some of the supervisors interviewed, was a level of independence that could not be demanded of all students, also applies to the final aspect of independence that emerged in our focus group material: the ability to generalise and synthesise. These aspects of student independence involved pulling together all the threads of the degree project, drawing conclusions and placing one's own study in a wider context. Unlike many of the other aspects of independence, this was something that was assumed to be expressed primarily in the finished thesis text, more specifically in the discussion or conclusion sections:

> I'm thinking the discussion... when they're going to tie all these pieces together... Then I think it usually becomes quite obvious how independent they are.
> *Focus Group Interview 4*

Since most of the supervisors involved in our research project came from the humanities and social sciences, generalisation was not primarily a question of statistics and significance, but rather the ability to contextualise and place one's own study in a larger context, such as education or media policy, media debates about school and education, and so on. If students were able to do this in the concluding parts of the degree projects, they were perceived as having come far in their independence.

Pedagogical Implications of an Elusive Concept

In the focus group interviews, supervisors described how they tried in different ways to communicate to students what was expected of them in terms of responsibility, making their own choices and being able to argue for them, the originality of the degree project, and so on, although they did not always talk about this in terms of independence. This can be seen as an example of the developing of students' academic literacies, in the sense that it highlights how much more than writing techniques is required of students, as well as in the sense that supervisors seek to illuminate the epistemological understandings that students need to be able to manage in different academic contexts (cf. Lea and Stierer 2000). It also became clear that many of the supervisors found it difficult, sometimes even frustrating, to try to encourage student independence, as the following examples from our focus group material show:

> Those students who are not interested in working independently. Who just want to know if this is right or wrong… The supervision resources that I have are not enough to get them to think about or see this in any other way.
> *Focus Group Interview 2*

> We have to distinguish between what we expect and what actually happens. Of course, we expect a maximum of independence, starting with the choice of the topic and ending with the attempt to find out the methodology, producing a ton of ideas and so on. What actually happens /…/ is that independence often ends at the stage of deciding on a topic at best.
> *Focus Group Interview 10*

As described by supervisors, the difficulties and frustrations stem in part from the need to strike a balance between allowing students to make their own decisions and follow their own ideas and whims, and the demands placed on the form, quality and timeframe of degree projects. This is also partly related to the fact that independence is an elusive and multifaceted concept, which makes it difficult to know, for example, which aspects are most important to encourage and at which stages of the supervision process this should be done. Not least given that students tend to be at very different levels when they start the degree project process and thus have varying preconditions for achieving the expected goals, something that the interviewed supervisors were also well aware of:

> You know, students are different. There are those who are motivated to do research and those who are not. /…/ In terms of independence and the relationship between a supervisor and a student in BA programmes, of course you expect some independence from a student because it is their work. However, sometimes students expect you to tell them what to write, or even better, to offer them something that's already been done, so that

they can make something worthwhile out of it. You know, because it takes hard work to do something on your own.
Focus Group Interview 7

Another aspect of this was that supervisors in the focus groups often defined independence in terms of what it was not. By far the most common was to explicitly state that independence is not about working alone or all by yourself, as the following example illustrates.

> Independence doesn't mean working alone. You can work independently even if you work with someone. For me, independence means thinking for yourself. And as a student, you have the supervisor to relate to, but perhaps also if you are writing together with another student.
> *Focus Group Interview 3*

Since this kind of negation of student independence, i.e. an emphasis on what it is not, was formulated by so many of the supervisors who participated in the focus groups, it can be concluded that there is an implicit or taken for granted norm or notion that student independence means working alone, which the supervisors explicitly positioned themselves against. This can, thus, be seen as an example of taken for granted norms or notions that researchers in the field of academic literacies believe need to be made visible (cf. Lea and Stierer 2000). Such a notion is also at odds with a relatively accepted and widespread ideal of teaching and a view of learning in which learning takes place in interaction (cf. Dysthe 1999).

Cases where students for some reason chose to work entirely on their own, what one supervisor described as total independence, were also explicitly raised as problematic by supervisors. In their eyes, this usually meant students who had gone astray and were too free in their interpretation of what academic work required, or students who did not feel that they needed to learn anything new at all. As can be seen from the examples given earlier in this chapter, grading criteria for degree project courses can include the requirement for students to demonstrate the ability to respond to the advice and recommendations of supervisors, which is not possible if students are working entirely on their own without any supervision. In addition to this being a pedagogical stance in the sense that it is seen as a key skill to be able to work with and develop comments from the supervisor, the inclusion of such aspects in the grading criteria for degree project courses may also be motivated by the rather significant risk that students who appear to be avoiding supervision are in fact not doing the work they are supposed to be doing. In other words, that they are using prohibited aids or methods to produce the degree project, such as specific, non-allowed AI writing tools, plagiarism or getting someone else to write it for them. In this respect, student independence is also tied to the ethical aspects of the research and degree project process.

Highlighting perceptions and interpretations of key concepts within higher education, such as student independence, may also be essential to address any lack of consensus that has implications for the supervision process and the assessment of student performance. For example, a lack of consensus among supervisors about what constitutes student independence may affect how much or what kind of help students receive in working on their degree projects. Furthermore, lack of consensus on key concepts in relation to assessment is obviously problematic for the equal treatment of students. It is also problematic in terms of transparency, for example in that students' and supervisors' perceptions of what student independence entails and how it is demonstrated may differ. In a couple of smaller surveys that we have conducted, students at the beginning of a degree project course at a Swedish university were asked how they perceived and understood the requirements for independence. The absolute majority of students responded with different versions of 'working alone', which is significantly at odds with how the supervisors we interviewed reasoned about independence, as we have shown. Many of the supervisors who participated in the focus group discussions also said that they rarely or never explicitly discussed independence and the related expectations and norms with the students they supervised.

The focus group material also showed that independence is not usually perceived as something that students do or do not have in an absolute sense. Rather, supervisors discussed independence in terms of degrees and levels. As we have seen in the previous examples, they could speak of little or basic independence and minimum levels of independence, as well as great or maximum independence, or independence at a more advanced level. For example, a minimum or basic level of independence that all students had to achieve might involve choosing a topic for the degree project, while a maximum or advanced level of independence that only some students were expected to achieve might involve critical thinking, positioning, and so on.

Supervisors also distinguished between several types of independence, further illustrating the complexity of the concept. In this example, for example, a distinction is made between independence understood as (critical) thinking and doing.

> I think there are two different parts in the degree project. One is the actual doing, like actually going out and searching for literature. /.../ And the other part is the critical thinking. And I feel that students can be very independent in their doing, but not so independent in their critical thinking. Or vice versa. Some students are very independent in their critical thinking, but they don't get to the actual doing.
> Focus Group Interview 4

Several supervisors discussed in different ways a division of the concept of student independence based on this contrast between cognitive thinking and practical doing. Taking initiatives, planning one's work and making choices could be examples of doing, while critical thinking and creativity were examples of thinking. This kind of differentiation or division makes the concept more tangible and concrete. It becomes a way of structuring a complex concept, which may provide an opportunity for discussion and, in the long run, more consensus on how to understand it.

A Model to Start With

As we have shown and discussed, independence is one of the key concepts associated with the supervision of degree projects, at the same time as it is a concept that is multifaceted and can be understood in many ways. According to the supervisors interviewed, independence can manifest itself at different stages of the degree project process—from the planning of the work, through the literature search and writing, to the submission of the finished text and the defence of the final product. There are also differences in perceptions of where independence is to be found: in the brain, in the text, in speaking or in doing, in the process or in the product. Furthermore, the concept can be described as relative, as supervisors did not talk about independence as something that students have or do not have, but rather that independence can occur to different degrees. From the perspective of equal treatment and students' rights, it can be problematic if different supervisors, departments or higher education institutions use significantly divergent definitions and criteria of such concepts in the practice of supervision and in the assessment and examination of degree projects.

Table 3.2 Independence matrix

	In the process	In the finished text	During the defence
Taking initiatives	X		
Demonstrating originality, creativity, and enthusiasm	X	X	
Relating to sources and context	X	X	
Arguing, motivating, and making choices	X	X	X
Taking responsibility	X		X
Demonstrating critical thinking and reflection	X	X	X
Ability to generalise and synthesise		X	

In other words, there may be a need for a collegial discussion in which supervisors' different perceptions of independence can be made explicit and visible for discussion and comparison with others. In such a collegial discussion, the matrix we present in Table 3.2 can serve as a tool. In the table, we have grouped along one axis the different perceptions of independence that emerged in our material, and along the other axis the different contexts or stages in which independence was described as emerging: during the supervision process, in the finished text, or during the final discussion or defence of the degree project. We would like to emphasise that process and product (the finished text) do not function as opposites, but as different parts or perspectives of the same competence. According to some supervisors, the process, or parts of it, can also be identified in the final product.

The marked crosses indicate how the different contexts were referred to by the supervisors in the focus group interviews, but where they should be put is, of course, open to discussion according to the experiences and perceptions of those involved in the supervision and examination of degree projects in a particular setting. As can be seen from the matrix, several aspects of independence may be identified either during the process, in the finished text or in the defence of the final product. Here, we would like to particularly emphasise that many aspects of independence can be related to the process of the degree project and then indirectly to the supervisors and what they enable, encourage, identify and assess in their supervisory practice.

From an academic literacies perspective, it is emphasised that higher education is characterised by different epistemologies and norm systems, which means that what is perceived as valuable and good varies not only between but also within different local academic contexts such as departments and disciplines (see e.g. Lea and Stierer 2000; Lea and Street 2006; Lillis 2001; Lillis and Scott 2007; Shanahan and Shanahan 2012). The independence matrix we present here should consequently be viewed from the perspective that there are no inherently better or worse criteria for student independence, and that there is no specific criterion that is the 'right' one to refer to in supervision. Rather, it is a matter of trying to articulate existing epistemological norms as a supervisor, to be able to verbalise and discuss one's own perceptions and thinking, and to discuss them with colleagues. For this purpose, a model of this kind could be a starting point.

* * *

The fact that there may be different understandings and interpretations of concepts that are central to the degree project process is significant for individual supervisors and students, as well as for supervision practice in a particular context, and for the ideals and expectations of academic writing that are dominant in a local academic context. The view of independence, for example, may be important for the tools that supervisors use in their supervision practice, as well as for perceptions of what the relationship between supervisor and student should be. In the next chapter, we will discuss this relationship in more detail, based on the recorded supervision conversations from our research project.

References

Agencia Estatal Boletín Oficial del Estado. 2023. BOE 133 Código de Universidades. Madrid: Agencia Estatal Boletín Oficial del Estado. Accessed November 29, 2023. www.boe.es/biblioteca_juridica/.

Almulla, Mohammed Abdullatif. 2023. Constructivism Learning Theory: A paradigm for Students' Critical Thinking, Creativity, and Problem solving to Affect Academic Performance in Higher Education. *Cogent Education* 10 (1): 1–25. https://doi.org/10.1080/2331186X.2023.2172929.

Aprianti, Fitri, and Eline Rozaliya Winarto. 2023. Learner Autonomy in the Context of MB-KM Policy: University Teachers' Beliefs and Practices. *English Review: Journal of English Education* 11 (2): 589–598.

Australian Qualifications Framework Council. 2013. *Australian Qualifications Framework*. Australian Qualifications Framework Council. Accessed November 29, 2023. www.aqf.edu.au.

Bartholomew, Scott R., and Matthew D. Jones. 2022. A Systematized Review of Research with Adaptive Comparative Judgment (ACJ) in Higher Education. *International Journal of Technology and Design Education* 32 (2): 1159–1190. https://doi.org/10.1007/s10798-020-09642-6.

Brew, Angela, and Constanze Saunders. 2020. Making Sense of Research-based Learning in Teacher Education. *Teaching and Teacher Education* 87 (1–11): 102935. https://doi.org/10.1016/j.tate.2019.102935.

Brodin, Eva. 2020. Development of Critical, Creative, and Independent Thinking. In *Doctoral Supervision. In Theory and Practice*, ed. Eva Brodin, Jitka Lindén, Anders Sonesson, and Åsa Lindberg-Sand, 165–204. Lund: Studentlitteratur.

Council of Ministers of Education Canada. 2007. *Ministerial Statement on Quality Assurance of Degree Education in Canada*. Council of Ministers of Education Canada. Accessed November 29, 2023. https://www.cmec.ca/9/Publication.html?cat=35&search=degree%20education.

Cukurova, Mutlu, Judith Bennett, and Ian Abrahams. 2017. Students' Knowledge Acquisition and Ability to Apply Knowledge into Different Science Contexts in Two Different Independent Learning Settings. *Research in Science & Technological Education* 36 (1): 17–34. https://doi.org/10.1080/02635143.2017.1336709.

Davies, Martin. 2011. Introduction to Special Issue on Critical Thinking in Higher Education. *Higher Education Research & Development* 30 (3): 255–260. https://doi.org/10.1080/07294360.2011.562145.

Davies, Martin, and Ronald Barnett. 2015. *Palgrave Handbook of Critical Thinking in Higher Education*. New York: Palgrave Macmillan.

Duff, Patricia A. 2012. Identity, Agency and Second Language Acquisition. In *The Routledge Handbook of Second Language Acquisition*, ed. Susan M. Gass and Alison Mackey, 410–426. London & New York: Routledge.

Dufva, Hannele, and Mari Aro. 2015. Dialogical View on Language Learners' Agency: Connecting Intrapersonal with Interpersonal. In *Theorizing and Analyzing Agency in Second Language Learning: Interdisciplinary Approaches*, ed. Ping Deters, Xuesong Gao, Elisabeth R. Miller, and Gergana Vitanova, 37–53. Bristol: Multilingual Matters.

Dysthe, Olga. 1999. Dialogue Theory as a Tool for Understanding Interactive Learning Processess. *Literacy and Numeracy Studies* 9 (1): 39–64.

Federal Ministry of Education, Science and Research. 2002. Federal Act on the Organisation of Universities and their Studies (Universities Act 2002 – UG).

Federal Ministry of Education, Science and Research, accessed 2023-11-28, https://www.bmbwf.gv.at/en/Topics/Higher-education---universities/Higher-Education-Legislation.html.

Kuzminov, Yaroslav, and Maria Yudkevich. 2022. *Higher Education in Russia*. Baltimore: Johns Hopkins University Press.

Lau, Ken. 2017. 'The Most Important Thing is to Learn the Way to Learn': Evaluating the Effectiveness of Independent Learning by Perceptual Changes. *Assessment & Evaluation in Higher Education* 42 (3): 415–430. https://doi.org/10.1080/02602938.2015.1118434.

Lea, Mary R., and Barry Stierer. 2000. *Student Writing in Higher Education: New Contexts*. London: Society for Research into Higher Education.

Lea, Mary R., and Brian V. Street. 2006. The "Academic Literacies" Model: Theory and Applications. *Theory Into Practice* 45 (4): 368–377. https://doi.org/10.1207/s15430421tip4504_11.

Lee, Anne. 2019. *Successful Research Supervision: Advising Students Doing Research*. 2nd ed. London: Routledge.

Lillis, Theresa. 2001. *Student Writing: Access, Regulation, Desire*. London: Routledge.

Lillis, Theresa, and Mary Scott. 2007. Defining Academic Literacies Research: Issues of Epistemology, Ideology and Strategy. *Journal of Applied Linguistics* 4 (1): 5–32. https://doi.org/10.1558/japl.v4i1.5.

Magnusson, Jenny, and Maria Zackariasson. 2018. Student Independence in Undergraduate Projects. Different Understandings in Different Academic Contexts. *Journal of Further and Higher Education* 43 (10): 1404–1419. https://doi.org/10.1080/0309877X.2018.1490949.

Meyer, Bill, Naomi Haywood, Darshan Sachdev, and Sally Faraday. 2008. *What is Independent Learning and What are the Benefits for Students?* Research Report 51. London: Department for Children, Schools and Families.

Ministry of Education and research. 2008. *Standard of Higher Education*, Republic of Estonia Ministry of Education and Research. Accessed November 30, 2023. https://www.riigiteataja.ee/en/eli/524092014013/consolide.

Ministry of Education and Research. 2019. *Higher Education Act*. Republic of Estonia Ministry of Education and Research. Accessed November 30, 2023. https://www.riigiteataja.ee/en/eli/529082019022/consolide.

Ministry of Higher Education and Science. 2013. *Ministerial Order on Bachelor and Master's (Candidatus) Programmes at Universities (the University Programme Order)*. Ministry of Higher Education and Science. Accessed November 28, 2023. https://ufm.dk/en/legislation/prevailing-laws-and-regulations/education/universities.

Moore, Tim John. 2011. Critical Thinking and Disciplinary Thinking: A Continuing Debate. *Higher Education Research & Development* 30 (3): 261–274. https://doi.org/10.1080/07294360.2010.501328.

NOKUT Norwegian Agency for Quality Assurance in Education. 2023. *Norwegian Qualifications Framework for Lifelong Learning.* Accessed November 29, 2023. https://www.nokut.no/en/norwegian-education/the-norwegian-qualifications-framework-for-lifelong-learning/.

van de Pol, Janneke. E. (2012). *Scaffolding in teacher-student interaction: exploring, measuring, promoting and evaluating scaffolding.* [Thesis, fully internal, Universiteit van Amsterdam]. https://dare.uva.nl/search?identifier=640b82ba-c27b-42d3-b9f8-fe08b1e0081f.

van de Pol, Janneke, Monique Volman, and Jos. Beishuizen. 2010. Scaffolding in Teacher–Student Interaction: A Decade of Research. *Educational Psychology Review* 22: 271–296. https://doi.org/10.1007/s10648-010-9127-6.

Reitsma, Lizette. 2023. Complexities of a Hypothetical Co-supervision Case: On roles, Expectations, Independence. *Journal of Teaching and Learning in Higher Education* 4 (2): 1–8. https://doi.org/10.24834/jotl.4.2.882.

Rico, Heidy, Mario Alberto de la Puente Pacheco, Adrian Pabon, and Ivan Portnoy. 2023. Evaluating the Impact of Simulation-based Instruction on Critical Thinking in the Colombian Caribbean: An Experimental Study. *Cogent education* 10 (2): 1–15. https://doi.org/10.1080/2331186X.2023.2236450.

Rienecker, Lotte, Gitte Wichmann-Hansen, and Peter Stray Jørgensen. 2019. *God vejledning af specialer, bacheloroppgaver og projekter.* Frederiksberg: Samfundslitteratur.

Shanahan, Timothy, and Cynthia Shanahan. 2012. What Is Disciplinary Literacy and Why Does It Matter? *Topics in Language Disorders* 32 (1): 7–18. https://doi.org/10.1097/TLD.0b013e318244557a.

Stoten, David William. 2014. Are we there Yet? Progress in Promoting Independent Learning in a Sixth Form College. *Educational Studies* 40 (4): 452–455. https://doi.org/10.1080/03055698.2014.930342.

Swedish Council for Higher Education. 1993. The Higher Education Ordinance Annex 2, Svensk Författningssamling 1993:100. Ministry of Education and Research. Accessed November 29, 2023. https://www.uhr.se/en/start/laws-and-regulations/Laws-and-regulations/The-Higher-Education-Ordinance/Annex-2.

Wass, Rob, Tony Harland, and Alison Mercer. 2011. Scaffolding Critical Thinking in the Zone of Proximal Development. *Higher Education Research & Development* 30 (3): 317–328. https://doi.org/10.1080/07294360.2010.489237.

Wichmann-Hansen, Gitte, and Karl-Johan Schmidt Nielsen. 2023. Can hands-on supervision get out of hand? The correlation between directive supervision and doctoral student independence in a Danish study context. *Scandinavian Journal of Educational Research* (ahead-of-print): 1–16. https://doi.org/10.1080/00313831.2023.2204113.

Wittgenstein, Ludwig. 1958. *Philosophische Untersuchungen: Philosophical investigations*. 2nd ed. Trans. G.E.M. Anscombe. Oxford: Blackwell.

Wollast, Robin, Cristina Aelenei, Johann Chevalère, Nicolas Van der Linden, Benoît Galand, Assaad Azzi, Mariane Frenay, and Olivier Klein. 2023. Facing the Dropout Crisis among PhD Candidates: The Role of Supervisor Support in Emotional Well-being and Intended Doctoral Persistence among Men and Women. *Studies in Higher Education (Dorchester-on-Thames)* 48 (6): 813–828. https://doi.org/10.1080/03075079.2023.2172151.

Zackariasson, Maria. 2019. Encouraging Student Independence: Perspectives on Scaffolding in Higher Education Supervision. *Journal of Applied Research in Higher Education* 12 (3): 495–505. https://doi.org/10.1108/JARHE-01-2019-0012.

Zackariasson, Maria, and Jenny Magnusson. 2020. Academic Literacies and International Mobility. The Organization and Supervision of Degree Projects in Sweden and Russia. *Cogent Education* 7 (1): 1–12. 1855770. https://doi.org/10.1080/2331186X.2020.1855770.

Open Access This chapter is licensed under the terms of the Creative Commons Attribution-NonCommercial-NoDerivatives 4.0 International License (http://creativecommons.org/licenses/by-nc-nd/4.0/), which permits any noncommercial use, sharing, distribution and reproduction in any medium or format, as long as you give appropriate credit to the original author(s) and the source, provide a link to the Creative Commons license and indicate if you modified the licensed material. You do not have permission under this license to share adapted material derived from this chapter or parts of it.

The images or other third party material in this chapter are included in the chapter's Creative Commons license, unless indicated otherwise in a credit line to the material. If material is not included in the chapter's Creative Commons license and your intended use is not permitted by statutory regulation or exceeds the permitted use, you will need to obtain permission directly from the copyright holder.

CHAPTER 4

The Supervisor-Student Relationship

As we discussed in the introductory parts of the book, the relationship between supervisors and students is an essential part of the supervision process and the degree project work. The type of supervisor-student relationship that prevails in a particular supervision situation will affect, for example, the tools used by the supervisors and the demands and expectations placed on the students. How then can you, as a supervisor, contribute to this relationship being positive and constructive? In this chapter, we discuss several aspects of this, including the balance between the professional and the personal in supervision, and how the design of the supervision conversation itself can affect the relationship between supervisor and student.

Building a Relationship

Although a considerable amount of supervision time is usually spent on activities such as giving feedback on texts and drafts written by the students and students informing supervisors about the progress of their work and problems they have encountered (cf. Vehviläinen 2012), supervision also consists of interactions that contribute in several ways to the development of the student-supervisor relationship. As we discussed in the introductory parts of the book, the relationship between the supervisors and the students and their different roles in relation to each other is an aspect that is described as crucial in much of the research on supervision and in

© The Author(s) 2024
M. Zackariasson, J. Magnusson, *Supervising Student Independence*,
https://doi.org/10.1007/978-3-031-66371-0_4

many of the handbooks written on the subject.[1] It is of obvious relevance to the supervision of postgraduate students, not least because a doctoral thesis takes several years to complete and the work often involves a great deal of interaction and varying degrees of collaboration between supervisor and student (e.g. Fan et al. 2018; Hjelm 2015; Mainhard et al. 2009; Wichmann-Hansen and Schmidt Nielsen 2023; Jacobsen et al. 2021; Schneijderberg 2021). Although a master's thesis or degree project does not take as long and generally does not involve as much interaction or developed relationships, the supervisor-student relationship is also important in this context (e.g. Ädel et al. 2023; e.g. Agricola et al. 2021; Van Veldhuizen et al. 2021; Lee 2019; Vereijken et al. 2018; Rienecker et al. 2019).

Building a good relationship between supervisors and students in the context of degree project supervision can involve fairly basic aspects, such as how to greet students when you first meet, how to start and end supervision meetings, what questions supervisors ask students about things beyond the thesis work, and also what such questions students ask supervisors. If, as a supervisor, you have many students at the same time and not enough time to spend with each of them, this kind of interaction—chatting about the weather, summer plans or what you did last weekend—may seem unnecessary and like a waste of time. However, even such basic and seemingly trivial aspects can contribute to the development of a supervisor-student relationship characterised by students seeing it as possible or appealing to be active in the joint scaffolding work that the supervision process can entail (cf. van de Pol 2012; van de Pol et al. 2010).

It may also help the supervisor to gain insight into the students' preconditions and goals for the work, as well as the struggles and problems they encounter along the way. In other words, it helps to determine what level the students are at and to establish contingency, which makes it easier for the supervisor to decide how best to design the supervision and which

---

[1] Another interesting aspect is the relationship between supervisors in cases where more than one supervisor is involved in the supervision process. In doctoral supervision, this is quite common, with a main supervisor and co-supervisors, and the significance of their relationship has been discussed in recent research (Almlöv and Grubbström 2023; Padyab and Lundgren 2023; Reitsma 2023). In the degree project context, there may also occasionally be more than one supervisor involved in a degree project process or in supervision meetings, for example, when supervisors within the same programme or course coordinate their supervision meetings. As we do not have examples of this in our material, we will not discuss it further here.

parts or aspects are most important to spend time on (cf. van de Pol et al. 2012, 2015, 2019). In the documented supervision interaction in our project, it was evident that supervisors spent a considerable amount of supervision time trying to find out where the students were in the degree project process. For example, they could ask explicit questions, both during the supervision sessions and via email, about how students were progressing with different aspects of the degree project work: the collection of empirical material, the writing process, experiences from seminars within the course, or problems that students had encountered, and so on.

In the focus group interviews, several of the participating supervisors emphasised another aspect of providing contingent support in the supervision context—that students have different personalities, backgrounds and prior knowledge, and that supervision needs to be calibrated accordingly in order for it to be useful and constructive for the thesis work. In one of the focus groups at a Russian university, one of the supervisors described it as follows:

> Different people need different approaches. Although we are working on the same task, we always have to take into account [the student's] personality, abilities and level of responsibility.
> *Focus Group Interview 6*

The need to tailor your supervision to the students you are supervising, according to their backgrounds, needs, abilities and personalities, was highlighted in focus group interviews at different universities in both countries. In many cases, supervisors linked the need to adapt their supervision practice to the students they supervised to the goal of encouraging and enabling student independence. As in the following examples:

> Well, there are [policy] documents and there are students. They are human beings and they are all different. So, of course, it is difficult to work with just one given scheme. All students are different and each one requires a different approach. For example, I may spend more time with one student and less with another. Some students are more independent and self-sufficient, and all you need to do is give them the direction and that's it. Others need a lot more hours of work.
> *Focus Group Interview 8*

It is simply that students have very different starting points, both as people and in terms of experience and knowledge and so on, and you have to meet them where they are. In order to, where they are, help them to practice being independent
Focus Group Interview 2

The way in which supervisors talked about the need to adapt their supervision practice to students' needs, backgrounds and preferences could be understood to mean that they took student diversity into account in several ways when planning and conducting their supervision. One aspect of student diversity that has been discussed, for example in research on the internationalisation of higher education and international student mobility, is how cultural and linguistic differences can be central elements in how academic contexts and practices are perceived and experienced by students (e.g. Dall'Alba and Sidhu 2013; Furukawa et al. 2013; Sidhu and Dall'alba 2017; Laufer and Gorup 2018; Gregersen-Hermans 2016; Fotovatian and Miller 2014). Such differences, related to how thesis supervision always takes place in specific national and local academic settings, may also be significant for how the relationship between students and supervisors is perceived (Ding and Devine 2018; Doyle et al. 2018; Fan et al. 2018; Hellstén and Ucker Perotto 2018).

The relevance of students' national and local academic backgrounds was also mentioned in some of the focus group interviews in our project, for example by supervisors comparing their experiences of regular students within a programme with their perceptions of exchange students from other countries. However, as the interview quotes above illustrate, supervisors did not limit their recognition of the significance of student diversity to these characteristics, but also talked about how differences related to personality, competencies, and prior education and knowledge were relevant to the supervision interaction. The recorded supervision sessions also revealed how supervisors regularly received or asked for information about students' current life situations. This is potentially relevant to the degree project process and supervision, as it may influence how much time and energy students are able to devote to their thesis work at any given time. Although the expectation may be that students should prioritise their degree project work in order to complete it on time, in practice factors such as financial circumstances, part-time jobs, health issues, childcare or life crises may well mean that this is not possible, or is not perceived to be possible. An awareness of this might, perhaps, lessen some frustration on the part of the supervisor when the degree project work is not progressing as planned.[2]

A well-functioning relationship between supervisors and students can contribute to these various exchanges of information about the student's work process, life situation, preferences, skills and prior knowledge taking place in a constructive way. In this chapter we will continue to explore how the supervisor-student relationship can be influenced by the actions of both supervisors and students, as well as by the design and structure of supervision meetings. However, we begin by discussing the rather complicated issue of how and to what extent the relationship between supervisors and students should be characterised by being academic and professional, personal or even private.

Managing the Supervisor-Student Relationship

A good relationship between supervisors and students may thus be beneficial to the degree project process by contributing to students' willingness or confidence to participate actively in the supervision interaction, and by facilitating for supervisors to adapt their supervision to the needs and preferences of the supervised students. From an academic literacies perspective, it is worth emphasising that expectations of what the supervisor-student relationship should look like depend not only on the individual supervisor and student but also on the local academic environment of which they are a part, and the expectations and ideals that prevail there (cf. Lea and Street 2000, 2006; Lillis 2001; Lillis and Scott 2007). For example, in one local academic setting, there may be expectations that the supervisors should appear distant from their students and that the supervision relationship should be primarily professional and academic, whereas in other academic settings, there may be expectations that the relationship between supervisors and students should be more personal.

Expectations may also concern how hierarchical the relationship between supervisors and students is perceived or expected to be, which can be related to Dysthe's (2002) typification of how the supervisor-student relationship can be characterised by the supervisor being

---

[2] It is worth noting the potential risk that supervisors sometimes receive more information about students' private lives and problems than they may have intended, so that the main focus of a supervision meeting ends up being the student's personal problems rather than the thesis work. This is a dilemma that is not always easy to deal with, which we will discuss further here and in Chap. 5.

considered an expert or a master, or by a more equal partnership relationship. From a scaffolding perspective, it could perhaps be argued that a partnership relationship should provide the best opportunities for both supervisor and student to be active in the learning process (cf. van de Pol 2012; van de Pol et al. 2010). At the same time, it is necessary to keep in mind that the relationship between supervisor and student is hierarchical in nature. If there are differences and contradictions in how the students and the supervisors think the work should proceed, what choices are possible or best to make, the supervisors' opinions will generally carry more weight than those of the students. In most cases, this is as it should be, since supervisors, by virtue of their position and experience, typically know more about how to write a good degree project than the students can be expected to. This is not to say that supervisors always know best, but rather that even in a supervisor-student relationship characterised by partnership, there are issues and boundaries that are not and should not be negotiable.

Another aspect of this is that the supervisor-student relationship is influenced by where the students are in the process of writing the degree project at any given time. From a scaffolding perspective, the relationship between supervisor and student should be characterised by the students taking on increasing responsibility as the thesis work progresses, while the supervisors gradually take on a more subordinate role (cf. van de Pol 2012; van de Pol et al. 2010). But it can also be the case that the supervision is initially characterised by partnership, in the sense that the supervisor tries to encourage and enthuse the student so that the work gets started and the student becomes confident enough to take initiatives, while the relationship can become more hierarchical and the supervision more directive or characterised by teaching towards the end of the work, when there is time pressure and the question of whether the degree project will meet the quality requirements becomes critical (Zackariasson 2019).

There are studies and handbooks on academic supervision that emphasise how a more personal relationship between supervisors and students, which also takes into account social and emotional factors, may be valued by students and beneficial for thesis work (e.g. Rienecker, Wichmann-Hansen and Stray Jørgensen 2019; Lee 2019; Brodin et al. 2020). However, a healthy and well-functioning relationship between supervisors and students does not necessarily imply a personal or remarkably close relationship. There are certain risks associated with the supervisor-student relationship becoming too marked by friendship or too focused on the emotional or social, so that role confusion occurs or academic work is overshadowed (Basic 2021, 19f; Blåsjö 2010). Susan Clegg (2000) has discussed this in a study of how doctoral supervisors experience the supervision situation and the supervision relationship. She suggests that supervisors and students may have differing views on what constitutes an appropriate level of closeness between supervisor and student, and that it is not obvious that students would value an overly warm relationship, or that they would expect the relationship to be anything other than professional and distant.

It is thus far from obvious what constitutes an appropriately personal relationship in the supervision context. What may be seen as friendly questions by a given supervisor may be seen as inappropriately private by one student, but completely unproblematic to another. Conversely, what a particular supervisor may perceive as a professional, moderately detached attitude may be perceived by some students as callous and distant, while the same type of approach works perfectly well with other students. There are of course also ethical issues to consider when it comes to how private or personal the relationship between supervisor and student can or should be. With the me-too movement, it became obvious that sexual harassment occurs in the context of higher education, but even before that, various studies and surveys had highlighted this problem (see e.g. Husu 2001; Muhonen 2016; Fedina et al. 2018; Istead et al. 2021). Some studies suggest that the relationship between supervisors and students, both postgraduate and undergraduate, is particularly precarious in this regard (see e.g. Bondestam and Lundqvist 2018). This is partly due to the fact that students are in a position of dependency in relation to the supervisor. If conflicts or problems arise between them, this can have considerable negative consequences for the supervision the students receive and for the progress of the work. Compared to other forms of teaching, supervision is also more likely to be one-to-one. There is therefore a risk that students may end up in a particularly vulnerable position if supervisors overstep the boundaries of what is ethically correct or what a particular student or postgraduate is comfortable with.

The fact that students are so clearly in a position of dependence in relation to supervisors is relevant to consider not only in terms of sexual harassment, but more generally when it comes to the supervisor-student relationship (cf. Basic 2021; Löfström and Pyhältö 2012; Brodin et al. 2020). There is a certain grey area where the boundaries of what is perceived as too personal and intimate can vary considerably from person to person. For example, where should supervision meetings take place? Should they always take place at the university, or can you meet in a coffee shop instead? Is it unproblematic to have supervision in the office with the door closed, or should you book a meeting room with glass windows? Are there any problems with conducting a digital supervision meeting from your bedroom, with your children on your lap or your dog barking in the background? Is it advisable to invite students to your home, if you for instance think that this would create a more personal relationship that might be beneficial for the work process?

When it comes to these kinds of questions, there are of course no obvious answers that apply to all types of supervisor-student relationships and all supervision situations. However, since the choices you make as a supervisor, for example where supervision meetings take place, can affect both the formal nature of the supervision situation and the relationship with the student, it is useful to reflect on such factors. Given that supervision can be emotional in a number of ways, which we will return to in Chap. 5, it is also worth considering what might happen if a student becomes upset or inconsolable in a supervision situation that takes place away from the university. In some disciplines and programmes, there are guidelines on how supervision should normally be conducted, which may include, for example, how often the supervisors are expected to meet the students and in what way. By including in such guidelines aspects related to the boundary between the professional, personal and private, and by discussing these in various collegial contexts, supervisors' awareness of these issues and their ability to handle them when they arise may be increased.

Another consideration is how much of the supervisor's private life should be shared with the students. In some situations, it is necessary for students to be informed about events in the supervisors' personal life, as they may affect the supervision in one way or another. Such events may include illness, death in the family or other life crises that make the supervisors less available than before, or that may result in students having to find a new supervisor. In such circumstances, it is important and natural that students are given the information they need. How much and what kind of information students should receive is then a matter for the individual supervisor or, where appropriate, the course or programme coordinator to decide on a case-by-case basis.

Sometimes much less serious matters in the supervisors' personal lives affect the conditions for supervision, as in the following example from our material, where the discussion concerned the timing of the next supervision meeting:

Student O:	We said next Tuesday, didn't we?
Supervisor F:	That's right. Mm, in a week, yes. And it's always the case for you now that half past two is not a good time, huh?
Student P:	Well, it's that I…
Supervisor F:	No, but let's go with that today, so…
Student O:	Should we change the day or?
Supervisor F:	No, let's go with this, um, actually it's (laughs)… It's my daughter sitting out there. You know, she got sick so, uh, so she had to come along.
Student P:	Yeah, yeah.
Supervisor F:	Sit there and play instead.
Students O & P:	(laughing)
Supervisor F:	But… uh… But otherwise she actually has practice on Tuesdays, and I didn't think about that. Then she starts at five o'clock and then I'll have to get home to [place] and pick her up from school. Get home and eat something and then get to the sports hall. And it turns out (laughs) that it doesn't work. That is not possible.
Student P:	But then… Yes, well, it depends on whether I might…
Supervisor F:	But really, no. It's more important that… /…/ No, but let's go with three o'clock.

Supervisor F, Recording 6, Pair supervision

This excerpt from the recorded supervision interaction can be considered from several perspectives. On the one hand, it could be viewed as an example of how supervisors could try to contribute to a more personal relationship with the students, in this case by referring to a daughter when explaining to the students why a particular time was not optimal for supervision meetings. Talking about one's family in this way may help to show that supervisors are human and have lives outside of work and supervision. Giving students a glimpse of this can help them gain a better understanding of what the supervisors' work and life situation might be like. Thus, it can be said to contribute to a more equal relationship between supervisor and student, which may then be more easily characterised by partnership (Dysthe 2002).

On the other hand, the extract could be seen as an example of the supervisor's private life entering the supervision situation in a way that is not always entirely relevant. In the quote, the supervisor also backs away from the initial question and emphasises that supervision should take precedence over the daughter's leisure activities, which could be interpreted as a sign that the supervisor realises that this may not have been an entirely legitimate aspect to bring up in the supervision interaction. Ultimately, the example illustrates the constant balancing act that supervisors face in drawing the line between the professional, the personal and the private, and that it is far from obvious where these boundaries lie in any given situation.

Personal: In What Way?

While it is necessary as a supervisor to be alert to when a supervision situation or relationship becomes too close, it may be beneficial, as mentioned earlier, for supervision to be characterised not only by being academic and professional, but also by a degree of being personal. As we discussed earlier in this chapter, a good relationship between supervisor and student is relevant in relation to scaffolding (van de Pol 2012; van de Pol et al. 2010), as it can contribute to the students being able, willing and confident enough to be active in the scaffolding work that takes place in the supervision situation. But how can one attempt to create such an appropriately personal relationship in practice?

Describing the supervisor-student relationship in terms of being familiar or personal can be perceived as mainly involving inquiring about the student's hobbies or family circumstances. Trying to find common interests that can be discussed in a friendly way can certainly be a valuable tool for supervisors, providing an opportunity to build a more personal relationship and contributing to a less hierarchical relationship with a greater element of partnership (cf. Dysthe 2002). For example, Clegg's (2000) study showed that the most uncomplicated amicable relationships between supervisors and doctoral students consisted of all-male couples where both shared an interest in sport. At the same time, the benefits of finding similarities or common interests between supervisors and students should not be exaggerated. If too much emphasis is placed on this, there is a potential risk that students who are similar to the supervisor, or perhaps working on a topic that the supervisor finds particularly interesting, will be met with greater enthusiasm and interest than someone who has a different background, interests or academic focus from the supervisor. Similarly, asking questions about the students' family situation has the potential to make the relationship more personal, but at the same time there is a risk that problems the students may be having at home, such as illness, divorce or custody disputes, will enter the supervision situation in a less constructive way.

Another way of trying to build a relationship that goes at least somewhat beyond the academic and professional is, as mentioned earlier, to make use of everyday small talk. Talking about the weather, public transport or how the student got to the supervisor's office can play a role in making students less nervous and more comfortable with the situation, which in turn can help to lay the foundation for a good conversation during the supervision meeting. There are not many examples of this kind of initial small talk in our recorded material, which is probably partly due to the fact that the recordings were not started until everyone was seated. However, it was quite common for the recorded supervision sessions to begin with a question from the supervisor, either a social question or a general question about the degree project work. As in the following examples from various supervision sessions in our material:

- Fun topic. How did you come up with this?
- I've read your memo here, but can't you tell me yourself first? What are you thinking?
- Hey, sorry to hear about your foot. How do you think things are going?
- What's up? How is everything going? What has happened since you last sent this?

From various supervision sessions with supervisors A and F

The examples from our material are consistent with Svinhufvud and Vehviläinen's (2013, 155) study of how supervision discussions are opened, which revealed certain patterns in the interaction between supervisors and students, such as that it was common for supervisors to start the conversation with a question. On the basis of this, there seems to be a kind of genre convention when it comes to how supervision discussions are started, as is common in institutional discussions in general (cf. Linell and Luckmann 1991). Usually it is the supervisor who controls the conversation and is responsible for initiating it, but the genre convention also includes the supervisor often opening up for dialogue at the outset and showing interest in the students' activities and the current state of the degree project work.

In many cases, the answers supervisors received to these types of open-ended, initial questions were clearly focused on the degree project work, but other aspects could often also be captured that were more concerned with how students experienced or felt about the process. As in the following example when the supervisor asks the students how it feels:

Supervisor A:	Well, how does it feel?
Student B:	Well, yeah, I guess it feels good. A bit stressful. Tomorrow we are going to [name of school] because my old teacher has mentor time with their class and has already talked to them [about this]. But there were only two students who were interested, so we will crash their class and try to convince or motivate them to participate. So we don't know if we'll get any interviews, but we hope to appeal to them. We will bring coffee and stuff as a bit of bait.
Supervisor A:	Yes, well. That sounds good.
Student A:	Mm.
Student B:	Yeah, but I hope they will agree.
Student A:	Right.
Supervisor A:	Yeah, but if you tell them about who you are, that you went to their school and what you're doing now and this thing about journalism and things like that. Then you can try to… then they might be interested. They can see themselves in you in some way. The personal approach is very important.
Student B:	Yeah, that's true.

Supervisor A, Recording 4, Pair supervision

From a scaffolding perspective, this type of questions, which provide insight into how students are progressing in their work, can be seen as a way for the supervisor to achieve contingency by identifying where students are at so that the subsequent conversation can be adapted accordingly (see van de Pol 2012; van de Pol et al. 2010, 2019). As the supervisor in this example is specifically asking how the students are feeling, rather than how things are going or how the work is progressing, there is also a clear opening for the students to express their possible uncertainties and concerns, in this case in relation to the collection of empirical material. This gives the supervisor an opportunity to reassure and encourage them, as well as to offer advice on how to make the best of the situation.

Of course, asking how it feels need not be a carefully considered and deliberate strategy to find out more about how students are experiencing the degree project work, although in the example above it had that effect. It may simply be a way of expressing oneself. But that supervisors in our material were sometimes actively trying to find out not only how the degree project work was progressing, but also how the students were experiencing the process, is evident in the following example:

Supervisor B:	What's up?
Student H:	Well, yeah, it's fine.
Supervisor B:	What's up with *you*, I should say.
Student H:	Oh, yeah, no, it's… it's fine. It's still a bit confused with… This degree project, you know, is like… I don't like it when it's… Like this time of unstructured and it's like, fuzzy. Then I get quite stressed.
Supervisor B:	So like this reflection phase or what?
Student H:	No, that's not my thing at all. Then I get really stressed, so it's… But it is, it's good. Really, it is.
Supervisor B:	Can you tell me a little bit about what's happened since we last saw each other?

Supervisor B, Recording 3, Individual supervision

To the supervisor's first general question in this example, the student gives a short and neutral answer. It is only when the supervisor specifies that he or she really wants to know how the student is doing that the student gives a more detailed answer and also addresses what is perceived as hard. It should be noted that none of the supervisors in these two examples dwelt much on the students' expressions of stress and concern. They did not express explicit sympathy or understanding, but neither did they belittle the students' experiences and descriptions of the situation. Instead, they gave specific advice on how the students could deal with the perceived problems or redirected the conversation to the actual work of the degree project. At the same time, in both cases the students were given the opportunity to talk about how they experienced the work, not just how it progressed academically. Giving students the opportunity to express that they feel stressed, for example, may have a favourable effect on the degree project work itself. As the questions signal that the supervisors are not only interested in how the thesis work is progressing, but also in how the students are feeling, the supervisors in these examples can also be said to be contributing to a more personal relationship between supervisor and student that includes aspects other than the purely professional and academic.

Mutual Appreciation

Another possible approach that can contribute to a good relationship with students is to provide affirmation and encouragement in various ways. This may also contribute to a good atmosphere during the supervision meetings, which can be important in relation to the idea of scaffolding (van de Pol 2012; van de Pol et al. 2010). If the goal is for students, together with the supervisor, to be active in the scaffolding work that takes place in the supervision situation, this can be facilitated if the supervisor-student relationship is such that the student's contributions, thoughts and ideas are perceived as desirable and welcome. Claire Aitchison et al. (Aitchison et al. 2012) have discussed that this is not always the case, for example when students, in their case doctoral students, fail to meet supervisors' expectations of academic writing. As their study shows, this can lead to disappointment and frustration on the part of supervisors, which in turn can contribute to a negative atmosphere during a supervision meeting and strain the relationship.

Other factors that may contribute to hostile feelings in supervisors include when students are perceived to be arrogant towards the supervisors or not accepting of criticism and comments, or when they do not understand or adhere to the written or unwritten rules of the supervisor-student relationship, for example by repeatedly missing deadlines or not respecting the supervisors' workload (Clegg 2000; Han and Xu 2021). Such behaviour can have a negative impact on the supervisor-student relationship and the climate of the conversation, in the sense that it may force supervisors to intervene and be more directive and explicit in their demands on how the students should proceed, and more negative in their feedback. This may make it more difficult or less attractive for students to be active in the supervision interaction. Although supervisors need to be able to react when students have not done what was agreed or expected, there is thus a need for some emotional regulation on the part of supervisors, as it is unlikely to be conducive to further work if the supervision becomes mired in blame and frustration.

In our focus group material, we had numerous examples of supervisors talking about the relationship with students in terms of disappointment or frustration, and such frustration could at times be reflected in the supervision interaction. However, there were also many cases where the interaction between supervisors and students was characterised by a positive attitude and mutual appreciation. The following extract from the recorded supervision sessions is one example of what this could look like in practice:

Supervisor H:	I think it's absolutely brilliant. When we were talking with the whole group before, I was thinking that you could do something similar to how you make an interview guide …
Student A:	Yeah. Yeah, sure, exactly.
Supervisor H:	… or an observation guide and that's exactly what you've already done and you've done it very ambitiously. I think it looks great! So this is: "Just go for it!"[3] /…/
Student S:	Mhm.
Supervisor H:	And the thought that I get sort of… Because it's kind of fun for me, that your topic is by far the closest to my actual academic profession as a linguist. And that's kind of exciting. How do you imagine… To what extent will your research be linguistic?
	Supervisor H, Recording 2, Collective supervision

One reason why the supervisor in this case seemed so positive about what the student wanted to do was, as can be seen from the quote, that the student's choice of topic was close to the supervisor's discipline and area of interest. As mentioned earlier, other similarities between students and supervisors can also contribute to a relaxed, positive and friendly relationship between them. Age, gender and ethnicity can obviously play a role, but so can shared hobbies or other similarities (see Clegg 2000). Whilst this can be positive and beneficial in many ways to the degree project process, there is a potential risk that such factors may influence the degree to which different students are affirmed and encouraged, or the way in which

---

[3] The Swedish expression originally used by Supervisor H here is "Tuta och kör!", an idiomatic saying that would translate as "Honk and go!"

supervision is organised and conducted. It is thus relevant for supervisors to reflect on the extent to which their own approach and attitude to the students they supervise is influenced by shared academic interests or hobbies, or a sense of connection through other commonalities.

However, the fact that the student's chosen topic was close to Supervisor H's area of interest was not the only thing that contributed to the positive attitude in the example above. As can be seen from the extract, the supervisor's appreciation was also based on what the student had achieved—in this case, producing an 'observation guide' before the supervisor had suggested it. That the supervisor seemed to approve of this can be understood in the context of how taking initiatives was seen by supervisors in our study as a central part of student independence, as discussed in Chap. 3. Here, then, it was both the fact that the topic of the degree project was close to the supervisor's own area of expertise and the student's demonstrated independence that appeared to be valued by the supervisor.

As far as the relationship between Supervisor H and Student S was concerned, the appreciation was mutual. During the concluding supervision meeting, when the two of them discussed the final manuscript for the degree project together, the student expressed appreciation for the supervision received during the degree project course:

Student S:	You had a question in your comments on the last draft, which is… Because I've… I found your comments amazingly useful!
Supervisor H:	Well, that's great!
Student S:	And I've tried to go through [it] and both ask like this… "Yes, but is this a perfect fit?"[4] And then I have either… if you think that: "Yes, but it probably is if you think like this…". Or maybe I've just tested it like this or kind of: "No, it's not. I'll remove it. Or like that, sort of. And it's been a really good support and structure."
Supervisor H:	That's great!
Student S:	Yeah, but all these examples and comments… Or it feels like it was very good like universal… Like for example:

---

[4] The Swedish expression originally used by Student S here is "sitter som en smäck" (fits like a cap), which is an idiomatic expression that Supervisor H has used in previous supervision meetings.

"Keep this in mind when you are writing. This is what you need to know at this stage" and things like that.
Supervisor H, Recording 3, Individual supervision

Here, in other words, it is the supervisor who is validated by the student and receives evidence that the help and support provided during the process was appreciated and made a positive contribution to the degree project work. Although Student S is unusually detailed in the feedback on the received supervision, it was not uncommon in our material for students to give affirmation to the supervisor in a variety of ways, for example by emphasising that they found the supervision meeting they had just had to be worthwhile. As in the following example, taken from the final minutes of a supervision meeting between Supervisor F and two students writing together:

Supervisor F:	But listen… I think this is a very exciting topic. Like I said, you just have to think: "What is it really about?"
Student O:	Yeah.
Student P:	Mm. We've actually gained a lot of new insights today. I really feel that. About what we should focus on.
Student O:	Absolutely.
Student P:	Yeah.
Student O:	Because it's probably… My head has been buzzing a lot with that. More where the focus is (laughs) really.

Supervisor F, Recording 1, Pair supervision

This example of how the concluding part of the supervision session was characterised by a positive and mutually appreciative atmosphere may also be related to the fact that in many of the recorded supervision discussions there was a desire for consensus. In the conversation, supervisors and students often worked together to create a description of the situation that all could accept, even if it was one party who had introduced or highlighted the issue or problem in the first place. This idea of consensus often characterised the very end of supervision sessions, as above and as in the following example from the end of Supervisor A's first supervision session with two students writing together:

Supervisor A:	So,... concentrate on doing the other things instead. Select your materials so that you have like a pile of articles.
Students C & D:	Mm. Okay.
Supervisor A:	Feel free to start reading as well. Because when you make an... [analytical] tool like this... You also have to do it in interaction with the material you are going to examine.
Student D:	Exactly.
Student C:	Absolutely. (laughs)
Supervisor A:	So it's a kind of dialogue you have with the survey material. At first you think, "I'm going to find out these things". That's how you read it at first. Then you find other things as you read on.
Student D:	Mm. Yeah, exactly.
Supervisor A:	And then you have to go back and rewrite the questions. Then maybe you read a bit more, then you find other things. So it's a bit of a back and forth.
Student C & D:	Mm. Exactly.
Supervisor A:	So if you have done that, sort of, so that you have a tool that you believe in.
Student D:	That sounds really sensible.
Student C:	Yeah, that sounds good.
Student D:	And fun, I think! (laughs)
Student C:	I can't wait to start!
Supervisor A:	That's great.

Supervisor A, Recording 2, Pair supervision

Here it is evident that the supervisor is in many ways confirming that the students are on the right track, while at the same time making explicit recommendations about how they should think about moving forward with their work. The students, on the other hand, repeatedly confirm what the supervisor is saying and show that they are on board, for example by saying that the suggestions sound good and sensible and that it will be fun and exciting to get started. In this way, the supervisor receives confirmation that the students have absorbed what has been said during the supervision meeting. In addition, this concluding conversation sequence contributes to the entire supervision meeting ending in a good atmosphere and with a visible consensus, despite the fact that the supervisor had already made a lot of remarks about the students' preparations before the supervision meeting, as well as about their thesis idea and initial planning, in the discussions earlier in the meeting. In this way, a good foundation is laid for the next supervision meeting, in the sense that the students and the supervisor are on good terms when they part. This in turn may make it easier for the students to contact the supervisor if they encounter problems or have any questions before the next supervision meeting.

When Students Become Too Personal

It is not only how supervisors relate to students, but also how students relate to supervisors that affects the relationship between them and, by extension, the nature of the supervision. At times it is the students who actively bring their personal lives into the conversation or try to find points of contact with the supervisors. They may do this, for example, by talking about their family or personal interests, or by asking the supervisors about such things. This can also be seen as a way of making the relationship more personal, not just professional and academic, and can therefore contribute positively to the degree project work, for example by making the students feel safer and more comfortable during supervision meetings. At the same time, supervisors may resist this due to not seeking or not feeling comfortable with this type of relationship with students. Since supervisors not only have to encourage and enthuse the students, but also sometimes have to put a stop to ideas that are not expected to work, or point out that work that has been done is not of a sufficiently high quality, it is not self-evident that supervisors would want anything other than a strictly professional relationship with students.

In the recorded supervision sessions, we had several examples of students getting into personal issues or problems of a more sensitive nature, which had affected their thesis work and the writing process in various ways. Sometimes it could be that the students had been struggling with personal issues or their self-image, and that this affected how they perceived their ability to complete the degree project. In other cases, major life events, such as death or illness in the family or divorce, affected the student's life, as well as the degree project process, in a significant way. But other, less serious life changes or personal circumstances can also impact on the student's ability to work on the degree project, as in the following example from our material:

Supervisor F:	Are you working this Christmas, or?
Student Q:	I… er… was going to go away… (laughs)
Supervisor F:	Aaahh! I don't want to hear that! (laughs)
Student Q:	(laughs) So, well… ehm… But I'll have to bring some stuff with me, that's how it is. (laughs)
Supervisor F:	Where are you going?
Student Q:	To [place] /…/ I have friends or cousins and stuff that live there, so I thought I'd spend Christmas with them.
Supervisor F:	Okay. Yeah, that sounds good… You are allowed to take some time off as well.
Student Q:	Because my… uh, our children, they celebrated Christmas with us last year, and the grandchildren and so on. But now we don't have anyone this year, so we felt so alone. So I didn't want to stay. I couldn't stay at home then. Too lonely inside the walls. It's not possible (laughs). So it's best to get away.
	Supervisor F, Recording 4, Individual supervision

The supervisor begins this conversation sequence with a relatively neutral question about how much time the student will have to work on the degree project over Christmas. When the student apologetically presents the plan to go away for Christmas, which is right at the end of the degree project period, the supervisor spontaneously reacts quite negatively. This may contribute to the student going on to explain in such detail the decision to go away at this particular time. In other words, the conversation and what Wetherell (2012) would call the affective practices are initially characterised by a certain amount of apology on the part of the student and a certain amount of blame on the part of the supervisor. However, in the subsequent conversation, the supervisor also shows understanding for the student's choice:

Supervisor F:	No, no, but I guess it's simply better to… I will go to [place] for Christmas for the same reason. My partner also has children, but will not have them then either, and thought it would be hard to be here over Christmas, sort of. /…/ So we're leaving (laughs).
Student Q:	Mm. That's what I thought. Maybe this time one might… So it was my choice, really. But… eh… I realise now that there is still a lot to do here.

Supervisor F:	Yeah, well, writing a degree project, it does take its time.
Student Q:	Yeah, yeah, it does. But it should be possible... it should be possible, I hope.

Supervisor F, Recording 4, Individual supervision

By referring to oneself in this way, and by pointing to similarities in life situations and choices, the supervisor could be said to be contributing to the relationship with the student becoming more personal and the conversation climate more intimate. The two quotes also illustrate the balance that supervisors must constantly maintain between, on the one hand, keeping the focus on the work, which is a central scaffolding goal in supervision practice (cf. van de Pol 2012; van de Pol et al. 2010), and, on the other hand, acknowledging that students also have a life outside of their studies that may have an impact on the degree project process.

As mentioned earlier, it can be problematic if too much focus is placed on the student's personal life situation or problems of various kinds, not least because supervision time is usually limited, but also because there is a potential risk of the supervisor acting too much as a counsellor or therapist (cf. Strandler et al. 2014). In our material, there are several examples of supervisors trying to steer the conversation back to the degree project work when students got into these kinds of topics. This was particularly evident in one of the supervision processes we documented, where the student had a recurring tendency to describe themself in negative terms in all supervision sessions. Even when the supervisor asked questions that were directly related to the writing of the degree project and not at all focused on the student as a person, the student had a tendency to respond with a negatively charged self-characterisation. The student talked about having problems or weaknesses, being lazy, having difficulties with setting limits and so on.

At one point, the student highlighted several reasons for not completing the degree project the last time around and for finding it difficult now. These reasons were linked both to self-perception and to aspects of personal life:

Student G:	(laughs) Putting it a bit crudely: I think I'm two years behind my, my starting course. I mean, my former classmates... I started like in [year]. 'Cause some other things happened in my life. So that... for me it feels like... I just want to get through this now. Just to get

	my degree. Actually I wouldn't... like my boss said, "You don't even have to". She didn't even think I needed to do this. But I feel like I have to finish it. So... I'm not super motivated, I can say, to do it. But I only do it because... Well, maybe it's obvious? That I am taking some shortcuts to get through the degree project.
Supervisor B:	It's a course. I told you that in the collective supervision session as well. It is a course, eh... It's a writing exercise. It's absolutely right to think about it instrumentally and, like, just do the task. /.../
Student G:	And then I don't really have the confidence. I always think that what I'm doing isn't any good. So I don't really have... I don't really believe myself in what I write. (laughs)
Supervisor B:	Well, you have a great topic and... uh...

Supervisor B, Recording 2, Individual supervision

As mentioned before, it can be difficult for supervisors to deal with students becoming very personal in this way during supervision. While the main focus of supervision should be on the degree project and writing, factors or events in the students' personal lives may be of inescapable relevance to the degree project. One way of dealing with this kind of situation is to try to downplay the importance of the degree project and make it seem less fateful. In the example above, Supervisor B does this, for example, by describing the degree project as a writing exercise and something you can actually think instrumentally about. Trying to find something positive in the student's work and build on it, as Supervisor B does at the end of the quote, can also be a viable way of dealing with the situation. At the same time, it may be easier said than done in practice in the particular situation that arises, as illustrated by the fact that this type of conversation was recurrent in all of the documented supervision conversations with this particular student.

How the Design of Conversations May Affect the Relationship

Another way of looking at the supervisor-student relationship, and how it is created and maintained in the supervision interaction, is to start with the design of the supervision conversations, primarily in terms of the structure and content of the conversations. The form and organisation of the conversations is relevant in terms of student independence, in relation to the roles that students take and are given in the conversations, and in terms of the space that students are provided to take initiatives (see Chap. 3) and bring up things that they want to discuss and that they consider important. This is related to aspects of whether the conversations are characterised by teaching, partnership or apprenticeship, and thus to power relations and hierarchies in the relationship between supervisors and students (cf. Dysthe 2002). From an academic literacies perspective, and also in relation to scaffolding, this kind of student agency, that students have the opportunity to influence the learning processes, becomes essential (cf. Jones et al. 2000; Lillis 2001; van de Pol 2012; van de Pol et al. 2010). In institutional conversations, of which supervision meetings are an example, the form of the conversation rarely invites agency and partnership, which places particular demands on the supervisors' awareness (cf. Linell and Luckmann 1991).

The student's ownership of these processes is thus important, which makes the organisation of supervision conversations and who controls the conversations through the choice of topics relevant to examine. Both in terms of who controls the conversation at an overall level and in terms of the space for students' own perspectives and reflections at a more specific and subordinate level. On an overall level, supervision discussions can be described as either supervisor-driven or student-driven. What this entails can be defined in at least two ways, either by looking at who takes the interactive initiatives and initiates conversation topics and perspectives or by looking at who has or receives the most speaking space in a conversation—the students or the supervisors.

In student-driven supervision conversations, students have often prepared questions or topics for discussion, either submitted in advance or presented at the supervision meeting. In the recorded supervision material in our study, the discussions were primarily directed by the supervisors. In other words, it was usually the supervisors who led the conversations and initiated the topics to be discussed, and it was usually the supervisors who received or took most of the speaking space, although the variation between different conversations was considerable. In the following, we will take a closer look at what this looked like in our material in quantitative terms. The overview in Table 4.1 shows how speaking space, defined as word count, is distributed as a percentage in the different conversations we recorded in our study. It is a rather crude measure of speaking space and participation, but it can still give an overall picture of how the distribution of speaking space in supervision interaction often looks. Column 1

Table 4.1 Table of speaking space in supervision conversations (cf Magnusson and Zackariasson 2021, 79)

		Supervisor	Student/s	Conversation length
1	A	62%	38%	4544 words
2	A	55%	45%	4483 words
3	A	65%	35%	6928 words
4	A	57%	43%	5363 words
5	A	60%	40%	6350 words
6	A	46%	54%	8958 words
7	A	19%	81%	4858 words
8	B	44%	56%	12654 words
9	B	50%	50%	6899 words
10	B	51%	49%	6392 words
11	B	62%	38%	3988 words
12	B	61%	39%	7210 words
13	B	40%	60%	6103 words
14	B	44%	56%	5431 words
15	B	57%	43%	10532 words
16	C	45%	55%	8531 words
17	C	55%	45%	7947 words
18	D	58%	42%	3522 words
19	D	60%	40%	5828 words
20	D	53%	47%	6111 words
21	E	61%	39%	19318 words
22	E	65%	35%	7008 words
23	E	70%	30%	5312 words
24	F	64%	36%	5570 words
25	F	68%	32%	9002 words
26	F	77%	23%	9047 words
27	F	59%	41%	10200 words
28	F	54%	46%	5028 words
29	F	62%	38%	8612 words
30	F	73%	27%	9890 words
31	F	72%	28%	6315 words
32	G	64%	36%	8540 words
33	G	77%	23%	6366 words
34	H	65%	35%	19592 words
35	H	42%	58%	14524 words
36	H	48%	52%	9292 words

indicates which conversation it concerns, and column 2 which supervisor. Columns 3 and 4 show the percentage of speaking time for both supervisors and students, while column 5 shows how long the conversations are in terms of word count. The percentage of speaking time in the student column can include between one and four students.

As can be seen in the overview, the supervisors have the most speaking space in most cases, 27 out of 36 conversations. In purely quantitative terms, then, the conversations are far from equal and far from what one might imagine to be the ideal image of a supervision conversation characterised by partnership (cf. Dysthe 2002). In the nine conversations where the students' speaking time exceeds that of the supervisor, there is often more than one student present at the supervision meeting, where no single student's speaking time exceeds that of the supervisor. There is no discernible pattern when it comes to conversations where the supervisor's speaking time is less than that of the students. There is no particular supervisor who consistently has less speaking time, and there is no supervisor-student constellation where the supervisor's speaking time is consistently lower. In other words, the differences do not appear to be about more or less dominant supervisors.

Although the supervisors have the most speaking space, the students' speaking space is rarely very small. Thus, there seems to be real student participation and involvement in the discussions, in the sense that they do not only consist of monologues and teaching by the supervisors, but also include some form of interaction. It might have been expected that the students' speaking time would increase in the later stages of the supervision process, when the students are likely to be more confident, but such a tendency is not at all evident in this material. The few conversations in which the supervisors' speaking space is smaller than that of the students are found both at the beginning and at the end of the supervision process. Thus, in our material, the supervisors' speaking space is generally greater, which is in line with the institutional role that supervisors have, but it is difficult to see any fixed roles for supervisors and students, as it varies between different supervisors and students, and between different stages of the supervision process.

The way in which supervision conversations are structured is significant for what the supervisor-student relationship looks like and what the possibilities are, or appear to be, within that relationship. Thus, it is not only the distribution of speaking space between supervisors and students that is relevant, but also how supervision conversations are managed in more detail. A closer examination of the recorded supervision interaction in our study revealed how supervisor-led supervision conversations tended to differ from student-led conversations in terms of the principles on which they were organised and structured. For example, supervisor-led conversations, or parts of conversations, could be structured on the basis of a submitted draft text, and the conversation then tended to follow the structure of the text and the comments that the supervisor had made in the document. In addition, conversations led by the supervisor could be structured on the basis of more general perspectives in relation to more specific perspectives, a kind of macro to micro structure. Such discussions could, for example, begin with a discussion of the problem formulation and the purpose of the thesis and end with discussions of specific expressions and phrases or perspectives. A third, more unusual, form of supervisor-led conversation was structured around the criteria for degree project work within a specific course or programme, where, for example, at the end of the degree project process, the supervisor would go through the submitted final draft from the perspective of whether it met all the requirements set for the course. Our material showed that the nature of the conversations varied depending on where the students were in the process, with the first conversations tending to focus on overall perspectives and the last conversations tending to focus more on detail.

The student-led supervision conversations were often structured around problems and concerns the students had about their own work process: finding and choosing relevant theory, problems with material collection and so on. Student-led supervision discussions were also structured around problems and concerns with the supervisor's written feedback, especially when it was perceived as difficult to interpret. A third way of structuring supervision discussions, which was only partly student-driven, involved student narratives or descriptions, where students were asked to describe what they had been doing since the last supervision meeting, while the supervisor interjected these stories or descriptions with questions and problematisations. In these cases, it was usually the supervisors who initiated the structure, but the students' accounts or descriptions still guided the conversation.

In summary, we were able to identify a number of types of supervisor-led and student-led conversations or parts of conversations in our material:

Supervisor-led conversations

- structured based on written comments in text drafts
- structured based on the macro-micro structure of the degree project
- structured based on criteria for the degree project

Student-led conversations

- structured based on problems and concerns in the work process
- structured based on questions about ambiguities in written feedback
- structured based on the students' account of what they have done.

Supervisor-Led Conversations

In the following, we will take a closer look at some examples of supervisor-led conversation sequences structured on the basis of the student's text drafts, taken from our recorded supervision sessions. In the tables below, the columns with topic levels 1–3 indicate whether the topics discussed are superior or subordinate, while the dialogue boxes indicate who is initiating the topics. Dialogue boxes on the left mean that the supervisor initiated the topic and dialogue boxes on the right mean that it was the student(s). In the conversation sequence from which the first example is taken (Table 4.2), it was, as the dialogue boxes show, only the supervisor who initiated topics.

First, the supervisor opened the conversation by explaining that the first draft submitted by the student and read by the supervisor was to be discussed. The supervisor then asked what the student had done since submitting the draft (progress summary), which was a relatively open start to the discussion. In response to this question, the student did not mention anything in particular, but stated that everything was probably included in the submitted draft text. The supervisor and the student then went through the draft from beginning to end—introduction and

Table 4.2 Supervisor-driven conversation (cf Magnusson and Zackariasson 2021, 82)

Topic level 1	Topic level 2	Topic level 3
First draft		
	Progress summary	
	Introduction and background	
	Aim and research questions	
	Methods	
		Phrasing issues
		Content analysis
	Previous research	References
	Previous research	

Supervisor G, individual supervision

background, purpose and research questions, method and previous research. Sometimes specific aspects were discussed in relation to these different parts of the text. What the supervisor called 'phrasing issues' were discussed in the method section, as well as whether or not the student was planning to do content analysis.

When they reached the section on previous research, the discussion first concerned the use of references and then more general considerations about what the section on previous research should contain. Even though it was the supervisor who introduced all the topics discussed and who directed the conversation, the student's own thoughts and reflections were constantly solicited—so there was a continuous opportunity for the student to take a more active part in the conversation. It should also be noted that this supervision conversation was clearly divided into two parts, which followed completely different organisational principles. What is being discussed here is the first part of the conversation, while the second part was based on open questions aimed at the student to raise matters that he/she considered important, difficult, interesting, etc.

In the example, the submitted draft text thus played an integral role in the structure of the conversation. The supervisor directed the conversation on the basis of the student's text, which the supervisor had read and commented on before the meeting, read out parts of the text to illustrate something that needed to be discussed and also read their own notes in the text out loud:

1. Supervisor G: Let's have a look at your first draft then… a bit… and discuss some more things I've been thinking about.
2. Supervisor G: But when it comes to… Have you made any changes to the aim and research questions since I read the project plan?
3. Supervisor G: Then you go into method and then you introduce hermeneutics.
4. Supervisor G: Uh, I've thought a bit about some, like, phrasing issues here and there.
5. Supervisor G: Previous research, I think this section also works well.
Supervisor G, examples from individual supervision

In these quotes from the conversation, the supervisor introduces the intended structure for the conversation—to look at the first draft and discuss things the supervisor reflected on during the reading (quote 1). The supervisor then follows the text throughout raising questions around aim and research questions (quote 2), method/theory (quote 3), wording (quote 4) and previous research (quote 5). Phrases such as 'then you go into' and 'that section' indicate that it is the text itself that is being discussed together.

This way of structuring a supervisor-led supervision discussion is quite typical in our recorded conversations, although not always expressed as explicitly. This structure suggests that it is primarily the text, the specific product, that is the goal of the supervision session, rather than a more general discussion of academic thinking, etc. It thus creates a focus for the activity in question and at the same time involves a prioritisation in which the written text is given the most important role. When, as in this example, a text is used in a variety of ways to support supervision conversations, it can be understood as what Star and Griesemer (1989) call a boundary object. This means that the text can be seen almost as a participant in the conversation, delimiting and connecting activities and situations (Magnusson 2016). The fact that it is the student's text that guides the conversation could also be described as the student indirectly directing the conversation and gaining agency, as quotes from the text become the starting point for the discussion, which gives voice to the student. At the same time, it is the supervisor who controls what in the text is considered relevant to discuss.

Student-Led Conversations

Although it was generally uncommon in the supervision conversations recorded within our project, for conversations or parts of conversations to be controlled by the student(s), there were some instances of this, such as the supervision conversation from which the example below is taken. Here the student had prepared questions about a number of perceived problems or difficult choices before the supervision meeting and the conversation was largely structured around these questions. As before, dialogue boxes on the right indicate that it was the student who initiated the topics in question, and dialogue boxes on the left indicate that it was the supervisor (Table 4.3).

In this particular supervision conversation, the opening lines were not included in the recording, so we do not know if the student started the conversation with an explicit request or description of what they wanted to get out of the conversation. However, at the end of the conversation, the student referred to having prepared questions beforehand,

Table 4.3 Student-driven conversation (cf Magnusson and Zackariasson 2021, 85)

Topic level 1	Topic level 2	Topic level 3
Methods	What methods are relevant?	
Readability	Theoretical or central concept?	
	Issues	
	Textbooks	
	Composition	
	Approach	
	Selection	
	Work plan	
Alignment	Theory?	

Supervisor E, individual supervision

commenting, "Yeah, well, those were probably the questions I had, I think", suggesting that this was also raised at the beginning. These questions from the student clearly structured the conversation, even though the supervisor also touched on related aspects in connection with these questions. The following quotes from the discussion illustrate how the student could initiate different topics in the discussion:

(1) Student N: Yeah, what I got stuck on then was this with the method /…/ I don't know if there is like something general… Or can you kind of use different methods?

(2) Student N: But this with legibility, I have to bring it up somehow and then explain what it is and this 'lix' and that and then I wonder: Where does it go, is it a theoretical concept or is it just a central concept that you …?

(3) Student N: Yeah, but that's right… Alignment—is alignment a theory or what?
Supervisor E, individual supervision

The recording began with the student introducing the choice of method as the first topic for the supervision conversation, then proceeding to present a number of potential methods for the degree project, before ending the segment with a question as to whether they were expected to use one overall method or whether several methods could be used (quote 1). The same pattern was then repeated in the ensuing conversation, with the student usually introducing a topic that ended in a question to the supervisor. As in quotes 2 and 3 above, where the topics of legibility and alignment were introduced by the student, leading to questions about whether 'lix', a readability test, should be considered a theoretical or central concept, and whether alignment should be regarded as a theory. The conversation then proceeded on the basis of these questions. As mentioned above, the form and organisation of a conversation is relevant to student independence, and this particular way of structuring a conversation can be seen as particularly effective in this regard, as it gives students plenty of space to bring up things they want to discuss and that they consider important. The form of conversation is also effective in terms of student agency, as students have the opportunity to be active and to control their own learning and learning processes, which is also central from a scaffolding perspective (van de Pol 2012; van de Pol et al. 2010).

Although this kind of student-driven supervision conversation was rather unusual in the recorded supervision sessions in our material, there are other forms of communication between supervisors and students where student initiatives were much more common, for example, email correspondence between supervisors and students, which often plays a significant role in the supervision process. In an article by Magnusson and Sveen (2013), a review was made of all communication between a student and a supervisor during the supervision of a degree project. There were a total of 15 emails in 3 email threads, and in all cases it was the student who initiated the contact by asking a question. This question was answered by the supervisor and then the email thread ended with the student sending a message thanking the supervisor for the help. Here's an example of what this could look like:

Student R:	Hi! I have another question about references. /.../
Supervisor G:	Hi! In this case it definitely sounds like you should refer to [author X].
Student R:	Thank you! Then I think I know what to do. *(Supervisor G, email conversation)*

In this example, the student asked a question about references, the supervisor responded with a direct recommendation, and the student then thanked the supervisor for the advice. This exemplifies how student initiative and participation may differ between communication channels or modalities, as the supervisor may be the initiator in conversations, while the student may be the initiator in email communication. In other words, our results show how various types of relationships between supervisors and students can be established during a supervision process through different forms of communication, and that this can enable different types of student participation and independence, understood as taking initiatives (cf. Chap. 3). We would thus argue that supervisors should be willing to let the forms of communication complement each other in order to facilitate different forms of student independence, especially since not all students are equally comfortable with each type of communication, as one student may prefer email conversations to express thoughts and ideas, while another may prefer face-to-face conversations.

* * *

So, there are a number of different aspects that are important in terms of what the supervisor-student relationship will look like, both in terms of how individuals choose to behave towards each other when it comes to asking questions or how personal they choose to be, and the actual interaction during the supervision session itself. In addition, relationships with people outside of this constellation are also important to the degree project work and the supervision process, both students' relationships with their fellow students and supervisors' relationships with their colleagues, especially if these are examiners, seminar leaders or programme or course coordinators within the degree project courses. We will explore this in the next chapter, where we develop the discussion of the emotional aspects of supervision.

References

Ädel, Annelie, Julie Skogs, Charlotte Lindgren, and Monika Stridfeldt. 2023. The Supervisor and Student in Bachelor Thesis Supervision: A Broad Repertoire of Sometimes Conflicting Roles. *European Journal of Higher Education*: 1–21. https://doi.org/10.1080/21568235.2022.2162560.

Agricola, Bas T., Frans J. Prins, Marieke F. van der Schaaf, and Jan van Tartwijk. 2021. Supervisor and Student Perspectives on Undergraduate Thesis Supervision in Higher Education. *Scandinavian Journal of Educational Research* 65 (5): 877–897. https://doi.org/10.1080/00313831.2020.1775115.

Aitchison, Claire, Janice Catterall, Pauline Ross, and Shelley Burgin. 2012. 'Tough Love and Tears': Learning Doctoral Writing in the Sciences. *Higher Education Research and Development* 31 (4): 435–447. https://doi.org/10.1080/07294360.2011.559195.

Almlöv, Cecilia, and Ann Grubbström. 2023. 'Challenging from the start': Novice Doctoral Co-supervisors' Experiences of Supervision Culture and Practice. *Higher Education Research and Development* (ahead-of-print): 1–15. https://doi.org/10.1080/07294360.2023.2218805.

Basic, Goran. 2021. Ethical Issues in Doctoral Supervision: An Analysis of Inherent Conflicts and Roles in Supervision Practice. *Future Students' Perspectives on Higher Education* 3 (2): 17–48. https://doi.org/10.5281/zenodo.7492713.

Blåsjö, Mona. 2010. *Skrivteori och skrivforskning: en forskningsöversikt*. 2. extended ed. Stockholm: School of Nordic languages, Stockholm University.

Bondestam, Fredrik, and Maja Lundqvist. 2018. *Sexuella trakasserier i akademin: en internationell forskningsöversikt*. Stockholm: Vetenskapsrådet.

Brodin, Eva, Jitka Lindén, Anders Sonesson, and Åsa Lindberg-Sand. 2020. *Doctoral Supervision in Theory and Practice*. Lund: Studentlitteratur.

Clegg, Sue. 2000. Knowing Through Reflective Practice in Higher Education. *Educational Action Research* 8 (3): 451–469. https://doi.org/10.1080/09650790000200128.

Dall'Alba, Gloria, and Ravinder Sidhu. 2013. Australian Undergraduate Students on the Move: Experiencing Outbound Mobility. *Studies in Higher Education* 40 (4): 1–24. https://doi.org/10.1080/03075079.2013.842212.

Ding, Qun, and Nesta Devine. 2018. Exploring the Supervision Experiences of Chinese Overseas Phd students in New Zealand. *Knowledge Cultures* 6 (1): 62–78. https://doi.org/10.22381/KC6120186.

Doyle, Stephanie, Catherine Manathunga, Gerard Prinsen, Rachel Tallon, and Sue Cornforth. 2018. African International Doctoral Students in New Zealand: Englishes, Doctoral Writing and Intercultural Supervision. *Higher Education Research & Development* 37 (1): 1–14. https://doi.org/10.1080/07294360.2017.1339182.

Dysthe, Olga. 2002. Professors as Mediators of Academic Text Cultures: an Interview Study with Advisors and Masters Degree Students in Three Disciplines in a Norwegian University. *Written Communication* 19 (4): 493–544. https://doi.org/10.1177/074108802238010.

Fan, Luo, Monowar Mahmood, and Md. Aftab Uddin. 2018. Supportive Chinese Supervisor, Innovative International Students: A Social Exchange Theory

Perspective. *Asia Pacific Education Review* 20: 101–115. https://doi.org/10.1007/s12564-018-9572-3.

Fedina, Lisa, Jennifer Lynne Holmes, and Bethany L. Backes. 2018. Campus Sexual Assault: A Systematic Review of Prevalence Research From 2000 to 2015. *Trauma, Violence, & Abuse* 19 (1): 76–93. https://doi.org/10.1177/1524838016631129.

Fotovatian, Sepideh, and Jenny Miller. 2014. Constructing an Institutional Identity in University Tea Rooms: the International PhD Student Experience. *Higher Education Research & Development* 33 (2): 286–297. https://doi.org/10.1080/07294360.2013.832154.

Furukawa, Takao, Nobuyuki Shirakawa, and Kumi Okuwada. 2013. An Empirical Study of Graduate Student Mobility Underpinning Research Universities. *The International Journal of Higher Education Research* 66 (1): 17–37. https://doi.org/10.1007/s10734-012-9586-4.

Gregersen-Hermans, Jeanine. 2016. *The Impact of an International University Environment on Students' Intercultural Competence Development.* Milan: Universita Cattolica del Sacro Cuore.

Han, Ye, and Yueting Xu. 2021. Unpacking the Emotional Dimension of Doctoral Supervision: Supervisors' Emotions and Emotion Regulation Strategies. *Frontiers in Psychology* 12: 651859–651859. https://doi.org/10.3389/fpsyg.2021.651859.

Hellstén, Meeri, and Lilian Ucker Perotto. 2018. Re-thinking Internationalization as Social Curriculum for Generative Supervision: Letters from the International Community of Scholars. *European Journal of Higher Education* 8 (1): 36–51. https://doi.org/10.1080/21568235.2017.1381568.

Hjelm, Markus. 2015. Barriers Encountered by Doctoral Nursing Students During Their Research Studies and their Strategies for Overcoming Them: A Qualitative Study. *Nordic Journal of Nursing Research* 35 (3): 172–178. https://doi.org/10.1177/0107408315590764.

Husu, Liisa. 2001. Sexism, Support and Survival in Academia: Academic Women and Hidden Discrimination in Finland. *Social Psychological Studies* 6. Diss. University of Helsinki.

Istead, Jeremy, Catherine Carstairs, and Kathryn L. Hughes. 2021. Before #MeToo: The Fight against Sexual Harassment at Ontario Universities, 1979–1994. *Historical Studies in Education* 33 (1): 1–21. https://doi.org/10.32316/hse-rhe.v33i1.4895.

Jacobsen, Michele, Sharon Friesen, and Sandra Becker. 2021. Online Supervision in a Professional Doctorate in Education: Cultivating Relational Trust Within Learning Alliances. *Innovations in Education and Teaching International* 58 (6): 635–646. https://doi.org/10.1080/14703297.2021.1991425.

Jones, Carys, Joan Turner, and Brian Street. 2000. *Students Writing in the University - Cultural and Epistemological Issues.* John Benjamins: John Benjamins Publishing Company.

Laufer, Melissa, and Meta Gorup. 2018. The Invisible Others: Stories of International Doctoral Student Dropout. *Higher Education* 11: 1–17. https://doi.org/10.1007/s10734-018-0337-z.

Lea, Mary R., and Brian V. Street. 2000. Student Writing and Staff feedback in Higher Education: An academic Literacies Approach. In *Student Writing in Higher Education. New contexts*, ed. Mary R. Lea and Barry Stierer, 32–46. Buckingham: Open University Press.

———. 2006. The "Academic Literacies" Model: Theory and Applications. *Theory Into Practice* 45 (4): 368–377. https://doi.org/10.1207/s15430421tip4504_11.

Lee, Anne. 2019. *Successful Research Supervision: Advising Students Doing Research.* 2nd ed. London: Routledge.

Lillis, Theresa. 2001. *Student Writing: Access, Regulation, Desire.* London: Routledge.

Lillis, Theresa, and Mary Scott. 2007. Defining Academic Literacies Research: Issues of Epistemology, Ideology and Strategy. *Journal of Applied Linguistics* 4 (1): 5–32. https://doi.org/10.1558/japl.v4i1.5.

Linell, Per, and Thomas Luckmann. 1991. Asymmetries in Dialogue: Some Conceptual Preliminaries. In *Asymmetries in Dialogue*, ed. Ivana Marková and Klaus Foppa, 1–20. Savage, MD: Barnes & Nobles.

Löfström, Erika, and Kirsi Pyhältö. 2012. The Supervisory Relationship as an Arena for Ethical Problem Solving. *Education Research International* 2012: 1–12. https://doi.org/10.1155/2012/961505.

Magnusson, Jenny. 2016. Text i samtal: Hur texter används som resurser i handledningssamtal. In *Svenskans beskrivning 34, Lund, 22–24 oktober 2014*, ed. Anna Gustafsson, Lisa Holm, Katarina Lundin, Henrik Rahm, and Mechtild Tronnier, 343–355. Lund: Lunds universitet.

Magnusson, Jenny, and Hanna Sveen. 2013. Topikalitet i handledning. In *Svenska föreningen för tillämpad språkvetenskap Vårsymposium. Linköping, 11–12 maj, 2012*, ed. Christina Rosén, Per Simfors, and Ann-Kari Sundberg, 173–182. Linköping: Linköpings universitet.

Magnusson, Jenny, and Maria Zackariasson. 2021. *Handledning i praktiken - Om studenters självständighet och akademiska litteracitet.* Lund: Studentlitteratur.

Mainhard, Tim, Roeland van der Rijst, Jan van Tartwijk, and Theo Wubbels. 2009. A Model for the Supervisor–Doctoral Student Relationship. *Higher Education* 58 (3): 359–373. https://doi.org/10.1007/s10734-009-9199-8.

Muhonen, Tuija. 2016. Exploring Gender Harassment among University Teachers and Researchers. *Journal of Applied Research in Higher Education* 8 (1): 131–142. https://doi.org/10.1108/JARHE-04-2015-0026.

Padyab, Ali, and Martin Lundgren. 2023. Stress in Doctoral Supervision: A perspective on Supervisors. *JPHE: Journal of Praxis in Higher Education* 5 (2): 91–117. https://doi.org/10.47989/kpdc307.

van de Pol, Janneke. E. (2012). *Scaffolding in teacher-student interaction: exploring, measuring, promoting and evaluating scaffolding.* [Thesis, fully internal, Universiteit van Amsterdam]. https://dare.uva.nl/search?identifier=640b82ba-c27b-42d3-b9f8-fe08b1e0081f.

van de Pol, Janneke, Monique Volman, and Jos. Beishuizen. 2010. Scaffolding in Teacher–Student Interaction: A Decade of Research. *Educational Psychology Review* 22: 271–296. https://doi.org/10.1007/s10648-010-9127-6.

van de Pol, Janneke, Monique Volman, and Jos Beishuizen. 2012. Promoting Teacher Scaffolding in Small-group Work: A contingency Perspective. *Teaching and Teacher Education* 28 (2): 193–205. https://doi.org/10.1016/j.tate.2011.09.009.

van de Pol, Janneke, Monique Volman, Frans Oort, and Jos Beishuizen. 2015. The Effects of Scaffolding in the Classroom: Support Contingency and Student Independent Working time in Relation to Student Achievement, Task Effort and Appreciation of Support. *Instructional Science* 43 (5): 615–641. https://doi.org/10.1007/s11251-015-9351-z.

van de Pol, Janneke, Neil Mercer, and Monique Volman. 2019. Scaffolding Student Understanding in Small-Group Work: Students' Uptake of Teacher Support in Subsequent Small-Group Interaction. *The Journal of the Learning Sciences* 28 (2): 206–239. https://doi.org/10.1080/10508406.2018.1522258.

Reitsma, Lizette. 2023. Complexities of a Hypothetical Co-supervision Case: On roles, Expectations, Independence. *Journal of Teaching and Learning in Higher Education* 4 (2): 1–8. https://doi.org/10.24834/jotl.4.2.882.

Rienecker, Lotte, Gitte Wichmann-Hansen, and Peter Stray Jørgensen. 2019. *God vejledning af specialer, bacheloroppgaver og projekter.* Frederiksberg: Samfundslitteratur.

Schneijderberg, Christian. 2021. Supervision Practices of Doctoral Education and Training. *Studies in Higher Education (Dorchester-on-Thames)* 46 (7): 1285–1295. https://doi.org/10.1080/03075079.2019.1689384.

Sidhu, Ravinder, and Gloria Dall'alba. 2017. 'A Strategy of Distinction' Unfolds: Unsettling the Undergraduate Outbound Mobility Experience. *British Journal of Sociology of Education* 38 (4): 468–484. https://doi.org/10.1080/01425692.2015.1131143.

Star, S. L, and J. R. Griesemer. 1989. Institutional Ecology. 'Translations', and Boundary Objects: Amateuers and Professionals in Berkeley's Museum of Vertebrate Zoology 1907–39. *Social Studies of Science* 19 (3). https://doi.org/10.1177/030631289019003003.

Strandler, Ola, Thomas Johansson, Gina Wisker, and Silwa Claesson. 2014. Supervisor or Counsellor? - Emotional Boundary Work in Supervision. *International Journal for Researcher Development* 5 (2): 70. https://doi.org/10.1108/IJRD-03-2014-0002.

Svinhufvud, Kimmo, and Sanna Vehviläinen. 2013. Papers Documents and the Opening of an Academic Supervision Encounter. *Text & Talk: an Interdisciplinary Journal of Language, Discourse & Communication studies* 33 (1): 139–166. https://doi.org/10.1515/text-2013-0007.

Van Veldhuizen, Bert, Ron Oostdam, Mascha Enthoven, and Marco Snoek. 2021. Reflective Movements in the Professional Development of Teacher Educators as Supervisors of Student Research in Higher Education. *European Journal of Teacher Education* 44 (4): 452–467. https://doi.org/10.1080/02619768.2020.1777977.

Vehviläinen, Sanna. 2012. Question-prefaced Advice in Feedback Sequences of Finnish Academic Supervisions. In *Advice in Discourse*, ed. Holger Limberg and Miriam A. Locher, 31–52. Amsterdam & Philadelphia: John Benjamins Publishing.

Vereijken, Mayke W.C., Roeland M. van der Rijst, Jan H. van Driel, and Friedo W. Dekker. 2018. Novice Supervisors' Practices and Dilemmatic Space in Supervision of Student Research Projects. *Teaching in Higher Education* 23 (4): 522–542. https://doi.org/10.1080/13562517.2017.1414791.

Wetherell, Margaret. 2012. *Affect and Emotion: A New Social Science Understanding*. London: Sage.

Wichmann-Hansen, Gitte, and Karl-Johan Schmidt Nielsen. 2023. Can Hands-on Supervision Get out of Hand? The Correlation between Directive Supervision and Doctoral Student Independence in a Danish Study Context. *Scandinavian Journal of Educational Research* (ahead-of-print): 1–16. https://doi.org/10.1080/00313831.2023.2204113.

Zackariasson, Maria. 2019. Encouraging Student Independence: Perspectives on Scaffolding in Higher Education Supervision. *Journal of Applied Research in Higher Education* 12 (3): 495–505. https://doi.org/10.1108/JARHE-01-2019-0012.

Open Access This chapter is licensed under the terms of the Creative Commons Attribution-NonCommercial-NoDerivatives 4.0 International License (http://creativecommons.org/licenses/by-nc-nd/4.0/), which permits any noncommercial use, sharing, distribution and reproduction in any medium or format, as long as you give appropriate credit to the original author(s) and the source, provide a link to the Creative Commons license and indicate if you modified the licensed material. You do not have permission under this license to share adapted material derived from this chapter or parts of it.

The images or other third party material in this chapter are included in the chapter's Creative Commons license, unless indicated otherwise in a credit line to the material. If material is not included in the chapter's Creative Commons license and your intended use is not permitted by statutory regulation or exceeds the permitted use, you will need to obtain permission directly from the copyright holder.

CHAPTER 5

Emotional Dimensions of Supervision

One reason why relationship building is an important part of supervision practice, as we discussed in the previous chapter, is that both writing and supervision of degree projects can be emotionally charged processes, often characterised by uncertainty, worry and anxiety. Supervision of degree projects is therefore not just about how to improve a piece of writing, or getting students to consider and reflect on their choices, but also about getting students to feel confident about their potential to cope with the considerable amount of work involved in producing a piece of academic writing at this level. In this chapter we explore this further and discuss issues connected to the emotional dimensions of supervision for both students and supervisors.

Emotions and Academic Writing

In our recorded supervision material, there are a number of examples of how the supervision interaction can be positively charged and characterised by joy, understanding and mutual appreciation (see also Zackariasson 2018). However, it is also clear from the supervision conversations we recorded and the focus group interviews we conducted that the degree project work, and thus the supervision, was regularly characterised by students feeling or expressing uncertainty about how to proceed or concern about how it would all turn out. Our study is thus in line with other research in this area, which has shown that working on academic theses, whether at undergraduate, graduate or postgraduate level, can be emotionally turbulent for both students and supervisors, and is often characterised by feelings of insecurity, anxiety, worry or guilt (see, e.g. Castello et al. 2009; Cotterall 2013; Doloriert et al. 2012; Han and Xu 2021; Liu and Yu 2022; Strandler et al. 2014; Todd et al. 2006; Zackariasson 2020). As has been pointed out in research on supervision at postgraduate level, such emotions may have a negative impact on the work process and the likelihood of students completing the task, and supervisors may to some extent have a role in preventing this (Wollast et al. 2023; Weise et al. 2020; Aitchison and Mowbray 2013; Aitchison et al. 2012).[1] However, emotions can also play a positive and constructive role in supervision interactions and in the process of writing an academic thesis, as discussed, for example, by Collins (2021), Collins and Brown (2021) and Cotterall (2013).

From an academic literacies perspective, the insecurity and worry expressed by students in our material can be understood in relation to how the task of writing a degree project in many respects differs from the coursework students have done earlier in their education. When students embark on their first degree project course and thus produce a more substantial academic text for the first time, they are usually confronted with partly new expectations and demands in terms of, for example, academic writing and student independence. In other words, they can be said to be undergoing what Lea and Street (2000) have termed a 'course switching', a change of course from their previous studies, which can contribute to them feeling uncertain about what is expected of them.

In the focus group interviews we conducted, it was evident that supervisors were well aware that students might feel insecure and worried about the degree project, or certain parts of it, even though the ideal was that students should also be able to enjoy the process, as exemplified by the following quote from one of the focus group interviews conducted at a Russian university:

> They get very nervous during the defence of these short pieces [presentations of the degree project topic] because we invite a lot of people. The

---

[1] In some cases, such negative emotions may develop into more severe stress-related problems or even depression, and as Strandler et al. (2014) point out in a study of doctoral supervision, supervisors need to be aware of the differences between acting as or being perceived as a counsellor and being a supervisor. We will not explore this further here but would like to stress that supervisors are encouraged to refer students to professionals within the university's student health services if they see signs of more severe stress-related problems or depression in connection with the degree project process.

students worry for each other /.../. In the end, they always change their topic, make slight modifications. In any case, we want the students to start enjoying their work. /.../ The result won't be satisfactory if they do the work only with their heads.
Focus Group Interview 9

The following quote from one of the focus group interviews conducted at a Swedish university also illustrates how supervisors were aware of how degree projects were often associated with anxiety, yet at the same time, as supervisors, they knew that the work could potentially be very rewarding:

I usually bring this up at the beginning when I meet new groups of degree project students. Writing a degree project is a pain in the neck. It is often associated with anxiety, and many people think it is the most demanding course they have ever done. But then I usually add that many people also think it's the most enjoyable course they've done. And that's to do with the fact that there are so many choices. That it's up to the students themselves. They are the ones who write the degree project. It is that element of creativity and all the choices that are associated with anxiety.
Focus Group Interview 2

In this quote, the interviewed supervisor linked the description of degree project work as being associated with anxiety to aspects of independence, such as the expectation of a certain level of creativity and the need to make one's own choices (cf. Chap. 3). In both the Swedish and Russian focus group interviews, there were several supervisors who similarly emphasised the expectations associated with academic writing and independence as one of the things that could contribute to students feeling insecure or anxious:

I also think that independence can be a problem. Not for me as a supervisor and such, but for the students who know that there is a requirement for a certain form of independence. That they have to go in and analyse the material themselves, make their own interpretations. In a way they feel very insecure about that.
Focus Group Interview 4

There really are students who are afraid of independence and don't know how to work independently. In this case I use the power of choice. Choice gives a certain freedom and also develops creative thinking. But then again, talking about the relationship between creativity, independence and responsibility. Responsibility is when you have to accept the consequences of your choices.

Focus Group Interview 12

Indeed, it is not surprising that many students feel insecure and anxious about the task of writing a degree project, as it is usually a new experience for them. Nevertheless, it is in many ways desirable for them to have sufficient confidence in their ability to carry out the work in an appropriate way, as this can contribute to their active participation in the process, which is essential from a scaffolding perspective (van de Pol 2012; van de Pol et al. 2010). For example, if students are uncertain about their own abilities and competences, it may be much more difficult for them to find the courage to make the necessary initiatives, choices and decisions related to their degree project.

However, supervisors may also feel worried, anxious and insecure in the supervision situation, as research in this area has shown (Light et al. 2009; Todd et al. 2006; Han and Xu 2021; Vereijken et al. 2018; Almlöv and Grubbström 2023). Each degree project is to some extent unique, each student is different, and even with extensive supervision experience, it is impossible to know in advance what will happen during the degree project process. If the work is progressing as planned, supervision may seem relatively easy and carefree, but if the students you supervise are suffering from personal problems or life crises, are not submitting work on time or are not producing work of the required standard, it is not always obvious how you, as a supervisor, should act to best help the students. Supervisors may also find it difficult to answer all students' questions or to have sufficient competence in all the parts the degree project consists of, not least because they may supervise in different academic programmes and contexts.

At the end of this chapter, we will return to the concern and uncertainty that supervisors may feel and the implications this may have in supervision practice. However, we begin by discussing how supervisors might deal with students' insecurities and concerns about the degree project process and relate them to issues such as collective and group supervision, student collegiality and the issue of directive supervision versus ideals and perceptions of independence.

Handling Student Insecurity

It is not always obvious to supervisors when students are feeling insecure about different aspects of the degree project work, as students may in some cases try to hide their uncertainties, for example if they feel there is a risk of otherwise appearing unfavourably. However, in our recorded supervision material, it is evident that the affective practices (see Wetherell 2012) that emerged in the supervision interaction could in many cases be characterised by insecurity and uncertainties. The uncertainties that students expressed during supervision sessions could concern more general aspects, such as whether they felt they had sufficient competence to carry out all parts of the work and bring it to a successful outcome. In addition, they frequently expressed uncertainty about practical aspects of the work, such as the collection of empirical material, the organisation of the text or the reference system they were expected to use, and how they would manage it. Even when students had received written course information and perhaps listened to information from a course coordinator or seminar leader, they were not always sure how to interpret the instructions or whether they had understood the information they had received correctly. The following quote from a collective supervision session illustrates how such uncertainty could be expressed in supervision interaction:

Supervisor B: You were wondering if you were going to do interviews with teachers?

Student H: Yeah, well, and that was partly because I also didn't know if it was allowed to do a pure, like text analysis. Or if I have to bring in interviews. /.../ But most of all I would like to do a text analysis of teaching materials. /.../

Supervisor B: That's an important question you raise. Like, what kind of materials and methods you are going to use.

Student H: Yeah, because then, well ... I feel that it will be a turning point, that I will have to change perspectives.

Student V: Yeah, I'm uncertain too.

Student G: [laughs] Yeah, exactly. Well, what should I do then? I feel like ... I think I'm going to get a no on this, I feel. I don't know what to do now. (laughs) Yeah, well, it will work out!
Supervisor B, Recording 1, Collective supervision

When, in this conversation sequence, Student H mentions being uncertain about an aspect of the thesis work—what kind of empirical material they can use in the degree project—the other students in the collective supervision meeting join in and express that they too have felt uncertain about this issue. The supervisor's initial reaction, as can be seen in the quote, is to confirm that this is a significant issue. Later in the conversation, when the students had further developed what they felt uncertain about concerning the choice of empirical material, the supervisor returned to the question in a more developed way. At this point, the supervisor started by referring to the course coordinator and the seminar the students were due to attend to discuss their thesis plans, recommending that the students should write their plans according to their current thinking and then raise the issue in the seminar to get a response from the seminar leader. In addition, the students were advised not to send an email to the course coordinator asking about it, as they may have had to wait a few days for a response, which would take too much time.

Here, then, the supervisor did not resolve the students' uncertainty by providing an answer to their question but instead referred to the course coordinator and the seminar leader and their role in this. This makes it apparent to students that there are several people involved in the degree project work and the supervision process, and that the supervisor is not the sole expert on how things should be done. In other words, the supervisor's role as an expert is toned down (cf. Dysthe 2002), and the supervision of degree projects is presented as a collegial practice in which people in different positions complement each other. Another aspect is that although the supervisor offered the students a concrete suggestion on how to handle the obstacle they were facing, this suggestion placed the responsibility for dealing with the problem with the students. They were the ones who would have to raise the issue in the seminar and, depending on the answer they received, decide what to do next. In other words, the scaffolding work that could be said to be present in this supervision interaction was based on the students being active in the process, not on the supervisor giving them the answers (cf. van de Pol 2012; van de Pol et al. 2010).

What it could look like in our material when students expressed uncertainty about whether their competence in a given area was sufficient for what they were expected to do, is illustrated in the example below, where one of the students talked about feeling unsure about how best to conduct interviews:

Supervisor F:	But you have done an interview, you said?
Student O:	Yes. We've done two.
Supervisor F:	Two, mm.
Student O:	Yeah, but … What we … To be honest (laughs), it's like this, uh … These questions we had written. It's hard to, you know, expand them and go into … And then I'd love to … I feel like I'm a bit lacking in how to do an interview.
Supervisor F:	Okay.
Student O:	Like, how do you do an interview so that it is sort of … I'm not really fully studied on that.
Supervisor F:	No, and that's something that you can't really just give a lecture on how to do. You really have to practice it. Actually I think you can practise on each other or practise on somebody else to start with.

Supervisor F, Recording 1, Pair supervision

Again, the supervisor's first response to the student's uncertainty about how to conduct a good interview was to go relatively straight to a possible solution to the problem—that the students should simply practise conducting interviews before going out and interviewing the intended interviewees. However, when the conversation later in the supervision session continued to revolve around the difficult art of interviewing, the supervisor also explicitly confirmed the students' experience that it is difficult to conduct good interviews. At the same time, the supervisor continued to suggest workable solutions, for example how the students could improve their interviewing technique and how they should best use the interview guide and the questions they had formulated there.

The way in which the supervisor both acknowledged the students' experience that conducting interviews is difficult and offered specific suggestions on how they could improve their interviewing technique, contributed to the affective practices in this conversation sequence being characterised neither by an amplification of the uncertainty communicated by the students nor by a reduction or ignoring of their experience (cf. Wetherell 2012). The interaction between students and supervisor could thus be seen as clearly anchored in the supervisor's greater experience and competence in the field but at the same time including a recognition of the students' experiences. From a scaffolding perspective, this can be seen as an example of contingency, where the supervisor learns about the students' level and then gives advice and recommendations based on this knowledge (van de Pol et al. 2015, 2019). Emphasising that good interviewing techniques are not something that can be learnt during a lecture but need to be practised, also encourages student activity (cf. Barrineau et al. 2019). In this way, the responsibility for practising conducting interviews or otherwise improving their interviewing technique is primarily placed on the students, even if the supervisor makes suggestions on how to proceed.

Another aspect of degree project work that can make students feel insecure and confused, and which came up in both the supervision interaction and the focus group interviews, is when students feel that they are getting mixed messages in that different people are giving them different answers to their questions or different advice on how to proceed. In some cases it may be fellow students who share an impression of what their supervisors, or perhaps supervisors in previous courses, have said they should or must do. In other cases, students may feel that course coordinators and seminar leaders have recommended something completely different from what their supervisors advocated. This can be seen in the following example from a collective supervision session, where one of the students recounted what was discussed in one of the seminars of the degree project course:

Student X: Because [the seminar leader] wrote … She gave good examples of problem formulation and background and so on. And then she wrote: "One way could be like this: This is interesting since most of the research that exists …" blah, blah, blah. And then it is one part of the research that you bring up in the background. While in the other she wrote: "When I have observed and participated in classroom contexts during my placement …" blah, blah, blah. And then you go on.
Supervisor E: Yes, yes, that's right.
Student X: Can I then write that I have seen this problem in the classroom itself and then write the justification for the research in the background? Or should I … Well, I … It will be … I don't know what to do because everybody says different things.
Supervisor E: You're absolutely right. Unfortunately, so to speak (laughs). You are.
Student X: Yeah. (laughs)

Supervisor E: Now there are people from two different academic disciplines and that's ... But the basic structure would be agreed by all. That you should take on something here with some kind of aim and research problem and then we have previous research and so on. What has been done? So to that extent no one will ever disagree. At least here at the university. Then there is some disagreement about exactly how to do it.
Supervisor E, Recording 1, Collective Supervision

In this example, too, the supervisor acknowledged the student's experience and expressed sense of uncertainty by confirming that it is true that seminar leaders and supervisors within the degree project course may well say different things. Here, however, the supervisor did not offer solutions or tell the student what to do, but focused primarily on the fact that this is something to be expected in an academic context. The message conveyed to the students in the collective supervision session was thus that it is possible to do things differently in academic writing, and depending on who you ask, you will get different answers about what is the best way to do it. By not immediately providing the students with a straight-forward solution—this is how you should think, yes, you can write like this—but rather striving to give them tools to deal with this kind of double message and the uncertainty it can create, also in the future, the supervisor's practice here could be said to contribute to the development of the students' academic literacies in ways that go beyond writing skills or the tasks associated with this particular degree project course (cf. Lea and Stierer 2000). In Chap. 3, we described how the ability to make choices and to justify and motivate them was one of the central aspects in the understandings of student independence in a supervision context that emerged in our study. From this perspective, the supervisor's actions can also be said to promote independence in so far as they emphasise that there are generally several possibilities in academic writing and the degree project process and that it is ultimately the students who have to make the necessary choices.

In the continuation of the supervision session quoted above, the supervisor also expressed views on how to think about the background and motivation of the thesis topic. However, the supervisor continued to phrase this in a way that emphasised that there could be several ways of doing this, saying things such as "Many people think that, and I am one of them" or " if you look at degree projects in general, you can see that there is both this and" and so on. The supervisor also referred to the course description for the course and what the course coordinator might say about this, emphasising that it is difficult as a supervisor to know what, for example, a seminar leader might mean by a specific comment. In the end, the participants in the collective supervision session agreed on a certain understanding of how the background and motivation of the thesis topic could be handled, and Student X commented that it had all become clearer.

Here the supervisor largely took on the role of expert, but in a way that clearly placed their own opinions and approaches within a wider academic context and collegial practice that included seminar leaders and course coordinators. Furthermore, the supervision was not primarily characterised by the supervisor telling the students what to do. Instead, the group discussed the issue together until they reached an understanding that they could all agree on and that the students felt was consistent with what they had heard in other contexts. In other words, while it was evident in the interaction that the supervisor was an expert in the field to a greater extent than the students, there were also strong elements of partnership in the supervisor-student relationship (cf. Dysthe 2002).

When insecure students ask supervisors questions about various aspects of the thesis work, the first spontaneous reaction may be to answer their questions as best one can. However, as Vehviläinen (2003) points out, student activity and self-direction are influenced by whether teachers choose to provide them with ready-made solutions and answers or, on the contrary, avoid doing so. As shown, the examples from our material also suggest that other types of actions than directly answering students' questions may have greater potential to promote student activity and initiative. Handling questions in this way could thus potentially contribute to student independence and to the ongoing scaffolding work being based on both student and supervisor activity (cf. Magnusson and Zackariasson 2018; van de Pol et al. 2010; van de Pol 2012). At the same time, there are certainly situations in which it is most appropriate or constructive to give students direct answers to their questions, not only to help them progress in their degree project work but also because it might reduce their stress and anxieties.

Concerned Students

In our research material, it was evident that in addition to feeling insecure and uncertain about their thesis work, students could also feel worried and anxious. In the recorded supervision conversations, there are a number of examples of how the affective practices (Wetherell 2012) in the supervision interaction could be characterised by students' worry, fear or anxiety. Sometimes these kinds of emotional reactions were expressed more implicitly, but students could also talk quite explicitly about being 'really scared' or 'panicking', say that something was 'scary' or describe something as a 'horror' or 'nightmare'. Students used these kinds of words and phrases, for example, when supervision conversations concerned issues such as whether they would actually be able to complete the degree project before the due date, or the risk that, despite all the work they had put in, the degree project would not meet the requirements. They could express concern or fear that they had made choices that would prove detrimental to their continued work. There were thus several examples of how anticipatory emotions, that is emotions that arise when the individual thinks about or imagines the future, were articulated in the supervision interaction (see Barsics et al. 2016). This could be understood in the context that an important goal of supervision is to get students to think about and plan for the further work on the degree project.

In the supervision sessions we recorded, it was noticeable that supervisors could react in various ways when students expressed concern or worry about the thesis work and the final outcome, talking about being scared or panicking and so on. One response could be to reassure the students and emphasise that their concerns were exaggerated or unjustified. Another could be to acknowledge their concerns and try to be supportive, and yet another could be to use the students' concerns to make a pedagogical point. Obviously, how supervisors respond to students' concern and worry may also depend on how it is expressed by them. As mentioned above, there are examples in our material where students explicitly expressed their feelings of concern, such as in the following extract from a collective supervision meeting, where one of the students talked about the anticipated risk of the collected empirical material being inadequate, in terms of fear:

Student Y: /.../ I've come to the conclusion after this ... Because when I was like, "Oh my God, I can't do it", my sister

said, "But it's better that you do the work now". Because I'm trying to think ... If I have this question and I expect something like this answer - this or that. But then I get this instead. Like, then my whole degree project mustn't fall apart. /.../ Well, I don't know. At least that's how I felt. I'd rather do the work now than sit there and have collected material and got everything and then you sit there and write the degree project but your material doesn't fit at all. Nothing came of it. That's my fear anyway.
Supervisor H, Recording 2, Collective supervision

When students express their worries and anxieties explicitly and emphatically, it can be easier for supervisors to pick up on this and relate to these expressed emotions in the supervision interaction. The excerpt below is an example of how this could be done in practice in the recorded supervision sessions. Here, the supervisor began by affirming what the student had said in the immediately preceding part of the supervision session, regarding the plan for the further work:

Supervisor E: It's ... It seems ... Yeah, that seems to make sense.
Student X: That's good.
Supervisor E: Mm.
Student X: That's great! (laughs) Yeah, because that's what I was afraid of. That I might be completely off track.
Supervisor E: No, you're absolutely not.
Student X: Okay.
Supervisor E, Recording 1, Collective supervision

Allaying the students' concerns and giving a reassuring message, as the supervisor does in this example, could be seen as a way of helping to ensure that the students can continue with the work as planned, without getting caught up in worry or fear of making mistakes. At the same time, there are some risks with such an approach, such as students due to the reassurance may underestimate the potential difficulties and problems they might encounter during the degree project (Zackariasson 2019). In this particular quote, the supervisor began with a relatively open affirmation that the student had made the right choice—'that seems to make sense', but when the student then brought up having been afraid of being completely wrong, the affirmation became more definitive—'you are absolutely not'. This could be regarded as an effect of the affective practices in the interaction being influenced by the student's explicit expression of fear and concern about how things will go, which contributes to the supervisor reinforcing the reassuring message (cf. Wetherell 2012).

There are also examples in our material of supervisors ignoring or not responding at all to the worries and concerns expressed by students. The quote below is an example of this. In it, the students signal that they are worried about whether the survey they are planning will produce the results they need to write a good analysis and ultimately a good enough degree project:

Supervisor A:	Why are you interested in this particular thing that you …?
Student D:	Um, no, but … Because it's so interesting how people are described and portrayed differently depending on their gender. And then I think that journalism should try to be objective and, like, that depends on what you write. That is, what words and what facts you tell. But how objective will it be? Because as a journalist you're also coloured by everything that everybody else is coloured by.
Student C:	That's what we want to find out. Whether that's the case in [major Swedish newspaper] or not.
Student D:	Yeah.
Supervisor A:	Mm.
Student C:	It might be what we think. It could also be that it is not the case at all.
Student D:	So we sort of hope that it … That we will find something. (laughs)
Student C:	Two months and then we don't find anything. (laughs)
Student C:	(sighs) Yes.
Supervisor A:	What is objectivity then?
	Supervisor A, Recording 2, Pair supervision

In this conversation sequence, the supervisor chooses not to comment or build on the students' sighing and laughing comments that they might not find what they are interested in. The supervisor does not reassure the students that everything will be fine and does not otherwise indicate having noticed the students' concerns. Instead, the supervisor's response is to refer back to one of the things the students mentioned earlier in the conversation—that journalism is expected to strive for objectivity. The students' concerns are thus left hanging in the air while the conversation moves on to other things.

Based on the idea that frustration control can be an integral part of active scaffolding work that might help students move forward (van de Pol et al. 2010; van de Pol 2012), it could be argued that the supervisor in this particular conversation sequence is missing something essential by not capturing the concerns expressed by the students. At the same time, an approach such as that exemplified by Supervisor A here may be rooted in the perception that the interaction between supervisors and students should not focus on emotional aspects but rather on the joint work of producing a good degree project. In other words, that in such cases it is more important, and more relevant or beneficial to the degree project process, to focus on the text and the task, rather than risk getting caught up in emotional reactions and discussions. Another aspect of this is that the students here do not express their concerns nearly as explicitly as in some of the previous examples. Although they sigh and laugh about how they may not be able to get what they want after several months of work, thereby signalling that this is something they have been thinking about and worrying about, they do not present it as a major concern. As mentioned above, this can also influence the supervisors' reaction and response.

Another way for supervisors to manage when students express worry or fear is neither to ignore it nor to give reassuring feedback, but to confirm that there may indeed be valid reasons for concern. We have examples of this in our material, as in the following quote from a collective supervision session with Supervisor H, where students described what they were worried about or found 'scary' about the degree project work:

Student Y: I find it difficult that everything should be sustainable.[2] What you collect, your material and then you write. And then you have, "This - is this relevant?" But in the end nothing fits and then you want to pull your hair out like "Why doesn't it fit?". Before, it was other people's thoughts. Like, when we had classes and you did an exam and there was a right or wrong. Whereas now you're the one who's going to investigate something and make sure it's sustainable and I think that's scary.

---

[2] In the original quotation, the student used the Swedish word 'hållbart', sustainable, to mean more cohesive.

Supervisor H: Okay.
Student Z: I think it has to do with the fact that you have to make all the choices yourself. Like all the time you have to be like "OK ... well ... But then I choose to go in this direction because ..." So you have to keep making new choices (chuckles). Make up your mind.
Supervisor H: Mm.
Student W: It's the first time we're really standing on our own two feet.
Supervisor H: I think you're putting your finger on what's tough here, that is ... That the ball is in your court and it's very much about making decisions. To choose. You are free to do what you ... And I'm here as a supervisor. /.../ But the starting point is that it is entirely up to you to write the degree project. And it should be that it is you who choose the questions, the purpose, the empirical material. It is up to you to decide how to talk about your questions and your results in the degree project, in the text.
Supervisor H, Recording 1, Collective supervision

In this example, rather than reassuring the students or downplaying their concerns, the supervisor makes it clear that writing a degree project can be difficult or 'tough', not least when it comes to the expectations of making one's own choices and decisions. It may seem counterintuitive to acknowledge students' concerns that working on a degree project will be difficult and tough. However, this kind of response can serve as a scaffolding tool that can contribute to frustration control by giving students a realistic picture of what the thesis work will entail. If students are prepared for it to require a lot of work and that they will encounter difficulties during the process, this may lead to less frustration when they encounter problems (cf. van de Pol et al. 2010; van de Pol 2012; Zackariasson 2019).

In the quote, the supervisor not only addresses the potentially negative and problematic but also presents the expectation that students should make their own decisions and choices as something potentially positive, describing it as being free to do what they want. It is mentioned that the supervisor will be there to support them, but this is more of a passing reference without going into detail about how or to what extent. The supervisor's approach, with its consistent focus on the student's role and responsibility, can thus also be seen as a way of opening up for student activity and participation. In other words, the supervisor's choice of wording not only highlights that the expectation of independence can be fraught with difficulties but also strengthens and enhances the students' position by making it seem rather self-evident that it is they who should be doing the work. This could be seen as contributing to making the supervision interaction in the example characterised primarily by partnership (cf. Dysthe 2002).

As we have seen, there are several ways in which supervisors can react and relate to students who express more or less explicitly that they are worried or concerned about the degree project work. Depending on the situation, the personalities of the supervisor and the student, the stage of the student's work and the nature of the concern, different ways of dealing with these expressed concerns may be more or less appropriate. Hence, we would argue that it may be beneficial for supervisors to reflect on how they tend to approach this type of situation in supervision, and whether there may be times when their first spontaneous reaction may not be the most appropriate one. By listening to and responding to students' concerns in a more reflective way, supervisors may have a better chance of contributing to frustration control and of preventing students from becoming so caught up in negative emotions that their emotional well-being becomes an obstacle to their work on the degree project (cf. Wollast et al. 2023).

Student Insecurity in Collective and Group Supervision

Another interesting aspect of the example from the collective supervision session with Supervisor H in the previous section is how the students interact and relate to each other in the supervision situation. The premise of this book is that supervision should be viewed as a social and collegial practice, and this is one example where it becomes obvious that fellow students are also part of the local academic environment in which this practice takes place. In other words, peer feedback and discussion between students—within the same course, seminar group or supervision group—can be, and often is, an essential part of supervision interaction.

In Student Z's and Student W's comments in the above example, they supported and confirmed what Student Y said about the degree project work being frightening and difficult, which can be understood as a kind of student collegiality. But they also made their own suggestions about possible reasons why thesis work might appear daunting—that they were now forced to make their own choices and expected to stand on their own two feet. In this way, they elaborated and clarified the concerns expressed in Student Y's statement, and the supervisor's response focused on precisely these aspects. In this way, the students' contributions to the discussion thus influenced how the supervision interaction developed in the specific situation.

In the collective and group supervision sessions that we have documented in our material, there are further examples of students supporting and confirming each other's experiences and comments in a kind of peer feedback. The focus is often on difficulties or obstacles in writing the degree project and the uncertainty or concern felt by the students, as in the following example from a collective supervision meeting with Supervisor B:

Supervisor B:	Oh, I've read your … your texts for today. Thanks for the texts by the way.
Student G:	It was difficult to write informally.
Student H:	Yeah.
Student G:	Yeah, it was really hard.
Student V:	I don't even think I could do that. I don't know.
Student G:	No, I thought, "Damn, she's included a lot of …" I was like, "Wow, she's got a lot of stuff!" I thought "Oops, should we have done that?" I was a bit like that too … Yeah. (laughs)
Supervisor B:	Right, uh, but that … Exactly. You are on such a level that you can do what you want, really.
Student G:	Mm. But it was kind of hard.
Supervisor B:	But I've noticed that at certain levels in higher education it can be … It can be kind of liberating not to feel like this "I'm expected to have a lot of references, the theory should be ready" sort of. That it becomes a barrier.
Student H:	Yeah, it was kind of nice that it didn't feel like it was a requirement that things like that should be in the text.

Supervisor B, Recording 1, Collective supervision

Here again, students thus supported each other's emotional experiences, in this case that they found it difficult and somewhat confusing to write the kind of informal text that the supervisor asked for because there were so few guidelines. When not just one but several students in the collective supervision session express similar experiences, the pressure on the supervisor to respond increases. In the example, Supervisor B did this by explaining the pedagogical idea behind the wish that students should submit a more informal text rather than, for example, a project plan.

The student collegial aspect of supervision practice can also be seen in the example above, when Student G describes it as though it was seeing the other students' texts that caused uncertainty as to whether the assignment had been done in the correct or expected way. During the degree project process, students may find themselves in many situations where their own work is explicitly or implicitly compared with that of others. For example, in peer feedback groups at writing seminars and during collective supervision, but also in more informal discussion groups with fellow students or on social media. While it can be a valuable resource to receive peer feedback on your work, or simply to gain insight into how others have approached or resolved different aspects of thesis writing, it could also lead to stress and anxiety. This may be especially true for those students who feel that they have not progressed as far as their peers. In our material, however, it is primarily the positive aspects of this kind of student collegiality that emerge. By giving students the opportunity to air their problems and concerns in collective supervision sessions and to receive feedback from both peers and supervisors, questions and ambiguities were often resolved.

There are also examples in the recorded supervision sessions of students making concrete contributions to the supervision interaction, in relation to issues raised by fellow students. As supervisors may be involved in several degree project courses, within different academic programmes or at different levels, supervised students may sometimes have a better knowledge of the specific guidelines and recommendations that apply to their particular course or academic programme. This is illustrated by an example from the same collective supervision session as above:

Supervisor B:	Then I would say that you shouldn't use interviews, uh, except in that, you know, you can talk to people (laughs).
Student G:	Mm, yeah, I've had a meeting with these teachers.
Student V:	Can I just add something?
Student G:	Mm.
Student V:	I think this year there's a requirement that you have to use at least two methods. So if you do a survey then you have to have another one.
Student G:	Mm, yeah, I'm going to do observations. /.../

Student V:	Yeah, exactly. OK, then that's it.
Supervisor B:	OK, so there is one of those, uh, like …?
Student V:	Yeah, right, guidelines.
Student H:	OK, right. I hadn't realised that.
Student V:	I only found out a few days ago.
Supervisor B:	Well then … Methods are a difficult thing. There are some that are very concrete. Then there are these … yes, but as you mentioned, text analysis and comparisons, if those are two methods, well, then you've ticked off two.
	Supervisor B, Recording 1, Collective supervision

In this example, it appears that Supervisor B is unaware of the change in guidelines for the degree project that Student G refers to, which, as mentioned earlier, is not surprising given that many supervisors teach within several different degree project courses. When students bring such information into the conversation, the supervisors must, however, deal with that in the further supervision interaction, as Supervisor B started to do at the end of the quote above.

Collective supervision, where supervisors gather several degree project students for a joint supervision meeting, can thus also open up the possibility for supervision to become a student-collegial practice, in the sense that students have the opportunity to share their knowledge with their peers as well as with the supervisor. But also in the sense that the students can support each other emotionally, as they are in a similar situation, experiencing the joys and hardships of thesis writing at the same time, while the student perspective for the supervisor is something they must take on actively and through shifting perspectives (see Chap. 6). From an academic literacies perspective, this can be understood as the power relations between supervisors and students changing when there are several students present at the supervision meeting, as students can collectively raise questions, views or emotional experiences they are having, which in turn can lead to supervisors having to justify or explain their reasoning, advice and suggestions more clearly.

Power relations between supervisors and students are also affected when two or sometimes more students write a degree project together. This is illustrated in the following extract from a pair supervision meeting from our material, where the supervisor notes that the students have not done all the things that were agreed at the last meeting:

Supervisor A:	First of all, I just wanted to ask … Because there were a lot of things that I pointed out in our last supervision meeting that you haven't done anything about.
Student D:	There were?
Supervisor A:	Er, yes, some things. But with the theories … That maybe that part should come before the previous research, for example. We talked about that. You start with theories, but a theory is like the pattern. That is what you use …
Student D:	Okay.
Student C:	Mm
Supervisor A:	In order to eh … eh …
Student D:	Yeah, we probably forgot to move that …
Student C:	We've been concentrating mainly on the analysis.
Student D:	Yeah.
Student C:	That's taken a lot more time than we thought.

Supervisor A, Recording 7, Pair supervision

Even though the students here provide explanations as to why they have not done what the supervisor thought they would have done since the last supervision session, in this part of the conversation they do not appear particularly distressed by the supervisor's comments or remorseful for not doing what the supervisor apparently expected. Being two people in this kind of situation, sharing responsibility for the process of the degree project, and thereby responsibility for what has not been achieved, is a different emotional situation to being solely responsible for the degree project, with no one else to lean on or blame. In the example, the students also support each other in their response to the supervisor, taking turns to explain why things have turned out the way they have. Thus, the relationship between supervisor and students in pair or group supervision can be said to be less hierarchical than in individual supervision. It should be noted, however, that this is not always positive. For example, if students take the supervisor's comments more lightly than they would if they were solely responsible for the work, it may be more difficult for the supervisor to get them to acknowledge relevant feedback and criticism that could improve the degree project.

The examples in this section show how students can be a valuable resource in supervision interaction, as has also been noted in studies of collective and group supervision (e.g. Baker et al. 2014; Nordentoft et al. 2013, 2019; Rienecker et al. 2019; Wichmann-Hansen et al. 2015). They can be a resource for each other, supporting the experiences of their fellow students and clarifying and elaborating on thoughts and ideas that may not yet be fully developed and formulated, as well as for the supervisors, since students may have a better insight into exactly what guidelines apply to the course they are taking. Since thesis supervision at the undergraduate level, where there may be large cohorts of students, is often at least partly group-based or with students writing in pairs, it may be valuable for supervisors to reflect on and discuss how peer feedback and students' interaction with each other can be used for pedagogical purposes in the supervision context.

Emotions as a Supervision Tool

As we have seen so far, students could often express their uncertainty about how to proceed with their work, or their worries and fears about whether they had made the right choices and how it might all turn out in the end. However, there are also instances in our material where supervisors introduce elements into the supervision interaction that they know may evoke fear or concern among the supervised students, as exemplified by the following quote from one of the focus group interviews conducted at a Russian university:

> I have a principle - you don't come to me empty-handed. If a student writes to me: "Let's meet", I reply: "Just seeing your face is rather meaningless. Send me at least 5 pages of written work. I'll read it in advance and then we'll discuss it". /.../ In this way, I push them to do something, in a way. /.../ "There will be no discussion without the first chapter. Unless you send me at least something for the first chapter, I consider our meeting irrelevant". And that's OK. They are scared, but they do it.
> *Focus Group Interview 5*

Encouraging or pushing students in this way to do something that might seem daunting, such as submitting text to the supervisor, based on an assessment that it would be beneficial to the degree project process, can be a way of helping students to overcome the obstacles that fear and anxiety can become. It conveys the message that some things need to be done, regardless of how the students may feel.

Another way in which supervisors could consciously introduce aspects of worry or anxiety into the supervision interaction was by letting students know what to expect during the degree project process. Although conversations about what would await them often concerned the writing process or practical elements, they also regularly touched on affective aspects, with supervisors communicating to students what emotions they might experience later on. When supervisors in this way used their experience of academic writing and supervision to warn students about what might happen later in the process, it can be understood as the use of anticipated emotions (Barsics et al. 2016) as a pedagogical tool in the supervision interaction.

This was done by different means and to varying degrees by the supervisors whose supervision sessions we documented. The most common was for supervisors to refer to the timeframe of the degree project courses, pointing out that students did not have much time and that it would be quite difficult and stressful if they did not pick up the pace of their work or make sure that they did what they were supposed to do. But there were other examples in the material, for example in the recorded supervision sessions with Supervisor H, who generally tended to use expressive and engaged language and vivid descriptions, when trying to get students to prepare for what would come later in process. As in the example below, where Supervisor H emphasised the importance of choosing the right topic for the degree project, as the culmination of the process can be very stressful:

Supervisor H: You should /.../ find a topic that you feel: This is exciting. This is something that's interesting. This is something that I am motivated to work with, that I want to work with. It's really important. Because like I said … Many of you will be tearing your hair out in the last week and feeling like: "Why did I get into this?!" (pretend sobbing) "I'm leaving teacher education!" And then it's really important that you have a topic that feels like … Well, but this - this is still exciting.
Supervisor H, Recording 1, Collective supervision

In the quote, Supervisor H repeatedly talked about how it is 'really important' that students think carefully about their choice of subject and choose something they are genuinely interested in. In addition, Supervisor H used emotional aspects to emphasise the importance of this, using expressions such as the students "will be tearing your hair out", as well as feigned sobs and statements in a borrowed student voice (see Chap. 6) that conveyed resignation and a desire to leave the entire programme. In this way, the despair that students may feel towards the end of the degree project process was powerfully illustrated and contrasted with the potential excitement of having chosen a good degree project topic.

The same supervisor also used committed and emotionally charged language when discussing concrete, specific parts of the thesis work, such as referencing systems and reference management, and the importance of working diligently with them:

Supervisor H: Everything you write should be referenced according to the Harvard system. And then, when you're sitting there with your books open, it's so insanely, insanely easy to write a Harvard bracket. You put in a little Gustavsson 1994, page blabla (laughs). And then suddenly you realise that you're not going to use that reference, and then it takes a second to hit delete. But imagine the nightmare of having written a lot of text and then having to add references that you didn't put in before. And then you have returned the books to the library. (laughs) Or the person you borrowed the book from wants it back. And just going through the texts to find out which page it was? Never end up there! As soon as you have a book in front of you, write references in your notes.
Supervisor H, Recording 1, Collective supervision

Here the supervisor's message is reinforced by the use of expressions such as it is "insanely, insanely easy" to write a reference in the text and strong exhortations such as "Never end up there!" The message is also reinforced by portraying the fictive situation as a 'nightmare', a horror scenario that students risk experiencing if they do not follow the supervisor's advice. When supervisors in this way use anticipated emotions (Barsics et al. 2016) to get students to work in a certain way, it can be understood as a pedagogical tool that may broaden and develop the students' academic literacies and help them manage the course switching that is required of them at this stage (cf. Lea and Street 2000). Supervisors lend their wider experience of academic writing to the students, showing them that thesis work is not just about producing a text, but that it involves a range of emotional aspects such as stress, anxiety, uncertainty—as well as joy and pride when it is finished, and the student has completed what is for many a challenging task.

In their study of doctoral writing, Castello et al. (2009) argue that knowledge of the writing process tends to reduce students' levels of worry and anxiety, which in turn can have a positive impact on their work and performance. When supervisors draw students' attention to the problems they may encounter during the degree project process—and warn them of the possible consequences—it can be seen as one way to illuminate the writing process and could from this perspective potentially contribute to reducing students' experiences of stress and anxiety.

The use of emotional elements in supervision, such as anticipatory or anticipated feelings, can also make it easier for students to listen to and actually absorb what the supervisor wants to say. This can potentially help to decrease the risk that what the supervisor perceives as a direct request or requirement is perceived by the students as general advice or something optional. In this sense, this type of supervision can be perceived as more directive and controlling than supervisors simply telling students what to consider in the future (cf. Wichmann-Hansen and Schmidt Nielsen 2023; Wang and Li 2011). On the one hand, this can be beneficial for the degree project process, as it makes it more obvious when the supervisors are saying something that is particularly important. For example, when Supervisor H warned students that they could end up in a 'nightmare situation' if they ignored the advice. On the other hand, there is also the possibility that this could lead to students feeling that they have less room to make their own choices and decisions, at least if these go against what the supervisors have suggested, as there is also an emotional pressure on the students to do what the supervisors say. In this sense it might thus discourage student activity and independence.

Using Dysthe's (2002) concepts, we can describe this as the interaction between supervisor and student becoming more characterised by the supervisor acting as an expert, teaching the student not only about the academic aspects of the thesis process but also about the emotional elements. From another point of view, it could be argued that supervisors, by sharing their experience of thesis writing with students on an emotional level, contribute to an increased element of partnership, as they show students that anyone can feel stress and anxiety in this kind of situation. In other words, it becomes a kind of normalisation of the negative emotions that many students may experience at different stages of the thesis process (cf. Svinhufvud et al. 2017).

Students Seeking Affirmation

Preparing students not only academically but also emotionally for what they may encounter during the degree project process can thus be a scaffolding tool that has the potential to contribute to reducing students' frustration and anxiety during the process (cf. van de Pol et al. 2010; van de Pol 2012). Another possible scaffolding tool that can contribute to this is confirming that students are on the right track, for example by recognising and affirming their choices and actions. In our recorded supervision material, it was a recurring pattern that students sought affirmation in a variety of ways about whether they had understood correctly, had done things in the right way, or had made the right choices. When they received such confirmation, they often expressed feelings of relief or joy. Sometimes such exchanges between students and supervisors concerned broad, overarching issues, but in other cases they concerned small, seemingly insignificant details, as in the following example from Supervisor D with two students writing together:

Student M:	This is the smallest of the problems we have right now.
Student L:	Yes, it's the least of the problems, but we said that [supervisor's name] should decide what they think looks best and then we can move on.
Supervisor D:	Yeah? (laughs)
Student L:	(laughs) Let's see if I can find it. It's like, for example, when it says something like this: "Purpose and research questions". So either it says "and" like that, or it says "and" with one of these … (clicks computer mouse).
Student M:	An ampersand.
Supervisor D:	Oh.
Student L:	So it's just what you think looks best.
Supervisor D:	Oh … Should I have an opinion?
Student M:	Yes!
Student L:	Please!
Supervisor D:	Ah … Well, if you write like that, no one will notice, but if you write an ampersand, some people will react. And then they get hung up on the wrong things.
Student M:	So you say 'and' with letters?
Supervisor D:	Yes.
Student M:	Yes! It feels so good! Oh, I feel really good now!
	Supervisor D, Recording 2, Pair supervision

In this conversation sequence, Supervisor D is initially somewhat reluctant to give advice on whether 'and' should be written in letters or with an ampersand (&). However, when the students actively ask for help in making a decision, the supervisor decides to comply with their request and offers an opinion. Although Student M starts by saying that the question they want to raise is the smallest of their problems, the emotional reaction at the end of the conversation sequence indicates that the students have put a lot of energy and time into this issue. Here, clear and unambiguous advice from the supervisor seems to serve as a scaffolding tool for frustration control in the writing process (cf. van de Pol et al. 2010; van de Pol 2012), in the sense that by receiving an unambiguous answer from the supervisor, the students can put the question behind them and move on with their work.

Students in our recorded supervision material could also seek reassurance from supervisors in relation to more general assessments, such as the likelihood of completing the degree project on time. As in the example below, when students asked the supervisor a direct question about how they were progressing with their work:

Student D: But what ... Well, do you think we can do it in time?
Supervisor A: Yes.
Student D: Yes. Good.
Supervisor A: You will, because you know them, as you said. You know these texts by heart. You know exactly what they look like.
Student D: Mm.
Supervisor A: Now it's about taking it to another level.
Supervisor A, Recording 7, Pair supervision

In this example it is quite clear how the supervisor is both assigned and takes on the role of an expert in the supervision interaction (cf. Dysthe 2002). The students want reassurance that they will be able to complete the thesis on time, and the supervisor uses their experience and skills to provide this. As mentioned earlier, such reassurance can be highly relevant and positive for the degree project process, as it can help students to overcome perceived obstacles and barriers and to continue with their work. However, in relation to van de Pol et al.'s (2010), van de Pol's (2012) discussions on how scaffolding should be based on both teachers and students—in this case students and supervisors—being active in the scaffolding process, the supervisor in this situation could also have sought to invite students into the scaffolding work rather than immediately taking on the expected expert role. An alternative supervision tool in this type of situation could be, for example, to ask counter-questions rather than giving students a definitive answer: "What do you think? Do you think you can do it in time? What would you say you have left to do?" This might encourage student activity in a different way, requiring them to evaluate their process and how far they had actually progressed with the work. From the perspective that a critical approach to one's own work is an aspect of the understanding of student independence introduced in Chap. 3, this kind of response from the supervisor could also be seen as a way of encouraging student independence.

The idea of scaffolding, as discussed earlier, is also based on a gradual transfer of responsibility for the work to the students, which entails a certain fading out of the teacher or supervisor in order to create space for the students to take on the increased responsibility (van de Pol et al. 2010; van de Pol 2012). To contribute to such a gradual transfer of responsibility, one possible course of action for the supervisor in this particular supervision situation could have been to clarify to the students what is expected of them at the various stages of the degree project process and to relate this to the idea and ideal of student independence in the degree project context. In this particular situation, for example, the supervisor could have emphasised that the students had come so far in their work that they should be able to complete the final parts of the process on their own. This could be a way of promoting student independence by making it clear to the students that they are expected to take responsibility for both the timely completion and the quality of the degree project.

Although students in our material often asked for confirmation that they had made the right choices, were on the right track or would finish on time, it is not always easy for supervisors to make such assessments. This can be seen in the example below, which starts with the supervisor's response to the student who had just explained that it had been difficult to find the right theories:

Supervisor B: Well, I think it feels like you still have a firm grasp of what you're doing.
Student H: Well, that's good to hear.
Supervisor B: I feel very calm with, with everything.

Student H:	But you think it sounds like …
Supervisor B:	But I can't … Now that you haven't submitted any text for today, I don't have anything concrete to comment on either.
Student H:	No, I understand. No, and it was also a bit that I wanted to meet you just to explain and because I've felt so confused. And I needed and I've taken a little break. So I've … I've given it less time. But I still sit with it every day, sort of, and try to get through it, like, bit by bit.

Supervisor B, Recording 6, Individual supervision

At the same time as Supervisor B's initial response here is to confirm that the student appears to be on the right track and in control, the supervisor also notes that this assessment is made despite the fact that no text had been submitted to the supervision session. The supervisor's affirmation is thus not based on what the student has achieved so far but rather a hopeful reassurance that things are likely to go well, based on what the student has said during the supervision session.

Given that frustration control can be an important scaffolding goal in supervision, a reassuring and encouraging affirmation from the supervisor may be justified in many situations (cf. van de Pol et al. 2010; van de Pol 2012). However, if the supervisor downplays the students' concerns and questions too much and simply confirms that they are on the right track, there is a potential risk that students will leave a supervision meeting feeling that the degree project is progressing as it should, even though this may not be the case. When, as in the example above, the supervisor has no actual documentation of the process or text on which to base the assessment, but only insight into what the students are saying about their work and what they have achieved, it becomes particularly difficult to make such an assessment. This balancing act between offering encouragement and affirmation, on the one hand, and expressing necessary and justified concerns about the progress of the work or warning students that there is a risk that they will not succeed in completing the degree project on the other, is something that permeates supervision practice and work with degree projects in general (see also Zackariasson 2019).

In the focus group interviews at both Swedish and Russian universities, several supervisors also expressed that they found it difficult to maintain a balance between allowing students to make their own independent decisions, on the one hand, and ensuring that the thesis work is successful on the other. Some students are able and willing to take on the responsibility expected of them in connection with their degree projects, but this is far from the case for all. Many students need or want considerable support, as well as clear advice and guidance from the supervisor, in order to successfully complete the extensive and often difficult project of writing a major academic piece of work within the given timeframe. In other words, while it is important from a scaffolding perspective, as well as from an independence perspective, to emphasise students' responsibility and agency, more directive supervision is sometimes both desirable and necessary in order for degree projects to be completed on time and of sufficiently high quality (cf. Rienecker et al. 2019, 61ff).

Supervisors' Insecurity and Concern

Although, as we saw in the previous section, it is not uncommon for supervisors to downplay the concerns expressed by students and to confirm in various ways that they seem to be on the right track, there are also instances in our material where supervisors' comments and contributions signal that they are concerned about whether students have made the right choices or will be able to complete the degree project on time. One example is the following quote from a supervision meeting where the conversation centred on what the student had or had not done since the last meeting:

Student G: I haven't had time to meet these teachers. I'll do that after the autumn break. So I haven't got the empirical stuff yet, so, you know … eh … (sighs)

Supervisor B: /…/ What are the timeframes again, for the collection of these surveys?

Student G: I'm hoping for … like, everything should be in by the middle of November.

Supervisor B: So you won't have access to your empirical data until then?

Student G: Yeah … or if it is … because now … This week they don't have the time. And besides, I'm going away. In the middle of my degree project. But … and then the week after the kids have autumn break. So it won't be until the second week of November that I send out the survey, maybe. I'm coming back that week and then I'll try to catch up with the interviews, but the week after is sort of … (sighs)

	At the beginning of that week I hope to have everything ready, sort of.
Supervisor B:	It's very …
Student G:	Tight.
Supervisor B:	tight.

Supervisor B, Recording 2, Individual supervision

In the extract, the supervisor's concerned reaction to the student's timetable for collecting all the empirical material appears to be a contributing factor to the student and supervisor agreeing that it will be difficult to do it on time. It was not uncommon for supervisors to express concern about whether students would be able to complete within the timeframe, not least towards the end of the degree project process when it became apparent how far, or perhaps not so far, students had actually got. Another example of this can be found in the following extract. The student in question was combining studies with a part-time job and was therefore not able to devote as much time to the degree project, which the student and supervisor had discussed earlier in the supervision meeting. In addition, the student was planning to go away towards the end of the degree project period and the supervisor was concerned that the thesis would not be completed on time:

Supervisor F:	No, I'm thinking about… /…/ like, it's hard even for regular students to keep up time wise, even though they have forty hours a week and often spend even more than that doing [the degree project]. But, yeah, it'll just have to be delayed, you know. I really don't think we should hope that it will be ready in January. You were going away too?
Student Q:	Yes, but I will have my computer with me and write. I'm going to do that anyway. But maybe it won't be so easy to find the time. But I'll be able to sit for a couple of hours some evenings and so on.
Supervisor Q:	Mm. How long will you be away?
Student Q:	Eight days.
Supervisor:	When are you leaving?
Student Q:	Well, on Thursday. /…/
Supervisor F:	Well, no, it … I'm actually a bit worried about that part.
Student Q:	Yes, me too.

Supervisor F: And I, like, see this as well … I mean … You can also see it in the text when you don't … like that you haven't had the time to really sit down.
Supervisor F, Recording 7, Individual supervision

In this conversation sequence too, it is primarily the supervisor who highlights the risk that the student will not be able to complete the degree project before the January deadline. The student's first reaction to the supervisor's comments that it is unlikely that the degree project will be completed on time is to express the ambition to work on the degree project even during the holidays, and it is only when the supervisor again expresses concern about how this will work that the student agrees with this assessment.

When supervisors, through their reactions and feedback, draw students' attention to the possibility that they may struggle to complete their degree project on time, they take on the role of expert in a palpable way (cf. Dysthe 2002). As mentioned above, this can be both positive and necessary in many cases, as a more directive supervision style may at times be necessary (cf. Wichmann-Hansen and Schmidt Nielsen 2023, 61ff; Rienecker et al. 2019). Through their teaching and often also research experience, supervisors are familiar with a wide range of problems that students may encounter during the degree project process. They also know that the degree project period tends to pass by much faster than students expect, so that there is often a lack of time at the end, unless the collection of material and writing is started on time and carried out in an efficient and structured way.

However, taking responsibility for decisions that affect the degree project work—even if they relate to life outside of the course, such as travelling during the degree project period or combining studies with part-time work—can also be seen as part of student independence, in line with the understandings of the concept we presented in Chap. 3. In other words, if independence is a scaffolding intention in the degree project context, it is worth reflecting on how student responsibility could be emphasised in such cases (cf. van de Pol et al. 2010; van de Pol 2012). In the examples above, the supervisors signal that they are concerned about the choices made by the students, but they do not explicitly address this in terms of responsibility or student independence. An alternative way of acting in similar supervision situations might be to explicitly emphasise that it is ultimately the students' responsibility to complete the degree project on time and that if they choose to travel during the degree project period or to work alongside their studies, these are also choices that may affect the work.

In addition to the question of whether the degree project would be completed on time, supervisors in our empirical material sometimes expressed concern about whether the research or study that students had chosen to undertake had the potential to produce a degree project of sufficient quality. This was thus a concern or worry expressed not only by students, as we discussed earlier in this chapter, but also by supervisors. As in the following example, where Supervisor B questioned whether a student's planned investigation would actually be able to produce interesting results:

Supervisor B: /.../ But a question I had when I read this is ... In academia it's a bit of a letdown if you don't find anything. You know, especially at higher levels. And this particular study, I think, runs that risk. If there are no significant results, no difference between the classes that you are assessing.

Student G: Well, you never know.

Supervisor B: What are you going to do then?

Student G: Yeah, what am I going to do?

Supervisor B: Are you going to write something like: "I have investigated this and show that there is no difference"?

Student G: Mm, yes. What else would I write? I don't know, yes.

Supervisor B: I'm thinking, because it's one of those... Especially when you work for four or five years, it can make you really depressed. (laughs) Like: "Shit, I haven't come up with anything! There was no difference!" And that's also a result, but it's a result that's not so sexy to present at conferences and ...

Student G: Yeah, that's what happens sometimes.

Supervisor B, Recording 1, Collective supervision

Again, it is primarily the supervisor's questions and comments that contribute to the ongoing affective practices being characterised by a certain concern (cf. Wetherell 2012). The student, on the other hand, seems to take the supervisor's expressed worry about the risk that there will be no real results from the planned study rather lightly. Comments such as 'that's what happens sometimes' suggest that the student does not see this as a major problem. Moreover, in contrast to several of the previous examples, the conversation sequence does not culminate in a mutual understanding that what the supervisor is emphasising is something the student should take seriously.

In this example, too, the supervisor can be said to be assuming the role of an expert by explaining to the student the risks involved in the current choices being made in relation to the thesis. However, it is also possible to understand Supervisor B's actions as a way of actually increasing the element of partnership in the supervisor-student relationship by situating the student's thesis work in relation to academic writing in general and comparing it to research publications and presentations (cf. Dysthe 2002). By choosing to discuss the perceived problems with the degree project in these terms, the supervisor contributes to equating what the student should achieve during the degree project period with what is expected of doctoral students or researchers in their work. The message is that the potential problems exist for everyone, regardless of the academic level. At the same time as the feedback and comments are based on the supervisor's expertise and wider experience of academic writing, they thus also give legitimacy to the degree project as something more than just a writing assignment within a course and to the student as part of a wider academic environment.

The various examples in our material of supervisors introducing a certain concern or anxiety into the affective practices that take place in the supervisory interaction, for example by expressing concern or surprise about what the students have or have not done, or by giving students admonitions about what they should do, can be understood in terms of how important it is also for supervisors that students graduate on time and write degree projects that meet quality requirements. By reminding students that time flies, that they have to expect to work hard, that it's time to put in the extra effort if they want to finish, or that they need to think through both method, material and purpose properly so that what they intend to do is actually feasible, they may be able to avoid some of the potential problems and obstacles along the way. Hopefully this will contribute to preventing students from realising after a few weeks or months that they have done a lot of work that will lead nowhere. Supervisors' concerns and worries about various aspects of the degree project work can, accordingly, be valuable feedback for students to receive. However, the usefulness of such feedback depends on how the concern is expressed and at what stage of the work it is given. If supervisors express concerns about the progress of the work and whether it is actually possible to complete it as the student has planned, in a way that is not constructive for the student's work but rather increases the student's stress and anxiety, it may, on the contrary, become an obstacle, as stress and anxiety can be negative for the writing process (cf. Castello et al. 2009).

Insecure Supervisors: Strength or Problem?

In this chapter we have discussed several examples of supervisors taking on or being assigned the role of expert. As mentioned, this is in many ways a natural consequence of supervisors having greater experience and competence in the type of academic writing that the degree project involves, and it can be both important and necessary for supervisors to appear or act as experts at different stages of the degree project process. However, this does not mean that supervisors will always feel completely comfortable in this role or that they are in fact experts on all the issues that may arise during the degree project work. They may well feel uncertain or insecure at times in their role as supervisors, just as students may feel insecure when writing their degree project. This is related to the fact that the degree project process is imbued with emotional aspects not only for students but also for supervisors, who may experience feelings ranging from frustration and anger to pride and joy in relation to the degree project and the students they supervise (cf. Han and Xu 2021; Strandler et al. 2014; Clegg 2000; Todd et al. 2006). In this final part of the chapter, we explore this particular aspect of supervision—supervisor insecurity—in more detail.

For supervisors who are relatively new to their role and do not have much experience of academic supervision, many of the situations, dilemmas and challenges that may arise during a degree project process may feel new and unfamiliar, as discussed, for example, by Vereijken et al. (2018) and Almlöv and Grubbström (2023). More experienced supervisors may still feel insecure in certain situations, such as supervising degree projects that are outside their own research area or that apply methods they do not regularly use in their own research. Other reasons for supervisors' insecurity may be that they supervise within many different courses or programmes and therefore do not have a clear enough understanding of the guidelines and requirements that apply to each individual course, or that they find themselves in supervision situations that feel uncomfortable and which they do not really know how to handle, as we saw examples of in Chap. 4.

Like students, supervisors do not necessarily express the insecurity they may feel during the actual supervision interaction. Nevertheless, there were a number of examples in our research material of supervisors more or less explicitly communicating to students that they were not quite sure how to handle an issue or solve a problem. The following extract from a supervision meeting with Supervisor H is one example. The discussion concerned the course guidelines for the degree projects, about which a student had questions:

Student Y: But am I allowed to have that? Don't I have to have a (school) subject?

Supervisor H: Well, I'm not sure … It … I'll admit it: This is the first time I'm supervising since … this has been changed. This requirement that the degree projects should focus on subject didactics. Like, I'm in a learning process too.
Supervisor H, Recording 1, Collective supervision

Although Supervisor H in this example explicitly expressed uncertainty about what applied to a specific aspect of the degree project work, as the guidelines and requirements had changed in some respects, this does not necessarily correspond to feeling insecure in the role as supervisor. On the contrary, clearly articulating one's lack of knowledge or competence on a particular issue may be a sign that supervisors feel fundamentally secure in their role and therefore feel comfortable telling students which areas they have less expertise in.

Furthermore, as a supervisor, telling students that you do not know the answer to a specific question or that you do not have expert knowledge in a certain area can also be a way of enhancing and confirming students' knowledge and competence or of emphasising their role and responsibility in the process. In this way, the hierarchical distance between supervisor and student can be reduced, making the thesis work appear more like a joint project. The following extract from a supervision meeting with Supervisor A, in which one of the students raised the question of how to find relevant previous research, can serve as an example:

Student C: Well, they have to be anchored in it all the time. Both in the questions that they get and, like, how they are

	described. And then I think it would be interesting to find some previous research on this. I have no idea what one should be searching for then.
Supervisor A:	No.
Student D:	No, what kind of words should you search with?
Student C:	I tried, but it was like …
Student D:	It's hard.
Student C:	Yeah, identity … research sort of. I don't know.
Supervisor A:	No, I don't know either. I don't know any more about this particular research than you do.

Supervisor A, Recording 7, Pair supervision

When Supervisor A in this situation actively avoids taking on the role of expert by claiming to know no more about the specific area of research than the students, the responsibility is shifted to the students. The supervisor communicates that it is not self-evident that he or she should always provide the students with the information they need, but that it must be based on active work by both parties. It is up to the students to decide how to proceed and to find the previous research that they think would be interesting in this particular context. In this way, the partnership aspect of the supervision interaction is strengthened—and from a scaffolding perspective, the supervisor's actions can be seen as part of the process of making students active in the scaffolding work (cf. van de Pol et al. 2010; van de Pol 2012). This kind of attitude on the part of the supervisor, where supervision becomes explicitly non-directive, could also contribute to student independence if it is done in a conscious way.

Common to both of the above examples is that supervisors acknowledge, but do not excuse, their relative ignorance in a particular area or on a particular subject. In doing so, they also convey a message to the students that although supervisors are experts in many things, they do not know everything about everything. In our recorded supervision material, this message could also be conveyed by supervisors explicitly or implicitly referring to colleagues and highlighting the various competences and responsibilities of different actors in the degree project context. Earlier in this chapter, we gave examples of how supervisors might refer to course coordinators or seminar leaders, for example, when students raised questions that they did not know the answer to. In the relatively long quote below, Supervisor D instead refers to colleagues within the discipline when students ask questions that the supervisor cannot answer immediately:

Supervisor D:	What do you think you want to focus on?
Student L:	I ... We don't know because at the moment we're going with numbers. But I've started to think that maybe we should use percentages instead. Just because I think it's easier to see roughly how much of a difference there is and maybe it's easier to do. Even though we have so much fewer pictures in the second survey, it's easier to, like, /.../ compare.
Supervisor D:	That's great. Yeah, right, if you want to compare. /.../
Student M:	I think it's really hard.
Student L:	I think it's a bit difficult.
Supervisor D:	It might ... Maybe I'll ask someone here too. Who could comment on this.
Student L:	Yeah, I just think it's hard because I feel like I'm not very good at this (laughs) with percentages and stuff. /.../
Supervisor D:	No.
Student M:	Well, now we've solved it so that we have numbers in the graphs and then we've translated them into percentages underneath. That's what we've done now. And I'm a bit more in favour of numbers (laughs) so we have two different, sort of ...
Supervisor D:	Yeah, that's right. /.../
Student L:	I'm a bit confused.
Supervisor D:	Yes, but the thing is that if I ask my colleagues, there can be different answers. But ... eh, I can do that just to see what ...
Student M:	Yes, please!
Student L:	Yes.

Supervisor D, Recording 3, Pair supervision

The starting point for the supervision interaction here is again that the students express uncertainty about a particular part of the thesis work and want to get answers from the supervisor on how to proceed. In the discussion, the students come up with different suggestions on how to proceed, but the supervisor chooses not to give direct feedback on these suggestions. Instead, Supervisor D offers to ask colleagues about the issue at hand, stressing that this may not lead to a simple solution to the problem as the colleagues may have different views on how to continue.

An alternative response in this particular situation might have been for Supervisor D to emphasise, as in the previous examples, that it is ultimately up to the students themselves to decide what they want to do and how best to do it in relation to the purpose of the degree project, the research questions and so on. Another possible scenario would have been for the supervisor and the students to jointly discuss what might be the best solution and try to find a solution together. In this way, the students' responsibility for the degree project would have been emphasised and the initiative to find a solution to the problem would have been placed more firmly with them, which could have contributed to student activity and encouraged student independence.

One of our main arguments in this book is that supervision should be seen as a social and collegial practice, in which the supervisor need not or cannot be an expert in everything. However, if supervisors too often or too extensively claim not to know or not to be able to answer, and constantly refer to someone who knows better, be it colleagues in the discipline, the course coordinator or seminar leaders within the degree project course, there is a potential risk that the supervision interaction will be characterised by insecurity, which in the long run could leave students with the feeling of being alone in their work. At the same time, this is one of the most difficult parts of supervision—to be able to handle all the different questions and problems that students raise, and preferably to give relevant and useful answers. In order to avoid supervisors feeling that they have to deal with such dilemmas on their own, we would argue in favour of creating arenas for collegial conversation and dialogue where various issues and problems can be discussed, both the concrete guidelines and requirements for specific degree project courses and other pedagogical or content-related issues that supervisors may face. This would provide an opportunity for new supervisors to learn from those who have been in the game longer and perhaps address some of the uncertainties that supervisors may face.

* * *

Uncertainty and concern can thus characterise both students' and supervisors' experiences of the degree project process and the supervision interaction. As we have shown throughout this chapter, these types of emotions can be handled by supervisors in a variety of ways, ranging from directing the supervision interaction away from talk of worry, fear and uncertainty and towards more neutral ground, to actively using such emotions to communicate to students what they can expect during the course of the work. Depending on how supervisors relate to and manage the emotional elements of the supervision interaction, these have the potential to serve as supervisory tools that can help to encourage student activity and independence, and contribute to making the supervision interaction more of a partnership. In the next chapter we will look at a number of other scaffolding tools that supervisors can use in supervision practice to encourage and enable student independence.

REFERENCES

Aitchison, Claire, Janice Catterall, Pauline Ross, and Shelley Burgin. 2012. 'Tough Love and Tears': Learning Doctoral Writing in the Sciences. *Higher Education Research and Development* 31 (4): 435–447. https://doi.org/10.1080/07294360.2011.559195.

Aitchison, Claire, and Susan Mowbray. 2013. Doctoral Women: Managing Emotions, Managing Doctoral Studies. *Teaching in Higher Education* 18 (8): 859–870. https://doi.org/10.1080/13562517.2013.827642.

Almlöv, Cecilia, and Ann Grubbström. 2023. 'Challenging from the start': Novice Doctoral Co-supervisors' Experiences of Supervision Culture and Practice. *Higher Education Research and Development* (ahead-of-print): 1–15. https://doi.org/10.1080/07294360.2023.2218805.

Baker, Mary-Jane, Elizabeth Cluett, Lorraine Ireland, Sheila Reading, and Susan Rourke. 2014. Supervising Undergraduate Research: A Collective Approach Utilising Groupwork and Peer Support. *Nurse Education Today* 34 (4): 637–642. https://doi.org/10.1016/j.nedt.2013.05.006.

Barrineau, Sanna, Alexis Engström, and Ulrike Schnaas. 2019. *An Active Student Participation Companion*. Uppsala: Uppsala universitet.

Barsics, Catherine, Martial Van der Linden, and Arnaud D'Argembeau. 2016. Frequency, Characteristics, and Perceived Functions of Emotional Future Thinking in Daily Life. *The Quarterly Journal of Experimental Psychology* 69 (2): 217–233. https://doi.org/10.1080/17470218.2015.1051560.

Castello, Montserrat, Anna Inesta, and Carles Monereo. 2009. Towards Self-Regulated Academic Writing: An Exploratory Study with Graduate Students in a Situated Learning Environment. *Electronic Journal of Research in Educational Psychology* 7 (3): 1107–1130. https://doi.org/10.1016/j.system.2020.102312.

Clegg, Sue. 2000. Knowing Through Reflective Practice in Higher Education. *Educational Action Research* 8 (3): 451–469. https://doi.org/10.1080/09650790000200128.

Collins, Jo. 2021. Validation in Doctoral Education: Exploring PhD Students' Perceptions of Belonging to Scaffold Doctoral Identity Work. *International Journal of Doctoral Studies* 16: 715–735. https://doi.org/10.28945/4876.

Collins, Jo, and Nicole Brown. 2021. Where's the Validation? Role of Emotion Work and Validation for Doctoral Students. *Higher Education Research and Development* 40 (7): 1389–1402. https://doi.org/10.1080/07294360.2020.1833315.

Cotterall, Sara. 2013. More than Just a Brain: Emotions and the Doctoral Experience. *Higher Education Research and Development* 32 (2): 174–187. https://doi.org/10.1080/07294360.2012.680017.

Doloriert, Clair, Sally Sambrook, and Jim Stewart. 2012. Power and Emotion in Doctoral Supervision: Implications for HRD. *European Journal of Training and Development* 36 (7): 732–750. https://doi.org/10.1108/03090591211255566.

Dysthe, Olga. 2002. Professors as Mediators of Academic Text Cultures: an Interview Study with Advisors and Masters Degree Students in Three Disciplines in a Norwegian University. *Written Communication* 19 (4): 493–544. https://doi.org/10.1177/074108802238010.

Han, Ye, and Yueting Xu. 2021. Unpacking the Emotional Dimension of Doctoral Supervision: Supervisors' Emotions and Emotion Regulation Strategies. *Frontiers in Psychology* 12: 651859–651859. https://doi.org/10.3389/fpsyg.2021.651859.

Lea, Mary R., and Barry Stierer. 2000. *Student Writing in Higher Education: New Contexts*. London: Society for Research into Higher Education.

Lea, Mary R., and Brian V. Street. 2000. Student Writing and Staff feedback in Higher Education: An academic Literacies Approach. In *Student Writing in Higher Education. New contexts*, ed. Mary R. Lea and Barry Stierer, 32–46. Buckingham: Open University Press.

Light, Greg, Roy Cox, and Susanna Calkins. 2009. *Learning and Teaching in Higher Education: the Reflective Professional*. 2nd ed. London: Sage.

Liu, Chunhong, and Shulin Yu. 2022. Exploring Master's Students' Emotions and Emotion-regulation in Supervisory Feedback Situations: a Vignette-based Study. *Assessment and Evaluation in Higher Education* 47 (7): 1101–1115. https://doi.org/10.1080/02602938.2021.2005770.

Magnusson, Jenny, and Maria Zackariasson. 2018. Student Independence in Undergraduate Projects. Different Understandings in Different Academic Contexts. *Journal of Further and Higher Education* 43 (10): 1404–1419. https://doi.org/10.1080/0309877X.2018.1490949.

Nordentoft, Helle Merete, Rie Thomsen, and Gitte Wichmann-Hansen. 2013. Collective Academic Supervision: A Model for Participation and Learning in Higher Education. *Higher Education* 65 (5): 581–593. https://doi.org/10.1007/s10734-012-9564-x.

Nordentoft, Helle Merete, Helle Hvass, Kristina Mariager-Anderson, Søren Smedegaard Bengtsen, Anne Smedegaard, and Sarah Damgaard Warrer. 2019. *Kollektiv akademisk vejledning. Fra forskning til praksis.* Aarhus: Aarhus Universitetsforlag.
van de Pol, Janneke. E. (2012). *Scaffolding in teacher-student interaction: exploring, measuring, promoting and evaluating scaffolding.* [Thesis, fully internal, Universiteit van Amsterdam]. https://dare.uva.nl/search?identifier=640b82ba-c27b-42d3-b9f8-fe08b1e0081f.
van de Pol, Janneke, Monique Volman, and Jos. Beishuizen. 2010. Scaffolding in Teacher–Student Interaction: A Decade of Research. *Educational Psychology Review* 22: 271–296. https://doi.org/10.1007/s10648-010-9127-6.
van de Pol, Janneke, Monique Volman, Frans Oort, and Jos Beishuizen. 2015. The Effects of Scaffolding in the Classroom: Support Contingency and Student Independent Working time in Relation to Student Achievement, Task Effort and Appreciation of Support. *Instructional Science* 43 (5): 615–641. https://doi.org/10.1007/s11251-015-9351-z.
van de Pol, Janneke, Neil Mercer, and Monique Volman. 2019. Scaffolding Student Understanding in Small-Group Work: Students' Uptake of Teacher Support in Subsequent Small-Group Interaction. *The Journal of the Learning Sciences* 28 (2): 206–239. https://doi.org/10.1080/10508406.2018.1522258.
Rienecker, Lotte, Gitte Wichmann-Hansen, and Peter Stray Jørgensen. 2019. *God vejledning af specialer, bacheloroppgaver og projekter.* Frederiksberg: Samfundslitteratur.
Strandler, Ola, Thomas Johansson, Gina Wisker, and Silwa Claesson. 2014. Supervisor or Counsellor? - Emotional Boundary Work in Supervision. *International Journal for Researcher Development* 5 (2): 70. https://doi.org/10.1108/IJRD-03-2014-0002.
Svinhufvud, Kimmo, Liisa Voutilainen, and Elina Weiste. 2017. Normalizing in Student Counseling: Counselors' Responses to Students' Problem Descriptions. *Discourse Studies* 19 (2): 196–215. https://doi.org/10.1177/1461445617691704.
Todd, Malcolm J., Karen Smith, and Phil Bannister. 2006. Supervising a Social Science Undergraduate Dissertation: Staff Experiences and Perceptions. *Teaching in Higher Education* 11 (2): 161–173. https://doi.org/10.1080/13562510500527693.
Vehviläinen, Sanna. 2003. Avoiding Providing Solutions: Orienting to the Ideal of Students' Self-Directedness in Counselling Interaction. *Discourse Studies* 5 (3): 389–414. https://doi.org/10.1177/14614456030053005.
Vereijken, Mayke W.C., Roeland M. van der Rijst, Jan H. van Driel, and Friedo W. Dekker. 2018. Novice Supervisors' Practices and Dilemmatic Space in Supervision of Student Research Projects. *Teaching in Higher Education* 23 (4): 522–542. https://doi.org/10.1080/13562517.2017.1414791.

Wang, Ting, and Linda Y. Li. 2011. 'Tell me What to Do' vs. 'Guide me Through it': Feedback Experiences of International Doctoral Students. *Active Learning in Higher Education* 12 (2): 101–112. https://doi.org/10.1177/1469787411402438.

Weise, Crista, Mariela Aguayo-González, and Montserrat Castelló. 2020. Significant Events and the Role of Emotion along Doctoral Researcher Personal Trajectories. *Educational Research (Windsor)* 62 (3): 304–323. https://doi.org/10.1080/00131881.2020.1794924.

Wetherell, Margaret. 2012. *Affect and Emotion: A New Social Science Understanding*. London: Sage.

Wichmann-Hansen, Gitte, and Karl-Johan Schmidt Nielsen. 2023. Can Hands-on Supervision Get out of Hand? The Correlation between Directive Supervision and Doctoral Student Independence in a Danish Study Context. *Scandinavian Journal of Educational Research* (ahead-of-print): 1–16. https://doi.org/10.1080/00313831.2023.2204113.

Wichmann-Hansen, Gitte, Rie Thomsen, and Helle Merete Nordentoft. 2015. Challenges in Collective Academic Supervision: Supervisors' Experiences from a Master Programme in Guidance and Counselling. *Higher Education* 70 (1): 19–33. https://doi.org/10.1007/s10734-014-9821-2.

Wollast, Robin, Cristina Aelenei, Johann Chevalère, Nicolas Van der Linden, Benoît Galand, Assaad Azzi, Mariane Frenay, and Olivier Klein. 2023. Facing the Dropout Crisis among PhD Candidates: the Role of Supervisor Support in Emotional Well-being and Intended Doctoral Persistence among Men and Women. *Studies in Higher Education (Dorchester-on-Thames)* 48 (6): 813–828. https://doi.org/10.1080/03075079.2023.2172151.

Zackariasson, Maria. 2018. 'I Feel Really Good Now!' – Emotions and Independence in Undergraduate Supervision. *Learning and Teaching: The International Journal of Higher Education in the Social Sciences* 11 (3): 1–24. https://doi.org/10.3167/latiss.2018.110303.

———. 2019. Balansen mellan att uppmuntra och ställa krav. En reflektion över studenters uppsatsskrivande i relation till stress och stöttning. *Högre utbildning* 9 (2). https://doi.org/10.23865/hu.v9.1662.

———. 2020. Kun kaikki ei menekään niin kuin piti: Syylisyyden tunne ja häpeä tutkielmaohjauksessa [When Things Don't Turn out the Way Expected. Guilt and Shame in Academic Supervision]. In *Afektit ja tunteet kulttuurin tutkimuksessa [Affects and Emotions in Cultural Research]*, ed. Jenni Rinne, Anna Kajander, and Riina Haanpää, 275–309. Helsingfors: Ethnos.

Open Access This chapter is licensed under the terms of the Creative Commons Attribution-NonCommercial-NoDerivatives 4.0 International License (http://creativecommons.org/licenses/by-nc-nd/4.0/), which permits any noncommercial use, sharing, distribution and reproduction in any medium or format, as long as you give appropriate credit to the original author(s) and the source, provide a link to the Creative Commons license and indicate if you modified the licensed material. You do not have permission under this license to share adapted material derived from this chapter or parts of it.

The images or other third party material in this chapter are included in the chapter's Creative Commons license, unless indicated otherwise in a credit line to the material. If material is not included in the chapter's Creative Commons license and your intended use is not permitted by statutory regulation or exceeds the permitted use, you will need to obtain permission directly from the copyright holder.

CHAPTER 6

Scaffolding Tools for Student Independence

There are a number of different scaffolding tools that supervisors can use in the supervision process. These pedagogical tools can be used more or less consciously and reflectively by supervisors and can have different functions at different stages of the degree project work. In the following chapter we will discuss in more detail some of the scaffolding tools we identified in our empirical material—questions, praise and active voicing—and how supervisors' use of them in supervision interaction can help to enable and encourage student independence.

Supervisors' Scaffolding Tools

While there are a variety of scaffolding tools that supervisors can use in the supervision process, these need to be adapted to each student's situation, background and abilities, as well as to the stage the student and the degree project are at. In other words, from a scaffolding perspective, it is important to strive for contingency, that is to try to clarify where the student stands in terms of knowledge, so that the supervision can subsequently be adapted (cf. van de Pol et al. 2012, 2015; van de Pol 2012). It can also be valuable to find out what students' ambitions are for their work and how much time they plan to spend on writing the degree project, in relation to competing demands such as family life or part-time work.

Different scaffolding tools also have different functions and can produce different types of outcomes, not least depending on how they are used. If a scaffolding intention in the supervision interaction is to promote student independence, then possible scaffolding tools and how supervisors use them need to be considered on the basis of their potential to contribute to this particular intention, for example regarding the extent to which they can promote independence in terms of student initiative and participation, making choices and so on. In this chapter we will discuss a number of such possible scaffolding tools, which, depending on how they are used, have the potential to encourage student independence. Using examples from our material, we will discuss whether supervisors expressed themselves in the form of *demands, recommendations* or *questions*, and the significance this may have in the supervision interaction, as well as how supervisors used the more specific scaffolding tools praise and active voicing, and how this can guide or support students in different ways.

Demands, Recommendations and Questions

When supervisors give feedback to students, they need to choose a particular form of expression, and this form of expression communicates to the students how to interpret and understand what the supervisors are saying. In a study by Eriksson and Gustavsson (2016), supervision practices are examined based on the types of feedback comments provided by supervisors in written supervision. The feedback comments given by supervisors are categorised according to whether they are demands, recommendations or questions. Eriksson and Gustavsson argue that these three types of feedback comments or forms of expression are, to varying degrees, directive or open to student independence, which they describe as the student's ability and opportunity to decide and choose what to do. Demands are presented as the most directive form of supervision and questions as the form of expression with the best potential for enabling student independence.[1]

The differences between these three types of feedback comments are mainly related to the level of commitment. Is it something the students should or must do, is it a suggestion to think about or something that might be useful, or is it a question that opens up for the students' own solutions? In other words, what is negotiable and what is not in the

---

[1] What Eriksson and Gustavsson (2016) want to get at with the three concepts of demands, recommendations and questions is something other than the differentiation of speech acts (Austin 1975). A speech act in the form of a question or a recommendation is therefore quite different from what is meant here.

supervisors' comments depends on how the feedback is framed in a particular supervision situation. The supervisors' underlying intentions with feedback comments and viewpoints are of course inaccessible, but what students hear and take part of is how these are expressed in the supervision interaction, and in this interaction norms and expectations of various kinds emerge. From an academic literacies perspective, the use of demands, recommendations and questions by supervisors in supervision conversations can thus be understood as the communication and expression of different academic norms (cf. Lea and Street 2000).

To Demand or to Recommend

What Eriksson and Gustavsson (2016) define as demands are requests and advice, which are often expressed explicitly in the supervision conversation with expressions such as 'must', 'shall' and 'need', although sometimes demands are also communicated implicitly. Recommendations, on the other hand, are expressed with phrases such as 'think about', 'maybe', 'I think' and 'you can think about it', which are more open to the students' own choices and points of view. In our recorded supervision material, there were many examples of supervisors using demands and recommendations in their interactions with students. As in the following example, where the supervisor gave advice in the form of demands, stating what the students should and must do in the work ahead:

Supervisor A: What I think you should do now, before you do the interviews and the interview guides, is to read up on the theory. Because you must have like … as a basis for the whole investigation, that this is what … Questions about trust in the media that you need to read up on. And I think you should also start writing. Introduction, aim, research questions and theory section, at the same time as you do the actual investigation.
Supervisor A, Recording 1, Pair supervision

Here, then, norms about how a scientific investigation should be done are addressed when the supervisor states that students should read up on the theory before conducting the interviews, in parallel with starting to write the text. Academic requirements relating to the writing of degree projects are also addressed in terms of the need for students to have a theoretical basis for their investigation. The use of 'must' or 'should' by the supervisor indicates that this is something that he or she sees as necessary for the work and rather non-negotiable. In other words, there are clearly stated requirements that students are expected to meet. However, by using expressions such as 'I think', the supervisor also communicates that other actions or solutions might be possible.

In another example from our material, the supervisor gave advice in the form of demands or requirements by using 'must' in connection with the choice of material:

> Supervisor E: Because then there will be a material selection in several stages. So you must choose a textbook, then you must make a selection of texts from this textbook, and this should be in the [section on] material.
> *Supervisor E, Recording 3, Individual supervision*

The academic norms expressed here by the supervisor, which through the choice of words and formulations appear to be non-negotiable, thus concern the order in which the work process should take place when it comes to the writing of the degree project—in the sense that the student 'must' choose a material at an early stage and make a selection from it, and that this 'should' be presented in a section on material in the degree project.

An example of how supervisors in our study gave advice in the form of recommendations comes from a supervision session where a particular theory had been discussed and the supervisor encouraged the students to use it as a model.

> Supervisor A: That's the way the mechanism works, so you could use that as a model.
> *Supervisor A, Recording 1, Pair supervision*

The difference with the previous examples is that the supervisor uses the word 'could' instead of 'shall' or 'must'. The wording signals an openness and that this is not something crucial or an absolute requirement but rather a recommendation that the students can choose to follow or not. Sometimes the recommendations are more implicit and seem even more like suggestions that students are free to consider. In the following example, the starting point was that the students felt that it would be too much to include a perspective that the supervisor had previously recommended, a qualitative analysis of images:

Supervisor D: I think you might want to wait to decide that, but be a bit prepared. It's a quantitative method you're going for, but if you sort of see that there are some things that deviate from a standard, so to speak, then maybe you should go for a more qualitative in-depth analysis of a few selected images. But that's the kind of thing you can be prepared for, rather than sort of always starting with what questions you want answers to. So I'm just thinking, don't forget it might be relevant. Just keep that in the back of your mind.
Supervisor D, Recording 1, Pair supervision

Here, then, the supervisor's recommendation was expressed through phrases such as 'you can be prepared' and 'it might be relevant', as well as cautionary expressions such as 'sort of', 'maybe' and 'so I'm just thinking', indicating that the advice was not categorical. The whole line of reasoning also ended with the phrase 'just keep that in the back of your mind', which also makes the recommendation appear less strict. This way of formulating feedback comments contributes to the supervisor not appearing as an expert or spokesperson for a particular set of academic norms but rather as one of several possible voices or perspectives to which students can relate in different ways. This can be understood in relation to the partnership model (Dysthe 2002) in the sense that the supervisor becomes a more equal discussion partner and that space is also given to students' choices and preferences.

Although there were distinct differences in how the supervisors in our material formulated their feedback comments, which signalled how directive their advice was to be understood, it is not self-evident that students always perceived such differences. Moreover, the way supervisors formulate their feedback comments during supervision meetings may also depend on personal differences in expression. That is, some supervisors may rarely express something as an absolute demand but still expect students to follow their recommendations, while others may be more authoritative in how they formulate advice and comments, regardless of how directive the recommendation is meant to be. In other words, supervisors might benefit from reflecting on their own way of formulating advice and comments, and clarifying to students when something is indeed non-negotiable and an absolute demand for the approval of the degree project.

Asking Questions
Demands and recommendations from supervisors can be considered as possible scaffolding tools from the perspective that one aim of scaffolding may be to reduce freedom, for example by taking over certain tasks that the student is not yet ready to undertake. Giving instructions that explain what the student should do next is also one of the scaffolding tools discussed by van de Pol et al. (van de Pol et al. 2010; van de Pol 2012). However, when it comes to encouraging and enabling student independence and participation in the process, questions are one of the supervisors' most important tools in the supervision interaction (cf. Eriksson and Gustavsson 2016). The function of questions has been examined in different contexts and in several ways (Freed 1994; Freed and Ehrlich 2010; Koshik 2010). Questions can be asked to obtain information but also to provide information, to instruct, to challenge and so on. As a supervisor it is therefore valuable both to be aware of your own use of questions and to make the use of questions a conscious choice. Wichmann-Hansen and Jensen, who also highlight questions as central to supervision practice, have, for example, introduced a supervision model they call 'the questioning wheel', which structures the whole process into phases based on questions adapted to each phase. They argue that it is important for supervisors to "familiarise themselves with the issues that students are concerned with before supervisors contribute their own views and advice" (Wichmann-Hansen 2021, 98).

By asking questions, supervisors elicit responses from the student rather than primarily provide feedback comments, which can create other opportunities to enable or encourage student independence. In our material, it was evident that many of the questions asked by supervisors had the potential to open up for student perspectives and participation, to allow students to make choices, to develop their ways of thinking or to think in new ways and so on. At the same time, however, it is not self-evident that the questions asked by the supervisors always contribute to enabling independence, as there are several types of questions that fulfil different functions in a conversation. Supervisors' questions to students can encourage activity, action and participation, and also influence and communicate what kind of activity, action and participation is expected. But questions can also silence a student and discourage participation and activity. It all depends on what questions are asked and how they are asked. Hence, for a supervisor who wants to develop an aware and effective supervisor role where student independence is encouraged, the role of questions in the supervision practice is highly relevant.

A central aspect of this is, however, that supervision discussions are asymmetrical in nature, given the different institutional roles of students and supervisors. The person who asks a lot of questions in a conversation is generally the one who also controls and is responsible for the interaction as a whole (cf. Freed and Ehrlich 2010). Using questions to open up and enable student independence in the form of participation would be in line with a general societal shift towards an ideal where hierarchical workplaces with authoritarian structures become increasingly equal and open to different forms of participation (see Freed and Ehrlich 2010). It would also be aligned with the supervisor model that Dysthe (2002) refers to as the partnership model. However, as long as it is only the supervisors who ask questions in the conversations and the students who answer, Dysthe's partnership model is difficult to achieve.

There are several ways of categorising questions, not least in educational research. At a general level, a distinction is often made between open and closed questions, and between high and low cognitive level questions (cf. Emanuelsson 2001). Open questions ask for productive, detailed answers from the students to questions that the supervisors do not know the answer to. In supervision meetings, questions such as "What have you done since we last met?" and "Is there anything in particular you want to discuss today?" are typical examples. Closed questions, on the other hand, are usually more controlling, with supervisors asking for short, specific answers, often with alternatives that are expected or given. Questions such as "Have you started working on the analysis yet?" and "Are you going to record or take notes of the interviews?" are typical closed questions, which can sometimes appear rather interrogatory and controlling (see further in the section on "Challenging and problematising questions").

Whether a question is at a high or low cognitive level depends on the type of answer it is trying to elicit. There is a difference between questions that ask for facts and reproduction of information and questions that ask for analysis, synthesis and evaluation (Emanuelsson 2001). Notwithstanding the various ways of defining and categorising questions, many researchers agree that several types of questions need to be used in educational communication and that it is not necessarily the case that some questions are better than others. At the same time, questions that require answers at a cognitively high level are crucial for supporting students' development of critical thinking and independence (cf. Ellis 1993). Sometimes a distinction is also made between questions that ask for new and unknown information and questions where the questioner already knows the answer or expects a particular answer. This can be discussed in terms of 'genuine questions' and 'test questions' or 'control questions', which are common in an educational context. The use of many test and control questions in supervision sessions would be an expression of a supervisor role in which the supervisor acts more as an expert and teacher than as a partner (cf. Dysthe 2002). However, this type of question was relatively rare in our recorded supervision sessions.

In analysing our material, we have identified some basic functions of questions with the potential to encourage and enable student independence through participation, and we will discuss three such types of questions in more detail below:

(1) Opening and transferring questions
(2) Developing and deepening questions
(3) Challenging and problematising questions.[2]

Opening and Transferring Questions
Opening and transferring questions aim to encourage students to control what the conversation is about, but this is achieved to varying degrees and in several ways. Questions that aim to open up for students' own perspectives and descriptions are mainly of three different types:

- Open-ended questions, often used as greetings, "What's up?", "How does it feel?", etc.,
- Open-ended questions that aim to get students to initiate their own topics, "Is there anything in particular you have been thinking about?", "What are you wondering about?", etc.
- Questions that aim to give students the opportunity to control what is to be discussed, but in relation to a specific topic: "How do you

---

[2] These terms correspond to some extent to the terms used by Wichmann-Hansen (2021) in relation to the questioning wheel model (clarifying, exploring, challenging and evaluating questions) but have a different definition and function in this context.

feel about the method?", "What did you want to investigate?", "Was there anything interesting you talked about in the seminar?", etc.

Open-ended questions such as these aim to open up to the students' own perspectives and descriptions, and can introduce new topics into supervision discussions, topics that the students can initiate and control. Such questions therefore have the potential to encourage student initiative and activity in the supervision interaction. In our recorded material, questions with this function are used by all supervisors.

If the purpose of open-ended questions is to increase student participation, it is also important to know how this works in practice, i.e. whether the questions actually lead to participation. In our material it was found that many of the open-ended questions used by supervisors did lead to participation but to varying degrees. Completely open questions, where students are expected to choose both a topic and a perspective, often worked less well than when the supervisor framed a topic but allowed the student to control the perspective. As in the example below, where a completely open-ended question was asked by the supervisor, giving the students the opportunity to direct the conversation, an opportunity they chose not to take:

Supervisor D: Well, what do you wonder about the most?
Student L: Oh, uh, I don't know if we're wondering so much right now, because we're just at the beginning, we're just getting started. We'll have problems later (laughs) but at the moment we don't have anything like that.
Student M: No, it feels like we just have to hit the books.
Supervisor D: Just think that you have a good structure, it feels like you have a clear idea that maybe can be specified when you have gone into the literature and so on.
Student L: Mm.
Supervisor D, Recording 1, Pair supervision

That the supervisor's approach in this particular example did not result in the students taking the opportunity to direct the conversation may be due to the question being too open. A question about what students are wondering about is perhaps generally more difficult to answer than, for example, questions about what they have done. It might also be related to where the students were in their process. In our material we could see that when students in the later stages of the degree project process were asked to describe for instance what they had done so far or since the last meeting, this tended to elicit quite detailed reflections and descriptions from the students, suggesting that both the clarity of the question and where in the process the question is asked may play a role in participation.

Developing and Deepening Questions

Developing and deepening questions are neutral and information-seeking questions where supervisors ask for information they do not already have. At the same time as the questions provide information for the supervisors, they give the students the opportunity to develop their thoughts and deepen their own thinking, and can thereby be understood to encourage student activity and participation. In the following example with the same supervisor and students, the supervisor initiated a topic by asking an opening and transferring question, which was then followed by developing and deepening questions.

Supervisor D: Mm, yeah, okay. Can you maybe tell me more [about your work]?
Student L: Yeah, we've started to read some background and stuff like that.
Supervisor D: Yeah.
Student M: Yeah, we started with, like, gender theory.
Student L: And pictorial rhetoric and things like that, to look at.
Supervisor D: Mm.
Student L: So this week we've added, like, reading. Next week we start designing, well it will be like a quantitative content analysis but with images.
Supervisor D: Yes, exactly, you could say that ... Is it one method or two? It's a quantitative content analysis of images instead of text, so to speak. If you look at it as one or two methods, you can ... But what kind of image do you have in mind? You were talking about pictorial rhetoric?
Student M: Mm.
Student L: Well, we've only just started to touch the surface of it, but we've been reading about how you choose to represent yourself through ... and certain choices of clothing and how you look at a picture, what angles you've used and how ...

Student M:	The composition …
Student L:	Yes, exactly, how the organisation has chosen to present its representatives and in what way. So it's a bit rhetorical.
Supervisor D:	So how they present their representatives?
Student M:	Yes, partly that and then a little bit about what images have been chosen in…
Supervisor D:	In the newspapers?
Student L:	Yes, exactly.
Supervisor D:	And by the photographer?
Student M:	Well, I don't know if I thought about that … I thought about how they were portrayed in the media.

Supervisor D, Recording 1, Pair supervision

Questions of this kind in our material often have the effect of developing and clarifying students' thinking. In the example above, the supervisor asks for a description of the students' working process and in the following interaction asks questions that lead the students to deepen and develop their description of this process. An initial opening and transferring question aimed at getting the students to lead the discussion: "Can you maybe tell me more [about your work]?", is followed by several developing and deepening questions about what the students have in mind when it comes to images and pictorial analysis, and confirmatory questions so that the supervisor can see that he or she has correctly understood what the students are saying: "So how they present their representatives?" and "In the newspapers?" and "And by the photographer?"

The role of the supervisor in this conversation sequence is thus to invite the students' viewpoint, to get them to deepen their perspective, to develop what they mean and to confirm that the whole thing has been understood correctly. If the supervisor is too quick with such developing and deepening questions, this can be perceived as negative, for example if the students feel that the supervisor is dictating what they should say or think, but in this example it does not seem to have that effect in the supervision situation. The students had submitted a draft text for supervision, but by asking these kinds of questions, the supervisor got them to go beyond what was in the draft and to motivate and explain their thinking about the choice of method and research design. This type of questioning therefore seems to be able to contribute to student participation by encouraging students to describe their choices and thinking in more detail. Students are constructed as competent participants and given the opportunity to both initiate the topic of discussion and to present their understanding and perspectives, which is vital from an independence perspective (cf. Chap. 3). In addition to being seen as a scaffolding tool that helps students develop their thinking, the supervisor's questions can be seen as a possible scaffolding tool for gradually transferring responsibility for thinking and reasoning to the students (cf. van de Pol 2012; van de Pol et al. 2010). The supervisor does this here, by suggesting which aspects might be relevant in the analysis; the context of the pictures, who selects the pictures to be published but also the role of the photographer in the process.

Challenging and Problematising Questions
In our material, challenging and problematising questions were by far the most common. Such questions have the potential to give students a deeper understanding, but also to give students a better view of what they have done and to be able to describe it in a new way, from a new perspective. There is a more or less implicit critique built into this type of question, in that it often concerns ambiguities or problems with what the students are saying or describing. These questions tend to start with the question words 'who', 'what', 'how' and 'why': "Who is the subject in your text?", "What can you read from it?", "How are you going to measure motivation?" and "Why are you interviewing teachers and not students?" and so on. The challenging and problematising questions are sometimes followed by explicit criticism or suggestions from the supervisor. Other times, however, challenging and problematising questions are asked without further elaboration, leaving students to draw the implications of the question in the way they think best.

In the following rather lengthy example, the supervisor first asks an opening and transferring question, but when the student has difficulty answering it, the supervisor switches to asking a series of follow-up questions, all of which are challenging and problematising.

Supervisor B: Um … but what are your thoughts on this concept of motivation?
Student G: Well, now it's kind of spinning all the time, so fast. Well, how does one think?
Supervisor B: Right, if I ask the question like this, based on your research questions, what is motivation, how do you …?

Student G:	It's an inner drive that you can get from within or with the help of external things that make you want to achieve something.
Supervisor B:	How are you going to measure motivation?
Student G:	Well, their experience. [Scholar] writes that it has to be like, the children's experience as well as how they, what they feel motivated by.
Supervisor B:	Mm.
Student G:	So to speak. Because it's never possible to know if they will be more or less motivated if you don't do the same thing in two different ways, I think, but that's the thing ... It's in the form of questionnaires, like, they will answer questionnaires, about motivation.
Supervisor B:	And if you then access their experiences, how will you know if it has had an effect?
Student G:	Mm. No, that's difficult.
Supervisor B:	I'm thinking like, how far will your results go?
Student G:	Mm, yeah, that's the question.
Supervisor B:	I ask questions to understand what will be your more ... like delimitation, definition, purpose formulation.
Student G:	I want more ... The question is a little bit about what they are motivated by in school so to speak. It's both digital tools, the teacher's teaching or group work or practical work or whatever. So to see which one ... if it is really motivating. Maybe it's not at all, we'll see. But in most of the studies that you read, motivation is like an internal motivational force to make it work or to achieve your goals. So I thought I'd interview the teachers and see if they get the same ..., if they experience the same thing as these surveys show, and then compare them.
Supervisor B:	But if they feel that they have been motivated, what do you think they have been motivated to do? Is it to play more computer games or is it to absorb the subject matter? Or?
Student G:	Yeah, yeah, a little bit more like that, that it's kind of /.../.

Supervisor B, Recording 2, Individual supervision

In this example the supervisor asks six different questions, all related to the same topic or area: how the student should measure or analyse motivation.

- What are your thoughts on the concept of motivation?
- What is motivation?
- How do you want to measure motivation?
- And if you then access their experiences, how will you know if it has had an effect?
- How far will your results go?
- If they feel they have been motivated, what do you think they have been motivated to do?

As the example shows, the student is not always able to answer the various challenging and problematising questions. On two occasions the student makes some attempts to motivate and explain, but the supervisor continues to ask the same type of questions, indicating that the answers are perceived as inadequate. In the ongoing conversation, the supervisor also explains the purpose or function of the questioning: "I ask questions to understand what will be your more … like delimitation, definition, purpose formulation". The fact that the purpose and function of the questions are described by the supervisor may also have the positive effect that the student finds it easier to accept and integrate the criticism implied in the challenging and problematising questions posed. The questions lead to brief comments on the various concrete suggestions made by the supervisor, but no new perspectives appear to emerge according to the documented interaction.

Challenging and problematising questions differ from the other questioning functions in that they do not necessarily lead to increased participation, but they may lead to deeper participation if students, through these questions, are able to consider their own thinking or writing from a new perspective. The questions often concern something that the supervisor perceives as insufficiently motivated or problematic, and through the questions the students have the opportunity to look at their choices and perspectives in a new way. However, it is often unclear from the documented supervision interaction to what extent this actually happens, as the students' responses are many times brief and not always very informative.

As mentioned earlier, all of the supervisors in our material used all of these types of questions in their supervision practice and through this created different forms of student participation. At a general level, then, it can be argued that the recorded supervisor interactions contained elements of Dysthe's (2002) partnership model through the questions asked of students and the participation created by these questions. However, there was a great deal of variation between different supervision interactions and parts of the interactions, and it is consequently difficult to discern any distinct supervisor models or styles in our material. Rather, we see it as a matter of supervisor strategies being used at different stages and in various ways in different supervision conversations, depending on the students' needs and the particular situation and interaction. For example, if as a supervisor you strive for equal participation where students' arguments and descriptions serve as a starting point and focus, the challenging and problematising questions may not be the most valuable scaffolding tool. On the other hand, if as a supervisor you want the students to undergo a course switching (cf. Lea and Street 2000) and adopt new perspectives, then challenging and problematising questions may be very useful.

Praise

Another potential scaffolding strategy or tool for encouraging and enabling student independence is to praise students, as all the supervisors in our recorded supervision interactions regularly did. At a general level, the function of praise is to show support, interest, commitment and solidarity (cf. Hyland 2000; Hyland and Hyland 2001). Praise has been shown to be important in educational contexts as it can lead to an increase in learning and to the learning situation being perceived as more positive and motivating (cf. Daiker 2011). Here, praise is defined as the supervisor's verbal acknowledgement of the students for some skill, attribute, something they have done, etc. that is positively valued by the supervisor (cf. Holmes 2011).[3] In supervision practice, praise serves different functions, such as acknowledging what the students have said, closing a topic or encouraging the students to continue along a suggested path (Magnusson 2020). Praise can furthermore be seen as a formative and forward-looking assessment of the students' work. There is thus an implicit asymmetry in praise in an institutional context such as higher education, in that the person giving the praise does so from a position of authority, where the praise can sometimes even be perceived as condescending. In other words, praise can have multiple functions and it is quite possible that the praise given in a particular situation may not have the desired or expected effect.

[3] Cf. explicit positive assessment (EPA) Waring (2008).

As mentioned before, our material shows that praise was a common tool for all the supervisors who participated in the study, often in the form of confirming what the students said or did. For example, supervisors praised what students had done and what students planned to do in terms of writing, carrying out and participating in activities related to the degree project work. This related to concrete activities, such as collecting material and searching for literature, but also to attitudes and choice of perspectives. Praise occurred both as a response to things that students raised and asked about, and as part of the supervisors' reflections on the students' work. Thus, the recorded supervision conversations contained both text-based and process-based praise. Below is an example of text-based praise, where students were praised for a modification they had made to the text:

Supervisor D: Then we've talked about the research questions. You made changes there too, right?
Student L: Yeah, exactly, to focus more on the organisation.
Supervisor D: Yes, and I think that's good too. Mm.
Supervisor D, Recording 1, Pair supervision

It is the changes in the research questions that the supervisor praises and confirms, "and I think that's good too", which has to do with the students' written text and the alterations made to it. Process-based praise is evident in this example where the student described what he/she had done since the last meeting:

Student Q: I've actually been to the library now and ... So I've borrowed some books.
Supervisor F: Yes, yes, mm. That's good.
Supervisor F, Recording 4, Individual supervision

The student described having borrowed some books from the library, which is a typical process-based degree project activity. This was praised by the supervisor by saying 'that's good', which is also an example of how praise can sometimes work as an acknowledgement rather than a compliment.

In addition to the way in which supervisors' praise can be both text-based and process-based, it has other functions, some of which can be linked to independence. All of the supervisors in the material regularly used praise with three main functions: praise as an affirmation of the student's suggestions, questions and ideas; praise as positive guidance; and praise as a counterbalance to criticism. Since the role of praise is relevant to how supervisors encourage and enable student independence, these features will be discussed in more detail.

Three Types of Praise

The most common role of praise in the recorded supervision sessions involved supervisors affirming and approving of what students described as having done or proposing to do in the forthcoming degree project work. This type of affirmative praise could be seen as encouraging and supporting student participation and initiative at a general level, which can be seen as way to enable and promote independence (cf. Magnusson and Zackariasson 2018). In the following example, the supervised student described what had been done since the last session, which was approved by the supervisor:

Student N: And then I've started to look at … what kind of questions are asked in the texts.
Supervisor E: That's great, and this one, is this text number one?
Student N: Yeah, exactly.
Supervisor E, Recording 3, Individual supervision

The student described working on an analysis of the collected material, by examining what questions were asked in the texts. The supervisor praised and validated this description of the analytical work with the words 'that's great', which also serves to encourage the student to continue with the analysis.

Another common function of praise used by supervisors in our material is what we have termed positively framed guidance, where praise is used in the supervisor's reasoning to support students and get them to move in a certain direction or pay attention to something particularly important. In the example below, the students described how one of their respondents reasoned about preschools with homogeneous or non-homogeneous age groups. The supervisor praised what the students were describing by highlighting what was seen as particularly interesting and useful for their further work:

Student O:	She says at the end of the interview that she thinks it's the one- and two-year-olds who are the losers in the new constellation because they usually want so much. She explained it like this, they often want to just look first and so on. And I imagine, she says, that sometimes they could simply have a box each, that there could be twenty boxes in a department, and in each box a child sits and looks at what is going on. In her image it looks like that, and I understand a little bit what she means. So that you just sit a little distance away and look at what the others are doing first. Before you do it yourself. That is how she describes it. And that is not possible today.
Supervisor F:	No.
Student O:	No.
Supervisor F:	Yeah, that's interesting, yeah. And it's good that you get a kind of counter-image. That maybe it's not just an idealisation, that everything will be fine and so on, that's what I think.

Supervisor F, Recording 3, Pair supervision

First, the interviewee's reasoning about the organisation of children's groups at the workplace is presented. Then the supervisor confirms what has been said, "no", before the praise comes—"interesting", "good". The praise indicates a specific aspect in the students' account that is relevant to continue, and the supervisor also justifies why: because it is important to get a counter-image to the previously reported positive descriptions from other interviewees in the students' study. The positive guidance here consists of the supervisor, by praise and by focusing on certain things that the students have mentioned, directing them towards a more complex picture with different perspectives as well as both positive and negative views on the topic studied.

The third most common function of praise in the recorded supervision interactions is to balance criticism given by the supervisor. Balancing criticism with praise is a general pedagogical strategy whereby one brings up something positive in order to be able to address negative criticism, something that Hyland and Hyland (2001, 194) call paired act patterns. In the following example, the supervisor begins with general praise of the draft thesis, followed by a description of things the student could work more on:

Supervisor G: If I'll start with a kind of, like, general assessment, I think you have a good degree project, a good foundation for the degree project. You've come a long way, but I think you should work through it one more time so that it becomes a better … There is still room for improvement, and this applies both to these quite basic things in a way, like language, punctuation, some references that are missing and so on. You've got quite a lot of "ibid".
Student R: Mmm.
Supervisor G, Recording 2, Individual supervision

The praise in this example consists of several parts—"a good degree project", "a good foundation for the degree project" and "you have come a long way". Then comes the criticism, marked by a 'but'. The criticism concerns how there is still 'room for improvement', exemplified by 'language, punctuation, some missing references and so on'.

Sometimes negative criticism is embedded between the opening and closing positive criticism or praise, which can be referred to as the sandwich method (Leibold and Schwarz 2015; Henley and DiGennaro Reed 2015). In the following example, praise is given both at the beginning and at the end, surrounding and somewhat mitigating the given criticism about the student's lack of collected empirical data:

Supervisor B: You've got a great topic, and …
Student G: Yeah, motivation, which this is part of.
Supervisor B: The difficult part is that you don't have your empirical data. I don't have any doubts concerning that you wouldn't manage it, when it comes to the study not being coherent. It looks great.
Supervisor B, Recording 5, Individual supervision

The supervisor first praised the student's choice of topic for the degree project, 'great topic', but then immediately addressed the critical part, 'the difficult part', the fact that the student had not yet collected the empirical data, even though there was relatively little time left in the degree project course at the time of the supervision meeting. Then came some praise, 'it looks great' and that there was no doubt that the student would manage to make the study coherent. Thus, it was mainly the student's chosen focus and plan that were praised by the supervisor.

Praise in the form of affirmation and positive guidance can be seen as a potential scaffolding tool for student participation, both to get students to move forward with their ideas and to help students realise which ideas might be worth moving forward with (cf. van de Pol 2012; van de Pol et al. 2010). Thus, when praise has these roles, it can be seen as a strategy for facilitating and enabling independence. The third role of praise, where criticism and praise are balanced in different ways, is not as obviously related to independence but could be said to support students by possibly making the negative criticism easier to absorb.

However, it is not entirely unproblematic for supervisors to use praise as a strategy in the supervision of degree projects, as there is also a future examiner of the degree project to consider. It can be difficult for students to distinguish between the formative praise of supervisors and the summative assessment of examiners, and students who feel that they have received a lot of formative praise may feel deceived if they then fail the summative assessment of the degree project by the examiner. In the recorded supervision sessions, it appeared that supervisors were dealing with this, consciously or unconsciously, by toning down the praise. Firstly, supervisors often hedged their praise. Supervisors would say that something was 'pretty good', 'sensible' or 'okay' rather than that it was 'great'. Secondly, it was common for supervisors to emphasise that it was their subjective judgement that they were expressing: 'I believe …', 'I think that …' or 'it feels like …'. This opens up the possibility of other potential perceptions and perspectives. Thirdly, it was often selected parts that were praised rather than the entire degree project. The aim, the description of the method and a single heading are examples of what could be praised. Linking praise and criticism could also be seen as a way of moderating and hedging the praise. In the following example, several types of hedging occurred.

Supervisor D: It feels like you've pretty much … as we say, so to speak. That's a good thing. There's a bit of time left to work so … You've kind of got the structure and the research questions and so on, I think. It feels like it's under control.
Supervisor D, Recording 3, Pair supervision

In the excerpt, hedging expressions such as "pretty much" or "kind of" were used, but also expressions indicating that the evaluation was based on the supervisor's subjective assessment: "I think ..." and "it feels like ...". All this hedging downplays the rather cautious praise that follows—"under control". The praise given thus expresses a positive assessment, but not at an absolute level.

As our discussion has exemplified, praise could, then, be regarded as a potential scaffolding tool that may be used to encourage and enable student independence. At the same time, it is important to clarify to students that any praise given is part of a formative assessment, not the final assessment of the completed degree project, as well as to be aware of what kind of praise you as a supervisor use—and why.

PERSPECTIVE TAKING THROUGH ACTIVE VOICING

A common perception of student independence that emerged from the focus group interviews we conducted is that it involves the ability to position oneself and relate to what one reads and hears (cf. Chap. 3). In order to be perceived as independent, students were expected to be able to relate to different sources and contexts, for which perspective taking is important (cf. Magnusson and Zackariasson 2018). In other words, this view of student independence requires the supervisor to enable and accommodate perspective shifts in the supervision interaction, but also to support the student in how to shift perspectives in the written text. In our recorded supervision material, it is clear that supervisors do this, among other things, through scaffolding tools such as modelling (cf. van de Pol 2012, 36; van de Pol et al. 2010, 277). Modelling means that supervisors demonstrate to students possible ways of thinking and acting, thus communicating what is typical or desirable in terms of attitudes, norms and strategies related to academic writing.

Students' ability to relate to different perspectives can be understood from a dialogical perspective, in which Bakhtin's (1981) concept of *voice* is central. Bakhtin argues that everything we say and do is part of a constant dialogue where what we say has been influenced by what others have said and will influence what others will say. We reuse words and expressions, and we respond to and oppose, agree with and question the statements and utterances of others. Our statements are never neutral and objective, and every time we speak we take a particular stance. This is, somewhat simplified, what Bakhtin calls voice. Our utterances are made up of other people's voices, and in our statements these traces of other people's voices are more or less evident. In order to describe and discuss how the supervisors modelled and illustrated perspective shifts in our material, Bakhtin's concept of voice, and more specifically *active voicing*, will serve as a starting point in this section (Hutchby and Wooffitt 1998, 225). The use of active voicing by supervisors means that expressions of other people's ideas or positions are more or less directly or consciously quoted or reflected by the supervisor. From an interactional perspective, active voicing is constructed and marked by changing intonation patterns, changing voice quality, or changing word or style choices.

Active voicing is thus a potential tool for supervisors to help students to distance themselves from their own individual perspectives and instead to adopt different stances in relation to their own investigation and their own text. In our material, supervisors used active voicing, for example, in relation to the different parts of the degree project, how concepts should be defined and how previous research should be described. It was largely general academic approaches that were modelled, such as taking a critical approach, problematising phenomena, describing phenomena from different perspectives and so on. The use of active voicing as a way of exemplifying or modelling academic norms is on one level close to the structure often used in academic writing, where claims are usually based on sources or empirical data. When results are to be presented in a (qualitative) degree project, this is often done through summary statements followed by examples to substantiate and illustrate, which is similar to how supervisors in our recorded material related to students' draft texts and degree project work. Active voicing can also be used to create authenticity—since the voices of informants, readers and students are heard in relation to the voice of the supervisor—or to create distance from what is being discussed.

In our recorded supervision interaction, both supervisors and students used several types of active voicing, but in the following we will focus on supervisors and how they used active voicing to stage and model different roles and perspectives during supervision conversations.

A Multi-voiced Enterprise

The use of active voicing by the supervisors emphasises to the students that the supervision context involves not only the students and the supervisor but also other participants in what could be seen as a kind of community of practice (cf. Lave and Wenger 1991; Wenger 1998). The actors made visible in this way by the supervisors included examiners, seminar leaders and students but also the imagined future readers of the degree projects. In what follows, we give some examples of how supervisors used active voicing in relation to these categories of actors in the supervision interaction, and discuss how this could be used as a scaffolding tool for modelling how students could or should think and act in their work on their degree projects.

The Student Voice
By far the most common voice used by supervisors in our material was the student's voice, or more specifically, two different types of student voice—a specific student voice and a generic student voice (cf. Sveen and Magnusson 2013). A specific student voice is when supervisors use the voice of the supervised student(s) to model or explain what students can or should do or write, or how they can or should reason. Through a generic student voice, supervisors instead explain or model how students often reason, which may indicate to supervised students what is likely to be expected of them later in the degree project process or show them that what they are doing or saying is not unusual in any way. In this way, supervisors can help to raise specific perspectives and individual experiences and make them more general and normalised (cf. Svinhufvud et al. 2017). Regardless of the type of student voice used, it can serve as a scaffolding tool by modelling how students can think, write or act (cf. van de Pol 2012; van de Pol et al. 2010).

Below is an example of how supervisors can use generic student voices to model different types of scenarios for supervised students—scenarios that are based on supervisors' experience of how students often or sometimes react or reason. In the example, where the supervisor was reminding the student to design a correct cover, the supervisor used a generic student voice, possibly to avoid the advice being perceived as criticism.

Supervisor G: Mm, and then you should have the correct front page eventually. Yeah, you probably know that, but just so that I've said it, so it's not like "Nobody told me that".
Supervisor G, Recording 1, Individual supervision

The active voicing in this excerpt, 'Nobody told me that', thus exemplifies a typical student comment or experience. This can be interpreted as the supervisor trying to mitigate the admonition that the front page needs to be designed correctly, by the shift in voice—showing that it is not this particular student who usually thinks in this way but other students who can generally think like this. In addition, the supervisor explains the reasoning behind the admonition by saying 'you probably know that, but just so that I've said it'. In other words, the supervisor used active voicing to remind the student of something that may seem obvious—to have a correct front page—possibly to avoid a face-threatening situation (cf. Brown and Levinson 1987), i.e. a situation in which the student feels questioned or criticised. The supervisor's use of previous student experiences as a perspective to justify a reprimand or instruction in a non-threatening way can be said to be in line with the pursuit of Dysthe's (2002) partnership model rather than the teaching model.

The use of a specific student voice was by far the most common among the supervisors we recorded. In a first example, the supervisor used active voicing several times to model and illustrate to the student how to think about academic concepts and how to describe them in the degree project.

Supervisor G: And you have different concepts, and you could have done that under "Identity". That you could start that section with something like: "The next concept that becomes central to my analysis is action dadadadadadada, where action is acts that have a purpose." So to tell me as a reader that ... like, "Now we're moving on to the next thing. So the first concept I'm going to talk about is identity. The next concept that becomes interesting or central to my analysis is action". So that's what I wrote [in the comments on the draft text]. But then I've given you suggestions here: "Identity is a manifold concept that has been understood and defined in many different ways: I'm going to start with what is called the mirroring theory". Because that's what you want to do, "this is the approach that" and so on. So that you sort of show the reader more clearly, like: "What am I going to do, what am I going to talk about and how am I going to use it?
Supervisor G, Recording 1, Individual supervision

The supervisor here scaffolds the student on how to make the use of concepts clearer by using several active voice shifts, concerning both the written text and how the student should think. This is done partly by modelling for the student how to use metalanguage to guide future readers of the degree project and partly by exemplifying how to think to achieve greater clarity. The examples given are presented through the student's voice:

> "The next concept that becomes central to my analysis is action, dadada-dada, where action is actions that has a purpose."
> "Now we're moving on to the next thing. So the first concept I'm going to talk about is identity. The next concept that becomes interesting or …"
> "Identity is a manifold concept that has been understood and defined in many different ways: I am going to start with what is called the mirroring theory."
> "What am I going to do, what am I going to talk about and how am I going to use it?"

The supervisor thus scaffolds the student through the active voicing shifts in two different ways, firstly by modelling concrete examples of how the student can describe his or her use of concepts meta-linguistically and secondly by modelling how the student can think in order to describe the concepts from several relevant perspectives. The scaffolding tool illustrates or models the same type of academic literacy skill, but in different ways.

In the next example, the supervisor used active voicing to model and show the students how to think and act when conducting interviews to collect their material, and how to get the informants to motivate and exemplify their statements, thereby gaining more depth in the interview responses.

Supervisor F:	And it's very much about showing a huge interest and curiosity and things like that. And then not to be focused on these questions, but just to say: "Now I want to know, actually I want to know everything about the introduction of the children". The questions are just a small tool, they are just a way in, "but I really want to know everything about your views on the introduction of children".
Student O:	Maybe we'll try it next time.
Supervisor F:	"And I want to know if, when you say that … Have you had any experience with it? Can you tell me about an occasion when …?" and so on. And if they say: "I don't think it's good for the children", "No, but why don't you think so?
Student O:	Yes, that's a question you ask.
	Supervisor F, Recording 1, Pair supervision

Through several different active voice shifts, the supervisor scaffolds the students by modelling two imaginary perspectives, the perspective that the informants might have, 'I don't think it's good for the kids', and the perspective that the students need to have during the interviews, 'No, but why don't you think so?' Here the supervisor scaffolds the students in how to ask their questions, and especially how to ask follow-up questions. Again, active voicing is used both to scaffold the students in terms of what they can specifically say, how the questions can be framed in this particular case, and to scaffold the students in terms of how they can think, "but I really want to know everything about your views on the introduction of children".

In another example, the supervisor used active voicing to scaffold the student by demonstrating two different approaches or perspectives the student might have when reading theoretical literature, only one of which was recommended by the supervisor.

Supervisor B: Because there's a difference to find, like: "and this is interesting, and this is interesting".
Student G: Yeah, that's exactly what I do. (laughs)
Supervisor B: You shouldn't do that, you should be able to differentiate: "Yes, this is interesting but not relevant, yes, this is interesting and relevant", so that you kind of try to …
Supervisor B, Recording 2, Individual supervision

The first approach to or perspective on the reading process that the supervisor demonstrates is that everything interesting is noted or included, "and this is interesting, and this is interesting", while the second approach to or perspective on the reading process is that only what is relevant to the purpose of the degree project is included. "Yes, this is interesting but not relevant, yes, this is interesting and relevant". The use of active voicing here can serve as a form of scaffolding for the student, by modelling a potential way of thinking or working (cf. van de Pol 2012; van de Pol et al. 2010).

In the next example, the supervisor used active voicing in relation to a specific student voice in a discussion about how previous research might be used to identify and justify a research gap in a degree project.

Supervisor B: And it's ... This is where you kind of come to the research gap, I think, this: "My study is pretty close to this study".
Student G: Mm.
Supervisor B: But unlike ...
Student G: It hasn't been done on young children or on ...
Supervisor B: No, exactly, "Unlike that study, I'm looking at young children and it can sort of complement or generate additional knowledge on this topic". Then poof, you have your research gap there, looking at how different researchers have dealt with it in the past.
Supervisor B, Recording 5, Individual supervision

The supervisor uses active voicing to illustrate how the student can think about the previous research and use it in the text: "Unlike that study, I am looking at young children and it can sort of complement or generate additional knowledge on this topic". The active voicing may thus be regarded as a scaffolding tool in the sense that a perspective or way of reasoning is modelled for the student (cf. van de Pol 2012; van de Pol et al. 2010).

In summary, the general and specific student voices are used to model different perspectives for the students—how they can think and do (write, speak), that there are many ways of thinking and doing, and how typical patterns have to do with academic writing norms. Through active voicing and modelling, this is concretised and made visible to the students and can be used by them as strategies and approaches in their further work process.

Other Voices
In addition to using specific and generic student voices, the supervisors in our material used active voicing in relation to other categories of actors in the supervision context, or the supervision community of practice, if we consider it as such (cf. Lave and Wenger 1991; Wenger 1998). One such category of actors consisted of the supervisors themselves. Whilst the supervisors were of course present in the supervision sessions, there were examples of active voicing in our material where the supervisors expressed themselves in their own voice from another time. In this sense, the supervision sessions could include voices from the supervisor in the present, the supervisor in the past and the supervisor in the future. To scaffold students in modelling different perspectives, supervisors could use a past voice— to show how they thought in the past, often when reading students'

drafts—or a future voice—to show how they would react or think if students did things one way or another. Such past and future voices require an active shift of voice from the present voice of the supervisor.

In our material, it was most common for supervisors to use a past voice, as in the example below, where the supervisor used active voicing to illustrate the thinking during the previous reading of the student's draft:

Student L:	Yeah, but I mean in addition to what fit in the draft, we do have more literature. But we can send it separately if you want?
Supervisor D:	Yes, please.
Student L:	Because we sat with it yesterday and wrote.
Supervisor D:	Yes, because I just saw that it was a little bit different. I thought: "Have you changed it or are you at least going to read a little?" You haven't locked it in yet, have you? You can get lots of ideas.
Student M:	No, no.

Supervisor D, Recording 1, Pair supervision

With the voice shift "Have you changed it or are you at least going to read a little?" and the subsequent question whether the students have "locked it in yet", the supervisor signals that the students' perspective might be too limited and that they might need to give it some more thought. The fact that the supervisor used active voicing, a voice from the past, can be interpreted as a cautious way of highlighting a perceived deficiency. The supervised students are presented with the same thought or recommendation twice in the form of questions, but only one of these is presented in the supervisor's present voice. In other words, it can be said that the supervisor guides the students on how to proceed by presenting the same wish or recommendation in a past and present voice, which helps to reinforce the impression that it is important.

Another category of actors that supervisors tended to use active voicing in relation to were the potential future readers of the degree projects. When supervisors used active voicing to express a reader's perspective, it often had the function of guiding students in their writing by drawing their attention to audience adaptation in the form of a focus on context and comprehensibility. As in this example, where it is context in the form of paragraphing that the supervisor focuses on when using active voicing and taking on the role of generic reader.

Supervisor G: And sometimes it's actually that it's quite clear that "Well, this should be a new paragraph because she's actually bringing up a new thing here". So one of the rules or guidelines that is usually suggested is that every time you bring up a new thing you should have a new paragraph.
Supervisor G, Recording 2, Individual supervision

In general, not dividing paragraphs clearly makes texts harder to follow. Here, however, it is also an academic writing norm that the student is introduced to, namely the convention where each 'new thing' gets its own paragraph. Writing rules or conventions can thus be conveyed with less explicit expertise and with a certain distance, as the supervisor takes on the role of a generic reader, while nevertheless marking the academic conventions clearly with the help of modal expressions such as 'actually' and 'should'. At the same time, however, the supervisor's approach can be seen as encouraging the student to adopt another perspective, that of the reader, in order to look at one's own text from the outside and to reflect on what is obvious to the intended reader and what is not. Thus, in this example, active voicing represents a softer way of expressing objections and introducing textual norms. The shift also concretises and illustrates the contexts in which the student's choices can be problematic, such as the fact that it is primarily when reading a text that different textual norms become important. Such a strategy also makes it clear that the student is not just writing for the supervisor or examiner but with the future readers of the text in mind.

Although relatively rare, there are examples in our recorded material of supervisors using active voicing to make the future or imagined examiner of the degree projects visible. In the few examples that exist, it is about the role of the examiner as assessor of the forthcoming degree project, where a difference between the role of the examiner and the role of the supervisor is clarified. In one example, the supervisor reminded the students that they should not dispose of all the material they have collected before the completion of the degree project, as the examiner may request the material in order to check that the project has been properly carried out.

Supervisor F: Just so you're aware of it after the exam ... So not when you're done with [the material collection] ... Because it could happen that the examiner comes and says: "Can I look at it, is it really there?" It happens that fictitious

results, very rarely, but I'm just saying it so you don't go and burn it beforehand. Then it can get silly.
Supervisor F, Recording 6, Pair supervision

The active voicing used by the supervisor in this example is aimed at helping the students understand the importance of handling and storing their collected material properly, by illustrating how the examiner may come and ask for it—"Can I look at it, is it really there?". The use of active voicing here may also be regarded as a way for the supervisor to create distance and place responsibility and authority elsewhere, either to clarify the roles between supervisor and examiner or to avoid the supervisor's own role becoming too controlling. Thus, it is both different perspectives on the material as such that are modelled through active voicing and the supervisor's perspective in relation to the examiner's perspective.

In summary, it is not only the student's voice that is used by the supervisor to support the supervised students but also, for example, the supervisor's own voice before and after the supervision session in question, as well as the voice of potential readers and the voice of future examiners. The different uses of active voicing model and illustrate different approaches and, in this sense, can be seen as potential scaffolding tools that supervisors can use in supervision to help students develop independence in the form of perspective taking (cf. van de Pol 2012; van de Pol et al. 2010).

* * *

In this chapter we have discussed some of the tools available to the supervisor in the supervision interaction—whether supervisors express themselves in the form of demands, recommendations or questions and how supervisors use praise and active voicing. These tools are related to the scaffolding process but also to the relationship between supervisor and student, not least when it comes to the balance of power. We have once again emphasised that supervision is a collegial and social practice and given examples of this. In the next chapter we will take a closer look at how the assessment of degree projects is also part of the supervision practice and how this too takes place in a collegial and social interaction.

References

Austin, John Langshaw. 1975. *How to do things with words: the William James lectures delivered at Harvard University in 1955* (2nd ed.). Cambridge, Mass.: Harvard University Press.

Bakhtin, Michail. 1981. *The Dialogic Imagination: Four Essays.* Edited by Michael Holquist. Austin: University of Texas Press.

Brown, Penelope, and Stephen C. Levinson. 1987. *Politeness: Some Universals in Language Usage.* Cambridge: Cambridge Univ. Press.

Daiker, Donald A. 2011. Learning to Praise. In *Concepts in Composition: Theory and Practice in the Teaching of Writing*, ed. Irene L. Clark, 168–174. London & New York: Routledge.

Dysthe, Olga. 2002. Professors as Mediators of Academic Text Cultures: an Interview Study with Advisors and Masters Degree Students in Three Disciplines in a Norwegian University. *Written Communication* 19 (4): 493–544. https://doi.org/10.1177/074108802238010.

Ellis, Kathleen. 1993. Teacher Questioning Behavior and Student Learning: What Research Says to Teachers. In *Annual Meeting of the Western States Communication Association*, Albuquerque.

Emanuelsson, Jonas. 2001. *En fråga om frågor: hur lärares frågor i klassrummet gör det möjligt att få reda på elevernas sätt att förstå det som undervisningen behandlar i matematik och naturvetenskap.* Göteborg: Acta Universitatis Gothoburgensis.

Eriksson, Anita, and Susanne Gustavsson. 2016. Krav, uppmaningar och frågor - en autoetnografisk reflektion över handledning av självständiga arbeten. *Utbildning och Lärande* 10 (1): 70–87.

Freed, Alice F. 1994. The Form and Function of Questions in Informal Dyadic Conversation. *Journal of Pragmatics* 21 (6): 621–644. https://doi.org/10.1016/0378-2166(94)90101-5.

Freed, Alice F., and Susan Ehrlich. 2010. *"Why Do You Ask?" The Function of Questions in Institutional Discourse.* New York, Oxford: Oxford University Press.

Henley, Amy J., and Florence D. DiGennaro Reed. 2015. Should You Order the Feedback Sandwich? Efficacy of Feedback Sequence and Timing. *Journal of Organizational Behavior Management* 35 (3–4): 321–335. https://doi.org/10.1080/01608061.2015.1093057.

Holmes, Janet. 2011. Complimenting - a Positive Politeness Strategy. In *Language and Gender - A Reader*, ed. Jennifer Coates and Pia Pichler, 71–88. Chichester: Wiley-Blackwell.

Hutchby, Ian, and Robin Wooffitt. 1998. *Conversation Analysis: Principles, Practises and Applications.* Cambridge: Polity.

Hyland, Fiona. 2000. ESL Writers and Feedback: Giving More Autonomy to Students. *Language Teaching Research* 4 (1): 33–54. https://doi.org/10.1177/136216880000400103.

Hyland, Fiona, and Ken Hyland. 2001. Sugaring the Pill: Praise and Criticism in Written Feedback. *Journal of Second Language Writing* 10 (3): 185–212. https://doi.org/10.1016/S1060-3743(01)00038-8.

Koshik, Irene Ann. 2010. Questions that Convey Information in Teacher-Student Conferences. In *Why Do You Ask?: The Function of Questions in Institutional Discourse*, ed. A. Freed and S. Ehrlich, 159–186. New York: Oxford University Press.

Lave, Jean, and Etienne Wenger. 1991. *Situated Learning: Legitimate Peripheral Participation, Learning in Doing*. Cambridge: Cambridge University Press.

Lea, Mary R., and Brian V. Street. 2000. Student Writing and Staff feedback in Higher Education: An academic Literacies Approach. In *Student Writing in Higher Education. New Contexts*, ed. Mary R. Lea and Barry Stierer, 32–46. Buckingham: Open University Press.

Leibold, Nancyruth, and Laura Marie Schwarz. 2015. The Art of Giving Online Feedback. *Journal of Effective Teaching* 15 (1): 34–46.

Magnusson, Jenny. 2020. "Jättebra, men" - Handledares beröm i handledningssamtal. *Språk och interaktion* 5 (3): 45–68.

Magnusson, Jenny, and Maria Zackariasson. 2018. Student Independence in Undergraduate Projects. Different Understandings in Different Academic Contexts. *Journal of Further and Higher Education* 43 (10): 1404–1419. https://doi.org/10.1080/0309877X.2018.1490949.

van de Pol, Janneke. E. (2012). *Scaffolding in teacher-student interaction: exploring, measuring, promoting and evaluating scaffolding*. [Thesis, fully internal, Universiteit van Amsterdam]. https://dare.uva.nl/search?identifier=640b82ba-c27b-42d3-b9f8-fe08b1e0081f.

van de Pol, Janneke, Monique Volman, and Jos. Beishuizen. 2010. Scaffolding in Teacher–Student Interaction: A Decade of Research. *Educational Psychology Review* 22: 271–296. https://doi.org/10.1007/s10648-010-9127-6.

van de Pol, Janneke, Monique Volman, and Jos Beishuizen. 2012. Promoting Teacher Scaffolding in Small-group Work: A contingency Perspective. *Teaching and Teacher Education* 28 (2): 193–205. https://doi.org/10.1016/j.tate.2011.09.009.

van de Pol, Janneke, Monique Volman, Frans Oort, and Jos Beishuizen. 2015. The Effects of Scaffolding in the Classroom: Support Contingency and Student Independent Working time in Relation to Student Achievement, Task Effort and Appreciation of Support. *Instructional Science* 43 (5): 615–641. https://doi.org/10.1007/s11251-015-9351-z.

Sveen, Hanna, and Jenny Magnusson. 2013. Handledningens vad, hur och varför: interaktionella mönster med fokus på röst. *Högre Utbildning* 3 (2): 87–102.

Svinhufvud, Kimmo, Liisa Voutilainen, and Elina Weiste. 2017. Normalizing in Student Counseling: Counselors' Responses to Students' Problem Descriptions. *Discourse Studies* 19 (2): 196–215. https://doi.org/10.1177/1461445 617691704.

Waring, Hansun Zhang. 2008. Using explicit positive assessment in the language classroom: IRF, feedback, and learning opportunities. *The Modern Language Journal* 92 (4): s. 577–594.

Wenger, Etienne. 1998. *Communities of Practice: Learning, Meaning, and Identity, Learning in Doing*. Cambridge: Cambridge University Press.

Wichmann-Hansen, Gitte. 2021. DUT Guide on Supervision. *Dansk universitetspædagogisk tidsskrift* 16 (31): 94–106. https://doi.org/10.7146/dut.v16i31.127292.

Open Access This chapter is licensed under the terms of the Creative Commons Attribution-NonCommercial-NoDerivatives 4.0 International License (http://creativecommons.org/licenses/by-nc-nd/4.0/), which permits any noncommercial use, sharing, distribution and reproduction in any medium or format, as long as you give appropriate credit to the original author(s) and the source, provide a link to the Creative Commons license and indicate if you modified the licensed material. You do not have permission under this license to share adapted material derived from this chapter or parts of it.

The images or other third party material in this chapter are included in the chapter's Creative Commons license, unless indicated otherwise in a credit line to the material. If material is not included in the chapter's Creative Commons license and your intended use is not permitted by statutory regulation or exceeds the permitted use, you will need to obtain permission directly from the copyright holder.

CHAPTER 7

The Supervisor as Assessor

At the same time, as supervision practice involves aspects such as relationship building and encouraging student participation and independence through a variety of tools, assessment is also an important part of the interaction in supervision. For example, when supervisors give praise or recognition to students, they are also making an assessment of what the students have achieved or the choices they have made. The same is true when supervisors provide negative critique or communicate in various ways that something the students have done or plan to do does not meet expectations and quality requirements. In this chapter we take a closer look at the supervisor's role as an assessor and how this too can be understood in relation to student independence, academic literacies and scaffolding.

WHEN FEEDBACK BECOMES ASSESSMENT

As we have discussed, supervisors have multiple roles and functions in relation to students. One of these roles has to do with assessment and evaluation, which is related to how a large part of the supervisors' work involves giving feedback on what the students have achieved or thought (cf.

Lundström 2016; Reid 1994; Rienecker et al. 2019).[1] Following the definition of van de Pol et al. (2010) and van de Pol (2012), giving feedback to students, that is providing students with information about their performance, may constitute an essential part of active scaffolding work in supervision.

Just as the teacher or supervisor needs to be aware of the students' level of knowledge and previous experience in order to be able to assess where they stand, the students need to be made aware of the extent to which their performance so far is sufficient to continue their work. This is particularly true in relation to independence, in the sense that degree project writers need some kind of indication as to whether what they have achieved is good enough, in order to be able to continue to make the choices and decisions that will allow the work to move forward. During a supervision session, this kind of assessment occurs continuously and in many different ways, which was clearly evident in our material. Sometimes it is done through short responses such as 'good' or 'ok', sometimes through repeated questions that force students to rethink what they have done or to think about their work in new ways, and in other cases through shorter or longer statements and comments with negative or positive critique on different parts of the degree project work.

In other words, supervisors' feedback and responses include positive assessments that encourage students to continue with their ideas and perspectives—such as the praise we discussed in Chap. 6—as well as negative assessments that cause students to step back, rethink and clarify. Supervisors' assessments can thereby be described as formative in relation to examiners' summative assessments. To a large extent, it is a forward-looking assessment, aimed at developing students' academic literacies and academic writing by identifying what seems promising and functional, as opposed to what seems problematic and unfruitful. But there are also summative aspects to supervisors' assessments, for example if, at the final stage of the degree project work, they inform students that the work is not up to scratch and advise them not to submit the degree project for examination, which we return to later in the chapter.

The formal organisation of the assessment of degree projects varies between disciplines, academic programmes, universities and higher

---

[1] Åsa Lindberg-Sand and Anders Sonesson argue that the circumstances of assessment in doctoral education are different from assessment in first- and second-cycle education. However, they also note that doctoral students are continuously assessed in a variety of ways and identify supervision sessions as one of the contexts in which this occurs (Lindberg-Sand and Sonesson 2020, 265).

education systems. In Sweden, supervisors are not supposed to be examiners of the degree projects they have supervised. However, there is often some kind of dialogue between supervisor and examiner, although this may be more or less formalised. In our material from Russian universities it was described how there was generally a formal examination committee or commission, at least at MA level but partly also at BA level, which in some cases could include representatives of stakeholders or representatives of the future professions (Zackariasson and Magnusson 2020). This made the assessment of the final product a collective decision involving several people (Focus Group Interview 5). Rienecker et al., who have written about the Danish context, discuss supervisors and examiners assessing degree projects together and the supervisor thereby having a dual role (Rienecker et al. 2019, 175f). Thus, the relationship between supervisors and examiners varies and can be relatively complex when it comes to the assessment of degree projects and whether the assessment is summative or formative.

When we discussed supervisors' positive assessments in the supervision interaction in Chap. 6, it mainly concerned praise and various functions that praise can have in the supervision context. As mentioned above, different types of negative assessment are also important for how students progress in their work, and in this chapter we will look more closely at how these can be communicated to students, orally during supervision sessions, but also in writing, as written comments on texts and drafts, and in e-mails.

Supervisor Versus Examiner

At the beginning of the degree project process, feedback from supervisors to students inevitably tends to focus on what students are planning to do. Comments on project drafts and ideas are given on the basis that they are something preliminary, which should maintain a certain standard, but which can also be expected to change as work progresses. When supervisors begin to have access to longer texts, feedback often concerns both what students have achieved so far and how they intend to proceed. In other words, in these early stages of degree project work, supervisors' assessments are to a high degree formative.

In the final phase of the degree project work, when time is running out and increasingly polished versions of the degree project manuscript are being discussed, there is less room for major modifications of the project and alternative choices. The supervisors' response therefore tends to focus on the presented texts. The assessments that are made are still largely formative, in the sense that they aim to enable students to develop and improve their texts, but they can also be summative, for example when the supervisor, having read a final manuscript, judges that it is not of a sufficiently high quality and therefore advises the student(s) not to submit the degree project. This may happen earlier in the degree project process, but then such advice is often based on what the students have not done, due to lack of time or for other reasons. For example, the supervisor may claim that there is not enough empirical material on which to base the degree project, or that the students have not progressed far enough in the writing process to make it realistic to complete the degree project within the timeframe. At the final stage, it is primarily what the students have actually done that is assessed, as it is the final manuscript that is the focus of supervision.

In the focus group interviews that we conducted as part of our research project, the participating supervisors rarely talked explicitly about making assessments in the sense of giving positive or negative critique to students during supervision discussions. What they did talk about on several occasions was their experience of colleagues examining and grading degree projects they had supervised, and how students might experience differences in assessment between supervisors and examiners. As in the following example from a focus group at a Swedish university:

> I have experienced very different tendencies for failing [degree projects]. Sometimes I think it's a bit scary. We are still quite similar, we who do the assessments. We have the same education and often the same age, but we think very differently. And this is also a problem that students often say: "You think differently depending on where you come from. No two people think the same." For example, if you have a supervisor and an examiner, or if you have had several examiners … There is a lot of talk about this and it also undermines legitimacy.
> *Focus Group Interview 2*

That supervisors are well aware that it can be very important for students what grade they obtain, especially when it is a question of pass or fail, was also evident in the Russian focus group material:

> Supervisor L: You know, usually we see discussions in cases when we decide whether to give a grade of 5 or 4 [good or excellent] according to our grading system, or 3 or 2 [satisfactory or failed]. Then there can be some heated debates. When it comes to something in between, colleagues usually come

to a consensus. But when you can fail a student by giving him a 2, and that student won't get a diploma and would have to come back next year, then the supervisor usually tries to protect his student, while the commission may disagree on the quality of the work.
Focus Group Interview 10

From an academic literacies perspective, it is not surprising that supervisors and examiners can make different assessments of the same text, especially if they come from different disciplines, considering how academic writing, and the expectations and assessments associated with it, from this perspective is assumed to differ between different local academic contexts (e.g. Lea & Street 2000; Lillis 2001, Shanahan and Shanahan 2012). At the same time, it is an aspect of degree project work that can be difficult for both supervisors and students to relate to, as the extracts above illustrate. From the students' perspective, it may seem that the supervisor's assessment is, or should be, equally important, even though the examiner or an examination board is primarily responsible for the final assessment. This attitude may also be shared by supervisors, not least from the perspective that, as noted above, they may in some cases make a kind of summative assessment of the final version of the work in order to determine whether the student should be discouraged from submitting the degree project—albeit in the knowledge that the examiners will then make their own assessment.

One aspect where supervisors in our material acknowledged difficulties was in relation to expectations or requirements of student independence. They could see challenges with encouraging students to make independent decisions and choices if examiners then had a relatively narrow view of how a degree project should be written and what choices are possible or desirable:

Then there is a kind of built-in contradiction in that we talk about independence at the same time as we want them to conform to certain folds. Some examiners are very, like, narrow and think it should be this way, and if it is not, then the student has to change it. While others might be a bit broader and accept other ways of ... arguing or other kinds of theories. And maybe you should have a somewhat self-critical discussion among examiners about this. That if on the one hand we're requiring independence, then at the same time we can't demand that they do exactly what I think (laughs) they should do.
Focus Group Interview 3

While supervisors in our material commented on the different roles of supervisors and examiners, and the potential conflicts that could arise, it is worth noting that several of the supervisors in our study were or had been degree project examiners. Thus, they had experience not only of having the degree projects they had supervised assessed and marked by others but also of assessing and marking degree projects supervised by colleagues. In many cases, therefore, they had experience of being 'on the other side', as in the following example from a focus group interview at a Russian university:

> Supervisor J: I have witnessed some conflicts as a member of [degree project] commissions. I think that in some cases, unfortunately, a supervisor does not see the difference between evaluation and attitude. The grade given has nothing to do with the student or the supervisor. It is an assessment of a specific piece of work. But some people take it as a personal insult and show resentment because they see a lower grade given by the reviewer as a sign that they do not value the supervisor or think badly of them. So we need to set ourselves a different task psychologically.
> *Focus Group Interview 6*

In addition to perhaps providing a better understanding of the roles of supervisors and examiners and the conditions under which they work, there may be greater opportunities for collegial discussion involving both categories if the examiners are also involved as supervisors in a particular course. If, on the other hand, there is a specific group of examiners who are not the same as the supervisors, something we also encountered in the course of the project, there is a certain risk that there will be a gap between these two categories unless arenas for joint conversation and collegial discussion are created. One way of creating such arenas is to include dialogue between supervisors and examiners as a formalised element in the organisation of the degree project course. That this can be fruitful was described in one of the focus group interviews at a Swedish university where this had recently been done:

> I feel that if you look at the course evaluations since we have introduced this [formalised dialogue], it appears much less in the course evaluations that: "Yes, that was really strange - how the examiner comes up with something completely different." Because that was quite common... so that's decreased significantly. But it still occurs. Because we have different traditions. We have different views. /.../ And we have different ways of ... If you have a

bad degree project, how do you save it? Then I suggest one way and you suggest another way and you suggest a third way, so to speak, and then the students may experience it as a conflict.
Focus Group Interview 4

Considering these potential issues, it may be helpful as a supervisor to actively discuss the role of supervisor versus examiner with supervised students, to raise their awareness of how these roles and categories relate to each other, and to give students a basic insight into the differences between formative and summative assessment and what this might mean for the supervision interaction. In addition, it can be valuable to reflect on how feedback and critique is given to students in relation to how student independence might be encouraged. This discussion is developed in the remainder of this chapter.

CRITIQUE AS FORMATIVE ASSESSMENT

As we discussed at the beginning of this chapter, formative assessment in supervision can take many forms and is often described as giving critique. In Chap. 6 we discussed positive critique in the form of praise, and here we develop the discussion of negative critique and how this also has the potential to be a scaffolding tool that can help students to progress in their work on the degree project. In this context, negative critique means that supervisors make judgements about students' written drafts or reasoning and descriptions of what they have done or plan to do. These assessments therefore concern things that, according to the supervisors, are missing or need to be developed.

How such negative critique is formulated may depend on whether it is given orally in a supervision session, in writing in commented drafts, or by e-mail. Critique that is formulated in writing by the supervisor, such as text comments on the students' various drafts, tends in our collected material to be relatively short and specific, in contrast to negative feedback that is given orally in the interaction.[2] This can be seen in the following examples from an annotated student text draft from our research material:

---

[2] The way in which responses and critique are formulated may also be influenced by the quality of the text, as noted in a study of written text response in Norwegian teacher education by Bauer et al. (2023).

- What paradigm is this? And what was it like before?
- It's very old research, is it really still relevant? A lot has happened with preschool since then.
- Shouldn't this go under 'definitions of learning'?
- Don't forget to include the word 'groups of children' when you write age-homogeneous and age-integrated. Otherwise it is unclear WHAT is homogeneous and integrated.
- Loose. It becomes fragmentary here when the different parts are not clearly connected - leading from one to the other. It is not clear what kind of approach you are talking about.

Supervisor F, examples from annotated draft text

These examples include both critical questions, recommendations to do or say something in a certain way and statements indicating that the student has chosen a less fruitful approach. All of these forms of criticism were common in the comments that supervisors made on different drafts in our material.

When supervisors provided feedback via email, they commented on specific wording and details as well as more general aspects of the texts or the degree project work. Not infrequently, their response to e-mails was a direct reply to students' questions about whether they were doing or thinking the right things, and sometimes the e-mail comments were linked to longer or shorter drafts of the text, which the supervisors also commented on and returned to the students. Negative criticism could be quite direct and straightforward, but it was often mixed with praise or encouragement, as in the following examples:

> Excellent work, it's starting to look good. Note that I am attaching a document with 'track changes' where I have corrected bits here and there. Think of my corrections as an indication of what you need to look at throughout the document. I have edited your abstract linguistically. Think of it as a help along the way, the abstract can still be worked on.
>
> There are still an incredible number of spelling mistakes, small errors and inconsistencies in the document. You need to go through your brackets: Sometimes you write (Author, year, p.), sometimes (Author year, p.), sometimes (Author: year:). There should be a long hyphen – between years and other numbers that are from – to. The headings are better, but still inconsistent. /.../ Watch your spaces and edit where they are doubled or missing.

I think the title is the best so far. See my rewritten suggestion.
There can't be too much of your own voice in the analysis.
Go for it - all the way to the top.[3]
Supervisor B, e-mail

In this case, the students specifically asked for feedback on their proposal for the title of the degree project and on how they should think about how visible they can or should be as authors in the text. However, the main focus of the response given is on the small details, which the supervisor had also noted in the annotated draft text.

Just like the conversations in the supervision sessions, the email responses can often be given according to the sandwich method (Henley and DiGennaro Reed 2015) that we discussed in Chap. 6, meaning that the response begins and ends with positive comments and encouragement, while the criticism is placed in the middle:

> Thanks for the exciting read!
> First of all, let's just say that you have an interesting take on an exciting subject and you write very well - so that bodes well! It's just a matter of not losing momentum and energy in the work – it's a matter of fighting to make the points (and what's good can always be even better)! I'm looking forward to reading more of the text analysis itself! The sample definitely left me wanting more!
> But I have one overall point. I think you have a remarkably good understanding of many of the advanced theories you refer to, and you have convinced me of the good point of using them. But you have a challenge in using your excellent writing to be pedagogical to your readers and to explain many things that are taken for granted in this version of the text without being so to those who will read your text. Tell your readers (= your classmates)! Illustrate with more examples what the point of this or that is (complicated concepts, for example). /…/
> Then you will probably be able to become more purposeful and economical in your presentation, thereby leading your readers on a straighter (but perhaps still somewhat wordier) path to the actual investigation. A win-win situation for your work!

---

[3] In the Swedish original, the phrase was 'in i kaklet', meaning 'all the way into the tiles'—a metaphor taken from swimming competitions.

> I look forward with excitement to the next progress report! Signal when you think it's time to meet and talk!
> For now: go, go, go!
> *Supervisor H, e-mail*

In both the above examples, the supervisors encourage student activity, thus emphasising that this is something they expect from the students. They address general aspects or recurring problems that students are encouraged to work on throughout the document. In the last example, the supervisor also makes it clear that it is the student who is expected to take the initiative for the next contact. From a scaffolding perspective, this can be seen as an example of how supervisors can gradually transfer responsibility for the degree project process to students over the course of the semester (cf. van de Pol 2012; van de Pol et al. 2010).

The tendency to give students more responsibility as the degree project work progresses was evident in several of the email conversations documented in our material. For example, it was usually the supervisors who invited the students to the first supervision meeting, often giving them specific instructions about the type of text they were expected to submit. By the end of the degree project period, however, the responsibility for keeping in contact or for the type of text submitted was placed more on the students, with the supervisors taking a more detached role. Since, as we discussed in Chap. 3, taking responsibility is a fundamental understanding of what student independence can mean in relation to degree project writing, this can be understood to mean that supervisors expected greater independence as the degree project work progressed. At the same time, this was based on the assumption that students would continue to make progress and take the supervisors' comments on board. Otherwise, the response in the final phase of the degree project period may again become more directive, which we also have examples of in the material (see also Zackariasson 2019).

While supervisors' comments via email were often a response to questions or requests for feedback from students, in the recorded supervision material it was usually the supervisors who initiated critical topics of conversation and pointed out problematic aspects of the drafts. In some conversations, however, the supervisors' criticism emerged partly in response to the students' questions, as in this example:

Supervisor A: Then you ask: "What do you think an article should contain to be relevant?" How do you answer that?
Student C: Mm, yes, maybe we should elaborate on that?
Supervisor A: Yes.
Student C: What we mean ...
Supervisor A: Yes.
Student C: ... with relevant.
Student D: Yes.
Supervisor A: Yes.
Student C: Do you think we're asking too broad questions?
Supervisor A: Yes.
Supervisor A, Recording 5, Pair supervision

In this example the supervisor reads out an interview question that the students have formulated in their interview guide, which the supervisor thinks is difficult to answer. The supervisor's initial criticism is implicitly formulated as a question, but then the students ask a counter-question, "maybe we should elaborate on that?", to which the supervisor answers "yes", as well as to the question the students ask later, "do you think we're asking too broad questions?". These two "yeses" confirm the students' self-formulated criticism.

In the following example it is the supervisor who initiates a topic relating to something they were critical of in the students' work, again introduced in the form of a question: "Media logic, is it really a theory that fits?"

Supervisor A: So I'm thinking about media logic, is it really a theory that fits?
Student D: Hm, yes, I guess that's mediatisation.
Student C: Mm.
Student D: I actually have a bit of a hard time telling the two apart sometimes, but ...
Supervisor A: Mm.
Student C: Those are the two that we've been thinking about anyway.
Supervisor A: Um ... media logic explains why the content of the media looks the way it does.
Student C: Mm.

Student D: Yes.
Supervisor A: Yes, but you're not going to examine the content.
Student C: No.
Supervisor A: You're going to look at how people perceive the content.
Student C: Yes.
Supervisor A: That's kind of the next step, isn't it?
Student D: But can you have that as a kind of background then?
Supervisor A, Recording 2, Pair supervision

The supervisor's initial question contained negative criticism in the form of a challenging and problematising question (cf. Chap. 6), which led to a discussion in which the students and supervisor worked through the issue together. In this way the students were actively involved in finding out what the problem was and how to deal with it.

In the following example, the supervisor criticised the students for not linking their results to theories and previous research, and for not having a section with a discussion and conclusion.

Supervisor A: Yes, that's what I'm missing so to speak, and that's what you have to do. Because then when you come to the conclusion and the discussion …
Student C: Mm.
Student D: Mm.
Supervisor A: There, what you're going to do there is link your results to theories and previous research.
Student C: Yeah.
Student D: Yeah.
Student C: Exactly.
Supervisor A: Because the thematic analysis is not conclusion and discussion, but it is …
Student D: No.
Supervisor A: It's part of …
Student C: Yeah, right, of the analysis.
Student D: Mm.
Supervisor A: Are you with me?
Supervisor A, Recording 5, Pair supervision

In the extract, expressions of lack and absence as well as negations are used to express the criticism. The supervisor points out what is missing and underlines that the thematic analysis is not the same as a discussion and conclusion.

Negative criticism can also be expressed through value judgements that are perceived as negative. For example, supervisors may suggest that students' research questions or aims are too vague and general or too broad. Opinions of this kind make it clear that it is often desirable and positive to make the degree project and the text more specific, limited and clear. However, the opposite can also be true, as in the following example where the supervisor described the students' description of the concept of media logic as 'a little too narrow'.

Supervisor A: You also write about media logic, there I think … You describe it a bit too narrowly. Like, media logic contains many different mechanisms, such as how it is about … Media logic is about how the working methods and working conditions of the media shape the content, so to speak.
Supervisor A, Recording 4, Pair supervision

Negations and value judgements are examples of explicitly formulated negative critique. There are also more implicit forms of negative feedback, not least the challenging and problematising questions, which by their very form can encourage students to think in new ways and change perspectives (see Chap. 6). These types of questions are often perceived by students as negative criticism, even though it is implied, as in the following example:

Supervisor A: That's why I think this question that you have: "What things do journalists tell in their own words and what things is the person allowed to say?" That question … What does it say? What do you think? Why do you include this question?
Student C: Yeah.
Student D: I don't really know. Like, it was one of those things that we thought was good in the beginning but now it might feel a bit superfluous, when we have done the analysis.
Supervisor A: Then you simply remove it.
Student C: Well, we'll remove it.
Supervisor A, Recording 5, Pair supervision

The students' reactions to the supervisor's questions indicate that they perceive them as criticism. When, as a result of the students' responses, the supervisor suggests that the research question be removed, the students agree. These types of challenging and problematising questions are quite common among all supervisors in our material and are the most common form of criticism. Using such questions to communicate criticism can offer more opportunities for students to explain and develop their thinking than explicitly and unambiguously stated negative criticism. However, the challenging and problematising questions are often combined with other expressions of negative criticism, although often the question comes first and other more explicit forms of criticism come second, as in the following example, where the supervisor asked the two supervised students several critical and challenging questions, followed by recommendations and criticism:

Supervisor C: What would you say … What is your main research question at the moment? Or rather … Now you write four different questions as well as some other questions in these two paragraphs that are there earlier [in the text]. So it's all connected, but it's a bit … The emphasis is sort of on different things.

Student J: Last time we probably just changed the questions and not the purpose itself.

Supervisor C: Yes, but what were your thoughts on the questions then? Or how … Why are they in the order they are and what is the most central thing you want to get answers to?

Student K: Well, it's really the comparison between the national tests and these different teaching materials. And that's why we've moved this question up because it was further down last time, right?

Supervisor C: Yes.

Student J: Right, or we … well, like a little bit the order in which it can be done. First of all, you might have to find out what kind of … What kind of writing discourses they contain before you can compare them. But maybe you could still put the questions in a different order.

Supervisor C: Well, it would be good if they were in the order that the most important or central thing that you want to get at is at the top and then it becomes, like, more precise or more

> detailed or whatever. Because now it's ... At first when I read this, both the aim and the questions, then it was a bit unclear to me what you think is most important.
> *Supervisor C, Recording 3, Pair supervision*

By using questions to provide critical feedback, the supervisor gives students the opportunity to develop their thinking and thus invites them to be active in the scaffolding work that can be said to take place during the supervision conversation (cf. van de Pol 2012; van de Pol et al. 2010). The students also respond by explaining their thinking and choices. This then becomes the basis for the supervisor's recommendation at the end of the exchange and the explanation of what would be the problem with the way the students have chosen to do it now—that it becomes unclear to the reader what is most important. At the same time as the supervisor's questions are mainly developing (see Chap. 6), it is clear to the students that they also contain criticism, as can be seen in Student J's comment that it might be possible to do things differently to the way they have done them now.

However, implicit criticism in the form of questions can also become a tool that is unclear or misunderstood by students. The following dialogue is an example of when it appeared as not entirely clear to the student what the supervisor was trying to get at by asking the questions. Instead of developing and explaining the thoughts and choices, the student reacted by expressing confusion and uncertainty:

Supervisor B:	How would you access the conceptions through your surveys, would you say?
Student G:	How I ... eh, to see which working method they ... which method the students find most motivating. Those are the research questions, yes.
Supervisor B:	So ... mm.
Student G:	I don't think I really understand. (laughs)
Supervisor B:	How did you set up these surveys?
Student G:	They answer from 1 to 5, like on a scale, from number 1 to 5 that they answer.
Supervisor B:	I think my question is this: How do you avoid, through the surveys, that you don't get a yes or no result? I've asked this before. Like, how do you get to this interesting

	question, "factors in the classroom environment that lead to increased motivation"?
Student G:	Mm ... I don't know. I don't have a good answer. /.../
Supervisor B:	Mm. Do you have any of these [survey] questions in the back of your head?
Student G:	Oh God, I am at a complete standstill. And I haven't ... it's on the other computer ...
	Supervisor B, Recording 5, Individual supervision

This quote thus illustrates the difficulties that can arise when using questions to convey negative critique to students, such that it may be unclear to them what the supervisors are actually trying to say. The student's reactions in the quote indicate that he/she perceives that the supervisor is being critical, but not what that criticism concerns specifically, which makes it difficult for the student to actively contribute to the ongoing scaffolding work. An alternative approach for the supervisor might have been to start by pointing out that there were problems with the way the student had designed the survey, explaining why it was problematic, and then asking the student to explain the choices made in terms of collecting material and what possible alternatives there might be.

If the intention is to increase student activity and facilitate greater student independence, such an approach may seem counterintuitive, as it may be perceived as more directive, making the supervision characterised more by teaching and less by partnership (cf. Dysthe 2002). At the same time, there are situations and stages in the supervision process when it may be both necessary and desirable for the supervisor to step in and provide a clear framework for the students in order to keep the work moving in the right direction. In the focus group interviews we conducted, it also emerged that clear frameworks and directiveness may in some cases promote student independence and participation in the degree project work. In other words, in situations like the one above, students may find it easier to develop their arguments and thoughts if it is clearer to them what the problems are, even if this means that the supervisor takes a more directive role in the discussion.

In Chap. 6 we wrote about how supervisors often hedged and moderated their positive assessments and praise in the recorded supervision sessions (see also Magnusson 2020). This can be understood in relation to the different roles of supervisors and examiners, that we discussed above, in the sense that overly positive assessments from supervisors could lead to students building up unrealistic expectations of the examiner's forthcoming assessments. Similarly, when it came to negative assessment or critique, supervisors in our material often used hedging and downplaying strategies. In the examples we have from our material, this seems to be related, for instance, to ensuring that the students did not experience the criticism as face-threatening (cf. Brown 1987). As in the following extract, where the supervisor tried to soften the criticism not only by how it is phrased but also by laughing and commenting on the students' diligent note-taking:

Student J: But then we want to take the opportunity to compare once we have the results from the different teaching materials. It feels like it could be relevant too, but it does become two different things sort of ... Like there will be two different investigations.

Supervisor C: Well, that's not really the case. You are doing a survey but you can draw several kinds of conclusions. You will get answers, or you already have a little bit, to both questions. But ... We talked about something similar last time we met, and it's good, as you say now, to have this "alignment" as the most central thing. And then it should come first in the aim. Then digitisation should not come first. (Silence, except for someone typing on a keyboard)

Supervisor C: (chuckles) You're taking so many notes! (laughs) But if we then look at the text itself or, say, in a little more detail. Because then I understand that this formulation of the aim is an older one, and here you have already rewritten the research questions. But when you then formulate the aim ... Now you are constructing it in a way that is quite difficult for the reader to follow. /.../ So it's much better to turn it around.

Student J: Absolutely.

Supervisor C: So that the reader first knows "What is the purpose? And then what methods you use to answer the purpose.
Supervisor C, Recording 3, Pair supervision

To sum up, there are many ways to give negative critique: implicitly and cautiously, or explicitly and in a more challenging way. Negative critique highlights gaps and the need for change, and we would argue that it is an important part of the scaffolding that students need to move forward in their work. However, it can also make students feel incompetent and vulnerable. In order for the negative critique to be constructive and formative, supervisors need to be aware of how it can be presented in the specific situation. This has to do with contingency—being able to adapt the supervision to the students' needs and conditions and choosing the scaffolding strategies accordingly (cf. van de Pol and Elbers 2013; van de Pol et al. 2015).

Assessing Independence

In the introductory parts of this book, it was discussed that independence is an aspect that is often addressed in the intended learning outcomes of the syllabus or in the grading criteria for the degree project. Where this is the case, student independence also needs to be assessed. Lecturers and seminar leaders, supervisors and examiners need to know and be in agreement about what is meant by independence in a particular course, and where and how this independence is to be found. The matrix introduced in Chap. 3 presented seven ways of understanding student independence that recurred in our focus group material:

1. Taking initiatives
2. Demonstrating originality, creativity and enthusiasm
3. Relating to sources and context
4. Arguing, motivating and making choices
5. Taking responsibility
6. Demonstrating critical thinking and reflection
7. Ability to generalise and synthesise

These different ways of understanding independence can serve as a basis for a collegial discussion, and by extension a common position, when it comes to how independence should be understood and therefore assessed. In the same matrix, the different contexts identified by the focus group participants as relevant in relation to independence were also presented:

- during the process of writing a degree project
- in the final text submitted for assessment
- during the defence of the degree project

Thus, it is in these contexts that the supervisors and examiners who participated in our focus groups believed that independence could be identified. However, it is not obvious how these different perceptions of independence can be found and evaluated in the different contexts. The different ways of understanding independence provide a starting point, but each of these conceptions or understandings of independence needs to be operationalised and broken down into concrete application in the respective context in order to serve as a basis for assessment. In the last part of the chapter we will discuss an example of what such operationalisation and application might look like. First, we would like to take a small detour to consider how artificial intelligence (AI) might influence the assessment of student independence, and what issues this might raise in the context of degree projects and supervision practice.

AI and Assessment in the Context of Independence

Every supervisor and faculty needs to consider AI and the opportunities and risks that new LLM models,[4] such as ChatGPT, offer in relation to student independence and the writing of degree projects. There are two perspectives that become particularly important in this context: the supervisor's role in assessing student independence and the AI writing tools that students are encouraged to use and those that become problematic for students to use in relation to independence. The role of the supervisors is to support students in writing a degree project, which includes support in the socialisation into an academic environment and the development of academic thinking (Brodersen 2009). For a long time, it has been possible for students to purchase a thesis from a ghostwriter or to have a degree project written for them by someone close to them. Today, however, the situation is quite different, as students can use AI tools to help them at all stages of the writing process: generating ideas, structuring ideas, formulating texts and editing texts according to different levels of style and various specified criteria.

One way of dealing with potential ghostwriting is to give the process a greater role and visibility in degree project courses. For example, course coordinators can require students to submit drafts in different rounds and to work on them based on different types of feedback. Giving more

---

[4] LLM models stands for Large Language Models and refers to the deep learning algorithms used in ChatGPT and other similar models.

importance to the process also means giving more importance to the supervisor as someone who has insight into the process and can assess its independence. The supervisor then becomes not only someone who supports but also someone who controls and evaluates the students' work and the process, which can have both advantages and disadvantages. The advantages include that as the process becomes more important than the product, supervisors and examiners are encouraged to collaborate in the assessment, making the assessment more collegial. The disadvantages include that the supervisors' role becomes more complex and partly conflicting when support and control are pitted against each other in even more ways.

With AI tools, the supervisor's task becomes even more complex and the supervisor's controlling role is further strengthened. Here, the supervisor needs to guide the students on which AI tools are acceptable to use and which are not, in relation to the expectations and requirements of independence. It becomes increasingly difficult to define what kind of independence is desirable and necessary in the writing of the degree project:

- Is it important for students to come up with the topic themselves or can AI tools be used to generate content and ideas?
- Is it important for students to write the text themselves or is it acceptable to dictate the text and have an AI tool or a classmate rewrite it?
- Is it important that students are able to spell for themselves or is it acceptable to use spell checkers?
- Is it important for students to summarise and compare text content (empirical evidence, previous research) themselves or can AI tools be used for this?
- Is it important that students are able to write in a second language by themselves (e.g. English if their first language is not English)?
- Is it important that all analysis is done by the students or can digital and AI tools be used to identify patterns, categories and relationships?

These are just some of the questions that course coordinators, supervisors and examiners need to discuss and agree upon, and which supervisors then need to address in their supervision practice. As indicated above, such questions may concern, in different ways, more or less all the main understandings of student independence that we identified in our focus group material, such as taking initiatives, taking responsibility, the ability to synthesise and generalise and so on. In other words, the role and significance of AI is one of the aspects of operationalising the different understandings of student independence in the degree project context, in order to provide a basis for assessing them. In the following, we will discuss other such aspects in relation to the understanding of student independence as the ability to relate to sources and context (cf Chap. 3).

An Example of Assessing Independence

Independence understood as students' ability to relate to sources and context is something that can be manifested both in the supervision interaction and in the written texts, and we will in the following look at both of these aspects. What constitutes sources and context here, includes, e.g. books and academic literature that the students have read, things that informants have said in interviews and that the students refer to or describe, as well as what the supervisors have said and recommended in supervision sessions.

Relating to Sources and Context in Conversations

To relate to something generally means to make an evaluation, and in this case it implies that a student makes an evaluation in relation to a source or context of some kind. In our material, students related to sources by evaluating them in a variety of ways: as good, fun and interesting, as useful and clear, or as difficult and so on (cf. Magnusson 2021). The ways of relating to sources varied considerably in complexity and specification, and in our material we could see two main levels of how students could do this:

- Relating to and evaluating something as good or interesting.
- Relating to and evaluating something as good or interesting and justifying this in relation to the degree project work.

Relating to a source by simply evaluating something as good or interesting has a low degree of complexity and specification and thus usually belongs to the first level. The same applies when students merely confirm what the supervisors say or recommend, without more developed reasoning or motivation, which was quite common in our recorded supervision sessions. As in the example below, where the supervisor suggested a reading strategy or workflow for the student—to read a particular researcher's work and choose a method based on what was written there:

Supervisor E: So read [scholar], but as quickly as possible, so that you jump down to the test and try to see: What do I choose?
Student N: Right, I want to read through all the texts and so on.
Supervisor E: Yeah, sure.
Student N: That sounds good.
Supervisor E, Recording 3, Individual supervision

It is perhaps not very surprising that positive affirmations, in this case 'that sounds good', are by far the most common student response to what supervisors describe or recommend in our material, as it can be perceived as face-threatening in the interaction to show a lack of appreciation or scepticism towards what supervisors are recommending and suggesting (cf. Brown 1987). In this example, the positive affirmation is not substantiated and the student does not show how he/she relates to what the supervisor brings up more specifically. Consequently, it can be considered as an evaluation of relatively low complexity and specification, corresponding to the first level of relating to sources and context. In another example, a student described and evaluated what an informant had said in a recorded interview:

Student Q: That was very interesting. I have to say that. Because I got quite a lot of material then.
Supervisor F, Recording 4, Individual supervision

The student here evaluates what the informant has said in the interview as 'interesting', but there is no justification or further specification of what is interesting about what the informant has described in the interview or how it can be related to the study the student is doing. Therefore, in terms of complexity and specification, this example could also be said to correspond to the first level of relating to sources and context.

In an example of more developed reasoning, the student evaluated and related to theoretical sources, in this case a theoretical work on language theory that the student had read:

Student S: It's kind of outside of the degree project itself when it comes to grammar and stuff like that, but in a way the same entry is super useful ... fundamental sort of ... kind of the same thing ... And that feels great.
Supervisor H, Recording 3, Individual supervision

The theoretical source is considered by the student to be 'super useful' in the degree project work, which is linked to the fact that it is 'fundamental'. The student also describes that it is "kind of the same thing", which in this case can be understood as the student perceiving that there are parallels between this theoretical source and other theoretical sources that the student has read before. That is, it is possible to link these sources and perspectives, one as a general starting point and the others as more specific in relation to the focus of the degree project. Evaluating aspects in relation to each other in this way, and relating them to one's own study and how they will be used there, can be seen as an example of relating to sources and context in a more advanced way.

In another, more complex example, the same student relates to different theoretical perspectives, comparing them and positioning them in relation to the degree project:

> Student S: Uh, and then … The way I interpreted it, social semiotics and multimodal discourse analysis, as I understand it, is also equivalent to the multimodal perspective, and it's the same perspective as [scholar], who has worked in both of them. And then, I've only read a little bit, but then I saw [scholar]'s functional grammar as a starting point for both, as well as critical linguistics and social semiotics. /…/ And then critical linguistics and social semiotics with discourse analysis as a kind of subheading to that, sort of, and then there'll be a bit of repetition. /…/ Because then it's a bit like this functional grammar, that it's like a bit more theoretical.
> *Supervisor H, Recording 3, Individual supervision*

The evaluative formulations used in the student's discussion of different theoretical perspectives and how they are relevant to each other and to the student's own study have to do with structure and hierarchy. It's about what should be a starting point, what should be superior and subordinate, what should come first and what should come later in the text. Word choices such as 'starting point', 'after that' and 'subheading' clarify how the student evaluates and relates to the different perspectives and how they might relate to each other in the forthcoming degree project. There are also phrases that compare the different theoretical perspectives, such as 'equivalent to' and 'same perspective'. These phrases can also be seen as evaluative, as they judge parts in relation to each other, what should come first and be most important in relation to other things, and which parts are equivalent and comparable. All this together means that the extract can be seen as an example of the second level of how students can relate to sources and context, in terms of complexity and specification.

Below is another example that can be seen as corresponding to the second level of complexity, where the student in question has come into contact with the notion of hierarchy of needs and is considering whether it might be a relevant concept or model in a study of which age groups teachers choose to work with:

Student R: Well, previous research. Then there was somebody who had brought up some sort of hierarchy of needs, which I initially thought sounded very far-fetched. I associate it with marketing, I think it was, like, far away from here. But then when I thought about it, it's a bit more and more like it makes sense. Because it's a bit like this ... It might explain why you choose to do something. How is it that you ... So I'll see if I can get hold of any [literature], so maybe I'll have a look at that too.
Supervisor G, Recording 1, Individual supervision

In this example, the student described a development of thought by explaining how he/she first perceived the theory in question as 'far-fetched', but then as 'making sense'. Both evaluations were justified in relation to the investigation the student was working on. The 'far-fetched' was justified by the student's description of associating the theory with marketing, which was far from what the student's study was about, while the 'making sense' was motivated by the statement 'it can explain why you choose to do something', which was closely related to what the student was investigating in the degree project.

If the supervision interaction is seen as an important setting for assessing student independence, which, as mentioned above, may be even more the case as a result of the increasing use of AI in the writing process, then, based on these examples, assessment criteria could be formulated so that on one level students are expected to refer to sources and context, but on another level they are also expected to be able to justify this explicitly. In a supervision discussion, the supervisor can then support the student in this, for example, by asking developing questions (see Chap. 6) that elicit motivation and specification: How do you think this will be relevant to your study? When you say it's interesting, what do you mean by that? How can this be useful for your analysis?

Relating to the Supervisor in Text
In order to see how students actually absorb and relate to the supervisors' demands, recommendations and questions in the supervision interaction, it is necessary to see how the students' text drafts are rewritten and developed. From this perspective, it becomes relevant to assess or evaluate the student's *remediation*. Remediation in a supervision context concerns how what is said or discussed in the supervision session is (re)used as text, another medium. Looking at how students process their texts in relation to the supervisors' recommendations and suggestions reveals how students relate to them, i.e. how they are remediated in the students' texts (cf. Magnusson and Sveen 2014).[5] The supervisors' recommendations and suggestions can be remediated by the students in different ways, for example as imitations or appropriations (e.g. Wertsch 1998). Imitation in this context involves students reproducing and repeating what the supervisors recommend, without showing that the understanding or knowledge has been fully integrated and without clearly relating to what the supervisors recommended more than by repeating it. If students have integrated the learning or knowledge and clearly relate it to the supervisor's recommendations, appropriation has taken place instead.

Based on these concepts, two different levels or degrees of independence can be distinguished:

- Following the supervisor's recommendations and writing exactly what the supervisor suggests (imitation).
- Following the supervisor's recommendations in several contexts and/or using them to find one's own solutions and formulations (appropriation).

In other words, these levels or degrees of independence could serve as a basis for supervisors to assess student independence, for example, in terms of their ability to relate to sources and context. Imitation is a necessary

---

[5] Remediation as a concept is closely related to other concepts such as *intertextuality* or *intertextual chains* (see, e.g. Solin 2001), *recontextualisation* (see, e.g. Linell 1998) and *text chains* (Holmberg and Wirdenäs 2010).

strategy in learning and should not be seen as undesirable or problematic in itself (e.g. Wertsch 1998). Rather, imitation may indicate that the student has not progressed so far in the learning process if the goal is student independence, understood as relating to sources and context. In a previous article by Magnusson and Sveen (2014), we have examined these different forms of remediation in a number of supervision sessions and in the text drafts written after the current supervision sessions. The supervisors' advice in the form of recommendations and suggestions has thus been followed up in the students' drafts, where it is possible to see if and how the students have remediated what the supervisors have said and suggested.

In the first example, taken from this article, the supervisor quotes and comments on a choice of words made by the student in the draft text, a choice of words that is taken out of its original context and could therefore be misunderstood:

Supervisor G: "That traditional methods of science such as measuring data and experiments do not provide relevant information" ... ehh and then you start with [scholar] and how she talks about traditional scientific methods. And then one is talking about positivism and natural science and so on, right? But here it's taken out of context and then you wonder: "What do you mean, 'traditional methods of science'?" At this point the social sciences are pretty traditional too.

Student R: Hmm.

Supervisor G, Recording 1, Individual supervision

In line with the definition by van de Pol et al. (van de Pol et al. 2010; van de Pol 2012), the supervisor could here be said to scaffold the student by explaining why the choice of words in question is problematic and by explaining it from a reader's perspective: "and then you ask yourself: 'What do you mean – traditional scientific methods?'" In the draft text that the student wrote after this supervision session, it was clear that the student had taken on board the point and made a modification in the text, changing 'traditional' to 'natural sciences':

When, as in this case, the purpose is to find out people's experiences and goals with their actions, the hermetic *(sic)* theorists argue that traditional

~~methods of science~~ natural science investigation methods, such as measuring data and experiments, do not provide relevant information (reference).

This can be described as imitation, as the student followed the supervisor's advice directly. The student was made aware of the risk of misunderstanding and given suggestions on what to write instead: "and then one talks about positivism and science", advise which was followed without further contributions or additions. This is thus a first, important and necessary step on the path to greater independence, where the student takes on board what the supervisors say at a basic level.

In another example from the same supervision session, the student relates to the supervisor's suggestions in a different way in the subsequent revision of the draft text. The supervisor's comments again concern a choice of words that might be misunderstood by readers. The advice offered by the supervisor moves from the general to the specific—from talking about formulations at a general level to giving specific examples from the student's text—and includes scaffolding in the form of modelling (cf. van de Pol et al. 2010; van de Pol 2012), by suggestions of what a potential formulation might be:

Supervisor G: And then there's another one of those wording things on the next page, under 'qualitative interviews'. At the beginning of the second paragraph there, you write: "By qualitative interviews one means interviews in which the interviewee makes up the answers" and there I would have used a more elegant phrasing, for example that they formulate the answers freely. Otherwise it sounds like they're making something up, and I don't think that's what you mean.
Supervisor G, Recording 1, Individual supervision

In the draft submitted after this supervision, the student took on board the supervisor's point of view and modified the sentence, for instance, by changing 'makes up' to 'decides' and 'determined' to 'defined':

Qualitative interviews refer to interviews in which the interviewee ~~makes up~~ decides the answers, unlike quantitative interviews where the researcher has ~~determined~~ defined specific alternatives (reference).

This can be seen as appropriation rather than imitation, as the student makes choices based on what the supervisor recommends, finding their own way of relating to and reformulating what the supervisor has commented on. The student did this even though, again, the supervisor had provided suggestions on how to write in order to avoid misunderstandings.

In another example from a later supervision session with the same student, the student's actions could also be seen as appropriation rather than imitation, as the student did not receive support in the form of specifically formulated suggestions but in the form of a broader and more general recommendation. The student was encouraged to think about what should be seen as more or less important to include in the text, given the space available in the degree project. The supervisor suggested, among other things, that the student should not write so much about hermeneutics.

Supervisor G: /.../ Then it would be good to put this topic in a scientific context and, like, that you want to interpret and understand and so on. And you don't do that so much, so extensively now. But I still wrote [in my comments] that you could still think about how much you need to discuss hermeneutics specifically and that the most important thing is, like, how you have done things and your reflections on it.

Student R: Yeah, it was also like I wrote everything I could think of in this first version and then I included everything I could put together, kind of. So I'm pretty much on the idea that I'm going to cut that particular part.

Supervisor G: That sounds good.

Supervisor G, Recording 2, Individual supervision

In the draft that the student wrote directly after this supervision meeting, nothing had changed, but in the final version of the degree project it seemed that the supervisor's recommendation had been taken into account, since the student had removed a large part concerning hermeneutics (see marked text).

> This study is qualitative and based on a hermeneutic ideal of science. Hermeneutics is a scientific tradition concerned with the interpretation of meaning and is mainly used in studies of people whose actions hermeneuti-

cians believe cannot be explained by measurable data (reference). The purpose of this study is to understand people's perceptions of the teaching profession and their goals in choosing teacher education in order to understand how they ended up where they are today. When researchers try to understand people's actions in this way, hermeneuticians believe that it is necessary to make interpretations of the collected material (reference). One of the most important theorists of hermeneutics, Hans Georg Gadamer, points out that interpretations are always influenced by the person who makes them, so that the knowledge it leads to is never universal. The results we arrive at, he argues, depend on the prejudices we have that form the framework for what is possible for us to understand (reference).

~~The hermeneutic research tradition, which states that research on people should be conducted by searching for and interpreting meaning in people's expressions (reference), formed the basis for this study. The method used was semi-structured qualitative interviews, which were analysed using content analysis.~~

~~When, as in this case, the purpose is to find out people's experiences and goals with their actions, hermeneutic theorists argue that traditional scientific methods such as measuring data and experiments do not provide relevant information (reference). In hermeneutics, one is instead interested in collecting different types of meaning content, such as stories or observations of actions (reference). When analysing meaning content, we are not interested in how many times the interviewees use certain sounds or words, but we are interested in what they say, the meaning they express. Therefore, in hermeneutic studies it is irrelevant to try to analyse the informants' narratives through measurements (reference).~~

The different levels at which students can relate to the advice or recommendations of their supervisors is thus reflected in these examples by the way in which they demonstrate in their written texts that they have understood and processed the recommendations and advice of their supervisors. Do students simply copy what the supervisors have said, or do they relate to and modify what the supervisors have said and formulate their own proposals and solutions? This, we believe, can be another tool to distinguish between a more or less independent way of relating to the supervisor's comments and advice.

To sum up, in these sections we have identified two different ways of accessing how students can relate to different sources and contexts, two ways in which this particular aspect of student independence can be operationalised, differentiated and broken down into levels or degrees:

1.

- Evaluating and thus positioning oneself in relation to a source.
- Evaluating and positioning oneself in relation to a source and justifying this in relation to one's own study.

2.

- Following the supervisor's recommendation and writing precisely what the supervisor suggests.
- Following the supervisor's recommendation by finding your own solutions and formulations.

These two types of differentiation of how students can relate to sources and the supervision context in which they and the supervisors are involved could, we would argue, be useful to supervisors as a basis for assessing independence. There are, of course, a number of other ways of identifying, differentiating and assessing different aspects of student independence, and it is up to each supervisor and each department to decide which are particularly relevant and desirable in their own activities and how best to access them. With the rapid development of AI, there will certainly be a need for further ways of accessing independence, as AI tools such as ChatGPT provide not only summaries of sources but also comparisons and positioning in relation to those sources.

Discussing and operationalising not only student independence but also other concepts and formulations that are included in grading criteria and assessment matrices, as a supervisor collective within an academic programme, degree project course or discipline, can be a fruitful way of trying to articulate the implicit norms and beliefs that exist around academic writing in different local academic contexts (cf. Lea and Street 2000; Lillis 2001). In this way, supervisors may become more aware of how to address the fact that assessment too is an essential part of supervision practice, as well as their role as an assessor in this context, and how this role relates to, for example, the role of the examiner. This kind of collegial discussion thus has the potential to contribute to the development of the individual supervisor's practice in this respect as well.

* * *

In the chapters of this book, we have discussed several aspects of degree project supervision and supervision practice, ranging from the relationship between supervisor and student and the emotional aspects of the supervision process to specific tools to scaffold students in their degree project work and encourage independence. As we have now also discussed different ways of understanding the supervisor's role as an assessor and given examples of how one particular aspect of independence—relating to sources and context—could potentially be assessed, all that remains is to tie the knot. We do this by presenting in the concluding chapter some of our main findings and some perspectives and approaches that we hope supervisors can take away from this book.

References

Bauer, Karen, Randi Farstad, Thea Selle Opdal, and Hildegunn Otnes. 2023. Responspraksiser i lærerutdanningen: Den skriftlige interaksjonen mellom lærerstudenter og deres lærere i seks skriveprosesser. *Acta Didactica Norden* 17 (3): 1–31. https://doi.org/10.5617/adno.9958.

Brodersen, Randi Benedikte. 2009. Akademisk vejledning og skrivning - for vejledere og studerende: Mere kollektiv og dialogisk vejledning giver mere laering of flere gode opgaver. *Millimála 1*: 173–217.

Brown, Penelope. 1987. *Politeness: Some Universals in Language Usage*. Edited by Stephen C. Levinson. Cambridge: Cambridge Univ. Press.

Dysthe, Olga. 2002. Professors as Mediators of Academic Text Cultures: an Interview Study with Advisors and Masters Degree Students in Three Disciplines in a Norwegian University. *Written Communication* 19 (4): 493–544. https://doi.org/10.1177/074108802238010.

Henley, Amy J., and Florence D. DiGennaro Reed. 2015. Should You Order the Feedback Sandwich? Efficacy of Feedback Sequence and Timing. *Journal of Organizational Behavior Management* 35 (3–4): 321–335. https://doi.org/10.1080/01608061.2015.1093057.

Holmberg, Per, and Karolina Wirdenäs. 2010. Skrivpedagogik i praktiken: textkedjor, textsamtal och texttypologier i tre svensklärares klassrum. NF 20. *Språk och stil. Tidskrift för svensk språkforskning* NF20: 105–131.

Lea, Mary R., and Brian V. Street. 2000. Student Writing and Staff feedback in Higher Education: An academic Literacies Approach. In *Student Writing in Higher Education. New contexts*, ed. Mary R. Lea and Barry Stierer, 32–46. Buckingham: Open University Press.

Lillis, Theresa. 2001. *Student Writing: Access, Regulation, Desire*. London: Routledge.

Lindberg-Sand, Åsa, and Anders Sonesson. 2020. The Concept of Quality and its Various Meanings. In *Doctoral Supervision in Theory and Practice*, ed. Eva Brodin, Jitka Lindén, Anders Sonesson, and Åsa Lindberg-Sand, 1–14. Lund: Studentlitteratur.

Linell, Per. 1998. Discourse across Boundaries: On Recontextualizations and the Blending of Voices in Professional Discourse. *Text & talk: an Interdisciplinary Journal of Language, Discourse & Communication studies* 18 (2): 143–157. https://doi.org/10.1515/text.1.1998.18.2.143.

Lundström, Markus. 2016. Handledningens potential, examineringens låsningar – om uppsatsmomentets konflikt mellan formativ och summativ bedömning. *Utbildning & lärande* 10 (1): 88–93.

Magnusson, Jenny. 2020. "Jättebra, men" - Handledares beröm i handledningssamtal. *Språk och interaktion* 5 (3): 45–68.

———. 2021. Positioning Oneself in Relation to Sources and Context – Enactments of Independence in Undergraduate Supervision. *Journal of Applied Linguistics and Professional Practice* 14 (3): 351–373. https://doi.org/10.1558/jalpp.19879.

Magnusson, Jenny, and Hanna Sveen. 2014. Handledningens effektivitet: En studie av remediering i självständiga arbeten. In *Förhandlingar vid trettiotredje sammankomsten för svenskans beskrivning, Helsingfors den 15-17 maj 2013*, ed. Jan Lindström, Sofie Henricson, Anne Huhtala, Pirjo Kukkonen, Hanna Lehti-Eklund, and Camilla Lindholm, 290–299. Helsingfors: Helsingfors universitet.

van de Pol, Janneke. E. (2012). *Scaffolding in teacher-student interaction: exploring, measuring, promoting and evaluating scaffolding*. [Thesis, fully internal, Universiteit van Amsterdam]. https://dare.uva.nl/search?identifier=640b82ba-c27b-42d3-b9f8-fe08b1e0081f.

van de Pol, Janneke, and Ed Elbers. 2013. Scaffolding Student Learning: A Microanalysis of Teacher–student Interaction. *Learning, Culture and Social Interaction* 2 (1): 32–41. https://doi.org/10.1016/j.lcsi.2012.12.001.

van de Pol, Janneke, Monique Volman, and Jos. Beishuizen. 2010. Scaffolding in Teacher–Student Interaction: A Decade of Research. *Educational Psychology Review* 22: 271–296. https://doi.org/10.1007/s10648-010-9127-6.

van de Pol, Janneke, Monique Volman, Frans Oort, and Jos Beishuizen. 2015. The Effects of Scaffolding in the Classroom: Support Contingency and Student Independent Working time in Relation to Student Achievement, Task Effort and Appreciation of Support. *Instructional Science* 43 (5): 615–641. https://doi.org/10.1007/s11251-015-9351-z.

Reid, Joy. 1994. Responding to ESL Students' Texts: The myths of Appropriation. *TESOL Quarterly* 28 (2): 273–292. https://doi.org/10.2307/3587434.

Rienecker, Lotte, Gitte Wichmann-Hansen, and Peter Stray Jørgensen. 2019. *God vejledning af specialer, bacheloroppgaver og projekter*. Frederiksberg: Samfundslitteratur.

Shanahan, Timothy, and Cynthia Shanahan. 2012. What Is Disciplinary Literacy and Why Does It Matter? *Topics in Language Disorders* 32 (1): 7–18. https://doi.org/10.1097/TLD.0b013e318244557a.
Solin, Anna. 2001. *Tracing texts: Intertextuality in Environmental Discourse*. Diss. Helsingfors: Helsingfors universitet.
Wertsch, James V. 1998. *Mind as Action*. New York: Oxford University Press.
Zackariasson, Maria. 2019. Encouraging Student Independence: Perspectives on Scaffolding in Higher Education Supervision. *Journal of Applied Research in Higher Education* 12 (3): 495–505. https://doi.org/10.1108/JARHE-01-2019-0012.
Zackariasson, Maria, and Jenny Magnusson. 2020. Academic Literacies and International Mobility. The Organization and Supervision of Degree Projects in Sweden and Russia. *Cogent Education* 7 (1): 1–12. 1855770. https://doi.org/10.1080/2331186X.2020.1855770.

Open Access This chapter is licensed under the terms of the Creative Commons Attribution-NonCommercial-NoDerivatives 4.0 International License (http://creativecommons.org/licenses/by-nc-nd/4.0/), which permits any noncommercial use, sharing, distribution and reproduction in any medium or format, as long as you give appropriate credit to the original author(s) and the source, provide a link to the Creative Commons license and indicate if you modified the licensed material. You do not have permission under this license to share adapted material derived from this chapter or parts of it.

The images or other third party material in this chapter are included in the chapter's Creative Commons license, unless indicated otherwise in a credit line to the material. If material is not included in the chapter's Creative Commons license and your intended use is not permitted by statutory regulation or exceeds the permitted use, you will need to obtain permission directly from the copyright holder.

CHAPTER 8

Concluding Findings and Reflections

Based on the analyses and discussions we have presented throughout the book, we will conclude by revisiting some of the key findings of our research project and offer some further reflections on how supervisors might think and work, both individually and collegially, to develop their supervision practice.

One of the main findings of our study, highlighted in this book, concerns the practical implications of how key concepts in higher education, in this case student independence, tend to be multifaceted, complex and not clearly defined. We have shown how a range of understandings and perceptions of student independence are articulated in governing documents at different levels, and that although there are many similarities in how supervisors understand independence in the supervision context, there are also differences within and between local academic contexts. As discussed in the book, student independence can be demonstrated at different stages of the degree project process—during supervision, in the final text or at the defence/examination—to different degrees and by different means, which has implications for individual supervisor practice, for the student-supervisor relationship, and for the assessment of degree projects and student performance.

A second main finding of our research project concerns how degree project supervision should be seen as a social and collegial practice, as it involves relationships at several levels with a number of people and in various contexts. We have shown how, in addition to individual supervisors and students, actors such as examiners and programme or course

© The Author(s) 2024
M. Zackariasson, J. Magnusson, *Supervising Student Independence*,
https://doi.org/10.1007/978-3-031-66371-0_8

coordinators, as well as fellow students and colleagues, are important actors in the degree project and supervision process, and what implications this may have for supervision practice. As a supervisor, you must manage a number of expectations from different directions: the students want the best, and perhaps the most, support possible to help them complete their degree projects, the examiners and the university want the degree projects to be of high quality, the programme directors and the university want as many students as possible to complete their degree projects within the timeframes and so on. In addition, supervisors need to be constantly aware of the various governing documents, guidelines and regulations associated with the writing of degree projects at a particular university and within the specific academic programme or discipline in which they are working. At the same time, for many university professors or lecturers, supervising degree projects is only one part of the overall workload, which has to be combined with all the other demands and responsibilities. In view of this, one might raise the question of how independent the supervisors are or can be.

From an academic literacies perspective, this can be understood in the context that academic writing is characterised by power relations at different levels (Lea and Street 2000, 2006; Lillis 2001; Lillis and Scott 2007). On the one hand, there is a power relationship between supervisor and student, which may be or appear more or less hierarchical, depending, for example, on whether the supervisor-student relationship is one marked by teaching, partnership or apprenticeship (Dysthe 2002). On the other hand, there are power relations at the institutional level, where universities have to comply with regulations such as Higher Education Acts and Higher Education Ordinances, and where individual students' performance in terms of academic writing and degree projects may be included in the periodic evaluations of and within higher education. In cases where completed and approved degree projects are used as quality indicators in such evaluations, the standard of students' work may, in the long run, have an impact on how whole disciplines or programmes are assessed. What individual supervisors do is thus both influenced by, and can have an impact on, the activities of the university as a whole.

In addition to complying with local and national expectations and regulations, individual supervision practice is also influenced by and needs to be adapted to the circumstances, aspirations and abilities of individual students. This is the third main finding of our study that we would like to highlight here. The need to tailor supervision to each student or group of students relates to how the relationship between supervisor and student(s) is established and what it looks like, for example, whether a particular supervision practice helps to create not only a professional or academic but also a more personal relationship between students and supervisors. In some cases a more personal relationship may be beneficial to the thesis work; in other cases it may be an approach that makes either the student(s) or the supervisor uncomfortable, or in other ways slows down the writing process rather than facilitates it.

The need to tailor supervision to each individual student or group of students also applies to the pedagogical tools that supervisors choose to use. Working with scaffolding in supervision practice, as we define it here, where students are expected to be active, where supervisors aim to base their supervision on knowledge of the student's background and circumstances, and where responsibility is gradually transferred from supervisors to students as the work progresses, with the supervisor fading somewhat, may work very well in some cases (cf. van de Pol 2012; van de Pol et al. 2010). In other cases, however, it may lead to the thesis never being completed, for example, because the transfer of responsibility from supervisor to student does not work as well as it would need to for the student to be able to complete the task.

Moreover, we have shown in the book how, for instance, emotions, praise, questions and active voicing can serve as potential scaffolding tools for encouraging and developing student independence and enhanced academic literacy but also how such tools need to be used consciously and deliberately in order to contribute to the intended goals. The use of these kinds of pedagogical tools can, at times, make things clearer to students and help them move forward in their work. However, sometimes these same tools do not work as intended. For example, an unreflective use of praise may lead students to believe that they have produced a better text than they actually have; certain uses of questions may lead to students not understanding the criticism being conveyed or the seriousness of it; and what is intended to be an engaged approach might in some cases lead to students losing the energy and desire to work on the degree project because they feel attacked and criticised.

In other words, supervision practices that work well for one student may be completely wrong for another, even if they are well intentioned and seem to meet all the requirements and expectations. Does this mean that it is not possible to say anything about how supervision practice can be developed to support and develop student independence and academic literacy? No, we hope that through the various chapters of this book it has become clear that although we strongly reject the idea that one model fits all supervisors and all students, there are certain things that we have seen in our study that we believe are important for supervisors to take with them in their work. We conclude by summarising these and presenting our visions for what we believe would improve academic supervision practice.

The Importance of Reflection

Firstly, we would like to emphasise the importance of reflecting on one's own supervision practice and the beliefs and ideals on which it is based, for example, in relation to the supervisor-student relationship and the kind of role one wants to take as a supervisor. As we have shown, supervisors can manage things such as the emotional dimensions of supervision, the boundaries between professional, personal and private, or how to respond to and critique students' work in different ways. While there is no single right or wrong way to do this, different supervisors' attitudes and approaches may be more or less appropriate or successful in scaffolding various aspects of students' academic writing and supporting them in their work, not least when it comes to student independence. In other words, it is important to find approaches and supervision practices that work for one's own personality, while at the same time having the potential to facilitate, for example, student independence. Furthermore, we would like to emphasise once again the need for flexibility. This applies both in relation to different students and their personal circumstances, abilities and needs, and in relation to the different stages of degree project writing and supervision. Supervisors need to be aware both that what appears to work for one student may be less appropriate for another and that different types of scaffolding may be needed at the beginning and end of the degree project process, as well as when things are going well and when things are going less well in the students' work.

In order to achieve this, it is valuable to consider your own supervision practice and the choices you make in it on an ongoing basis. One way of doing this might be to record some of your own supervision conversations and actively listen to them—after asking the student for permission to record, of course. Another way is to invite someone to shadow you during a supervision session and ask for their views on what could be developed. Shadowing one of your colleagues during one of their supervision sessions can also be valuable in gaining perspective on your own supervision practice.

Through this kind of self-reflection, we argue that it becomes easier for supervisors to work consciously with different supervision tools and strategies, for example to encourage student activity and participation in the supervision process, and to deal with the more or less unexpected difficulties and problems that often arise during the degree project process. This is true whether these problems concern students getting stuck in material collection or writing, students experiencing personal setbacks that affect the degree project work, or the potential contradiction between giving students the freedom to explore their ideas and aspirations, on the one hand, and ensuring that the degree project they produce is of a sufficiently high quality and completed within the given timeframe, on the other.

THE IMPORTANCE OF DISCUSSION

In addition to considering and reflecting on one's own supervision practice and approach to students, we would like to emphasise the importance of collegial discussion about academic writing and supervision. In the research study we conducted, it became obvious in several ways that there is a need to discuss both one's own supervision practice and the shared guidelines and approaches to academic supervision within the university or within a particular programme or discipline. In this book we have primarily taken student independence as an example of an aspect that is central to the process of the degree project, at the same time as there is often a lack of collegial discussion of, for example, how independence might be understood in this context, what it might mean in practice to encourage or enable student independence, or how this might be assessed. A collective discussion of what the requirements and expectations of student independence might mean makes it easier for individual supervisors to adapt their supervision practice to the ideals and perceptions that exist in the local academic context.

However, there are also other essential parts of the degree project work which are not obviously unambiguous and where there is not necessarily a consensus on how they should be understood and interpreted. An example of this is assessment criteria and assessment matrices, where the criteria given for different grades can often be understood and interpreted in several ways, which can lead to problems if supervisors and examiners do not communicate sufficiently. What does it mean, for example, to have a more or less developed research base, use of theory or analysis? How should such criteria be understood? Apart from the fact that this is important for individual students and the way their degree projects are assessed, it is necessary to have a reflected consensus on such questions among supervisors and examiners in order to ensure that professionalism pervades the degree project courses and that the quality of the education is maintained.

Collegial discussion can also be valuable when it comes to certain specific details of academic writing, which may not seem so important in the larger context but on which students can spend a lot of time and energy: for example, reference systems and formalities, linguistic conventions or how to interpret the instructions given in guidelines or manuals for writing student theses. If supervisors, course coordinators and examiners have good collegial communication about these kinds of issues, this can contribute to less uncertainty for both students and supervisors, and mean that less time and energy needs to be spent on them in supervision discussions.

It can, furthermore, be valuable to have a collegial discussion about the supervisor-student relationship. What are the expectations of this relationship and, not least, what are the limits in terms of an overly personal or private relationship? How do you manage when such boundaries are crossed, either by the supervisor or by the student, and how do you work to clarify the boundaries so that this does not happen? As we have discussed, students are in a situation of dependency in relation to the supervisors and a certain action may be perceived as inappropriate or as sexual harassment by a student without the supervisor in question being aware of this or sharing this view. Although ideally all students should have the right to change supervisors, it is far from certain that this can be done without serious consequences for the degree project work in terms of lost focus, time and energy, which makes it all the more important to try to prevent such situations from arising.

The Importance of Communication

Finally, we would like to stress the importance of communicating with students. Clearly describing central parts of your supervision practice to the students you supervise, and the reasons behind it, can help students to know what to expect in the future. This may include availability and practical issues, such as how quickly students can expect responses to emails and how far in advance they are expected to submit texts for supervisors to have time to read, or that supervisors' personal circumstances, such as childcare or commuting, affect the of supervision conditions. It may also include how you normally give feedback or express criticism and praise. For example, if students have been told that the supervisor rarely marks what is good and works well in a piece of writing, but focuses on areas for improvement, it may be easier for them to digest and absorb the comments they receive.

There were several examples in our material of how this could be done, such as a supervisor warning students that towards the end of the degree project process they were likely to perceive the supervisor as very negative and demanding, but that this was to ensure that they were not surprised by the examiner's criticism and assessment. Another example in our material involved a supervisor explaining the reasons for asking the student all those critical questions that seemed so difficult to answer. This kind of explicit explanation of the supervisors' tasks and approach, and the pedagogical idea behind their actions, can make it easier for students to relate to and cope with supervision.

Likewise, in relation to independence, there is value in communicating to students what this might mean in the degree project context. As there may be a discrepancy between how supervisors perceive independence in relation to degree project work and how students perceive it, for example whether it is a matter of working alone, there may be a need to clarify what the term means. This applies both to supervisors' views and to formulations in course syllabi and assessment criteria. Doing so can clarify what is expected of the student, for example, in terms of coming to supervision sessions prepared, actively participating in supervision discussions, and listening to and responding to the supervisor's comments, as well as in terms of who bears ultimate responsibility for the completion and quality of the degree project.

The same applies to academic literacies, although it may not be necessary for students to engage with the concept itself. But if supervisors talk not only about the content and structure of the degree project, or about language mistakes and reference systems, but also about the expectations and norms associated with academic writing, this can help students to cope better with the transition from the texts they have written earlier in their education to the larger and more advanced academic texts that a degree project normally involves.

* * *

As we have shown throughout this book, academic supervision is in many ways a complex process in which the relationship and interaction between supervisors and students is of great importance, whether in the sometimes rather short timeframes of academic work at undergraduate level, or in the longer timeframes of academic work at masters and doctoral levels. The process can be rewarding and educational for both students and supervisors, and can be fraught with emotions ranging from frustration and anger to pride and joy. In closing, we would like to emphasise that supervision practice has the potential to contribute not only to the production of the academic product itself, the degree project, master's thesis or doctoral dissertation, but also to the growth of the student in terms of aspects such as academic literacies and independence and potentially also to the growth of the supervisor, as each new student you supervise brings something new to the equation. You are, in other words, never complete as a supervisor, and we hope that this book will contribute in some way to the ongoing reflection and development of supervision practice, both at a collective and individual level, that we believe is therefore necessary.

REFERENCES

Dysthe, Olga. 2002. Professors as Mediators of Academic Text Cultures: an Interview Study with Advisors and Masters Degree Students in Three Disciplines in a Norwegian University. *Written Communication* 19 (4): 493–544. https://doi.org/10.1177/074108802238010.

Lea, Mary R., and Brian V. Street. 2000. Student Writing and Staff feedback in Higher Education: An academic Literacies Approach. In *Student Writing in Higher Education. New contexts*, ed. Mary R. Lea and Barry Stierer, 32–46. Buckingham: Open University Press.

———. 2006. The "Academic Literacies" Model: Theory and Applications. *Theory into Practice* 45 (4): 368–377. https://doi.org/10.1207/s15430421tip4504_11.

Lillis, Theresa. 2001. *Student Writing: Access, Regulation, Desire*. London: Routledge.

Lillis, Theresa, and Mary Scott. 2007. Defining Academic Literacies Research: Issues of Epistemology, Ideology and Strategy. *Journal of Applied Linguistics* 4 (1): 5–32. https://doi.org/10.1558/japl.v4i1.5.

van de Pol, Janneke. E. (2012). *Scaffolding in teacher-student interaction: exploring, measuring, promoting and evaluating scaffolding.* [Thesis, fully internal, Universiteit van Amsterdam]. https://dare.uva.nl/search?identifier=640b82ba-c27b-42d3-b9f8-fe08b1e0081f.

van de Pol, Janneke, Monique Volman, and Jos. Beishuizen. 2010. Scaffolding in Teacher–Student Interaction: A Decade of Research. *Educational Psychology Review* 22: 271–296. https://doi.org/10.1007/s10648-010-9127-6.

Open Access This chapter is licensed under the terms of the Creative Commons Attribution-NonCommercial-NoDerivatives 4.0 International License (http://creativecommons.org/licenses/by-nc-nd/4.0/), which permits any noncommercial use, sharing, distribution and reproduction in any medium or format, as long as you give appropriate credit to the original author(s) and the source, provide a link to the Creative Commons license and indicate if you modified the licensed material. You do not have permission under this license to share adapted material derived from this chapter or parts of it.

The images or other third party material in this chapter are included in the chapter's Creative Commons license, unless indicated otherwise in a credit line to the material. If material is not included in the chapter's Creative Commons license and your intended use is not permitted by statutory regulation or exceeds the permitted use, you will need to obtain permission directly from the copyright holder.

LIST OF MATERIALS

FOCUS GROUP INTERVIEWS

- Focus group interview 1–4, Sweden, 2016 and 2017, 60 minutes each, a total of 20 participants (in addition to moderators), 12 women, 8 men.
- Focus group interview 5–12, Russia, 2016 and 2017, 60 minutes each, a total of 38 participants (in addition to moderators), 25 women, 13 men.

DOCUMENTED SUPERVISION INTERACTION

Supervisor A

Recorded Supervision Meetings

1. Pair supervision student A and B, recording 1 and 2, spring 2016
2. Pair supervision student C and D, recording 1, 2 and 3, spring 2016
3. Pair supervision student E and F, recording 1 and 2, spring 2016

Email conversation spring 2016 with student E and F

Supervisor B

Recorded Supervision Meetings

1. Collective supervision, recording 1, autumn 2017
2. Individual supervision student G, recording 1, 2 and 3, autumn 2017
3. Individual supervision student H, recording 1, 2 and 3, autumn 2017
4. Individual supervision student I, recording 1, autumn 2017

Email conversations autumn 2017 with four students
A total of 22 student texts (thesis memo, work plan, text drafts, final manuscript, finished thesis) of which 11 with comments from the supervisor

Supervisor C

Recorded Supervision Meetings

1. Pair supervision student J and K, recording 1, 2 and 3, autumn 2017

Supervisor D

Recorded Supervision Meetings

1. Pair supervision student L and M, recording 1, 2 and 3, spring 2016

Supervisor E

Recorded Supervision Meetings

1. Collective supervision, recording 1, spring 2016
2. Individual supervision student N, recording 1 and 2, spring 2016

Email conversation spring 2016 with student N

Supervisor F

Recorded Supervision Meetings

1. Pair supervision student O and P, recording 1, 2, 3 and 4, autumn 2016
2. Individual supervision student Q, recording 1, 2, 3 and 4, autumn 2016

A total of seven student texts (text drafts, final manuscript, finished thesis), of which four with comments from the supervisor

Supervisor G

Recorded Supervision Meetings

1. Individual supervision student R, recording 1 and 2, autumn 2011

Email conversation with student R, autumn 2011
A total of six student texts (thesis memo, text drafts, final manuscript, finished thesis), of which four with comments from the supervisor

Supervisor H

Recorded Supervision Meetings

1. Collective supervision, recording 1 and 2, spring 2016
2. Individual supervision student S, recording 1, spring 2016

Email conversation spring 2016 with student S
A total of six student texts (thesis memo, text drafts, final manuscript), of which one with comments from the supervisor

Supervisor I

Recorded Supervision Meetings

1. Pair supervision student T and U, recording 1, spring 2016

OTHER MATERIAL

Student survey on students' perceptions of independence 2016 and 2017, student teachers; a total of 47 responses.

Study manuals, course guides, grading criteria and assessment matrices/templates from courses for degree projects, BA-level.

A total of 131 syllabi for degree projects at BA-level mainly in the humanities and social sciences, from Malmö University, Stockholm University, Södertörn University and Uppsala University, from 2013, 2016, 2017 and 2023.

Index[1]

A
Academic literacies, 1, 6, 14–17, 59, 60, 64, 73, 91, 108, 115, 125, 129, 153, 175, 185, 186, 189, 220–222, 225, 226
Academic norms, 53, 153–155, 172, 225
Academic writing, i, 13–17, 19, 26, 44, 64, 82, 107–110, 115, 128, 129, 139, 140, 171, 172, 177, 179, 186, 189, 214, 220, 222, 224, 225
Active voicing, 151, 152, 171–180, 221
Affective practices, 20, 21, 88, 111, 113, 117, 119, 138, 139
Agency, 37, 91, 97, 99, 135
Anticipated emotions, 20, 21, 128, 129
Anticipatory emotions, 20, 21, 117
Appropriation, 209, 212
Artificial intelligence (AI), 61, 203–205, 208, 214

Assessment, 37, 62, 132, 185, 219, 225
- criteria, 28, 52, 208, 223
- examiners vs. supervisors, 16, 186–191, 200, 201, 204, 223–225
- formative, 171, 191–202
- matrices, 28, 214, 223, 232
- summative, 170, 186, 189, 191

Autonomy, 38–41, 38n1, 41n2

B
Bologna declaration/process, 2, 2n3

C
Collective supervision, 13, 17, 26n4, 83, 90, 110–112, 114–118, 120–125, 128, 129, 138, 141, 230, 231

---

[1] Note: Page numbers followed by 'n' refer to notes.

Collective/collegial practice, i, 5, 13–14, 29, 112, 116, 122, 144, 219
Community of practice, 13, 172, 177
Contingency, 23, 70, 80, 113, 151, 202
Course switching, 15, 108, 129, 165
Critical thinking, 37, 41, 46, 47, 49, 56–58, 61, 62, 158, 202
Criticism/critique, 82, 126, 162, 164, 167–170, 173, 185, 186, 188, 191–202, 221, 222, 225

D

Demands, 14, 15, 19, 22, 23, 42, 45, 59, 69, 82, 91, 108, 151–165, 180, 189, 209, 220
Design of conversation, 90–100
Directive supervision, 17, 74, 82, 110, 130, 135, 137, 152
Disciplinary literacies, 15, 16
Diversity, 72
Documented supervision interaction (material/method)
    draft texts, 94–96, 161, 172, 174, 193, 210, 211
    e-mail conversations, 26, 26n5, 100, 194, 229–231
    recordings, 27, 77, 79–81, 83, 85, 86, 88–90, 97, 98, 111, 113, 115, 118, 119, 121, 123, 125, 126, 128, 129, 131, 132, 134, 136–138, 141–143, 153–155, 159, 161, 163, 166–170, 173–180, 195–197, 199–201, 206–208, 210–212, 229–231

E

Emotions in supervision, 20, 100, 107–145, 222
Ethical issues
    research project, 25n3, 61
    supervision relationships, 18, 75

Examiners, 5, 12, 16, 25, 47, 55, 100, 170, 172, 179, 180, 186–191, 200–204, 214, 219, 220, 223–225

F

Fading, 23, 133, 221
Focus groups/interviews (material/method), 3, 18, 24–26, 25n3, 28, 29, 48–63, 71, 72, 83, 107–110, 114, 127, 134, 171, 187–191, 200, 202–204, 229
Frustration control, 23, 120–122, 132, 134

G

Governing documents, 5, 12, 19n1, 24, 28–29, 37, 38, 42–48, 52, 57, 219, 220
Grading criteria, 28, 44, 47, 52, 60, 202, 214, 232
Group supervision, 13, 17, 46, 110, 122–127

H

Higher education policy documents, 37, 39–41, 41n2
    international comparison, 37, 41

I

Imitation, 209–212
Independence as
    creativity, 48–52, 62, 109, 110, 202
    critical thinking, 37, 41, 46, 47, 49, 56–58, 61, 62, 158, 202
    enthusiasm, 48, 51, 202
    making decisions/choices, 49, 53–56, 62, 152, 202
    originality, 48–52, 55, 56, 58, 202
    relating to sources/context, 49, 57, 202, 205–210, 215

responsibility, 46, 47, 49, 53–56, 110, 135, 137, 194, 202, 204
taking initiatives, 48–52, 62, 84, 100, 202, 204
theme of the book, 11, 29, 37–47, 219, 221, 223, 226
Insecurity
students, 108, 110–127
supervisors, 108, 135–145
Internationalisation, 18, 72

L
Learning outcomes, 37, 42, 52, 202
Local governing documents, 28, 42–47

M
Modelling, 19, 23, 171–177, 211

P
Peer feedback, 13, 122–124, 127
Personal relationship, 73–78, 82, 221
Perspective taking, 171–180
PhD students, *see* Postgraduate supervision
Postgraduate supervision, 17, 19, 70, 70n1, 75, 108, 108n1
Praise, 21, 22, 151, 152, 165–171, 180, 185–187, 191, 192, 200, 221, 225
Professional relationship, 73, 75, 87, 222

Q
Questions
challenging, 158, 158n2, 162–165, 196–198
developing, 158, 160–162, 208
opening, 6, 158–162

R
Recommendations, 22, 54–56, 60, 86, 100, 113, 124, 152–165, 178, 180, 192, 198, 199, 209, 210, 212–214
Relationship supervisors-students
ethical aspects, 18, 43, 43n4, 56, 61, 75, 224
personal relationships, 73–75, 82, 221
professional relationships, 73, 75, 78, 79, 82, 87, 221
teaching – partnership – apprenticeship, 19, 74, 77, 78, 91, 93, 112, 116, 130, 132, 137, 139, 140, 142, 155, 158, 220
Remediation, 209, 209n5, 210
Russian context, 28, 50, 55

S
Scaffolding
definition, 22
intentions/goal, 23, 89, 134, 137, 151
tool/means, 23, 121, 131, 132, 145, 151–180, 191, 221
work, 48, 51, 70, 78, 82, 112, 116, 120, 133, 142, 186, 199, 200
Speaking space, 27, 91–93
Student collegiality, 110, 122, 124
Student independence
assessment of, 16, 61, 165, 203
in governing (policy) documents, 5, 28–29, 42–47, 219, 220
matrix, 63, 64, 202
model, 64, 156, 157, 165, 171, 203
perceptions/understandings, 6, 24–26, 48–58, 61–63, 115, 133, 171, 194, 202, 204, 205, 219, 232
in relation to Artificial intelligence, 203–205

Student-led Conversation, 93–95, 97–100
Supervision
  criteria-based, 62, 94
  definition, 4, 62
  by e-mail, 187, 191–193
  ethical issues, 18, 43n4, 56, 61, 75
  text draft-based, 26n5, 94, 187, 191, 193, 209, 210
Supervisor-led Conversation, 93–97
Supervisor roles, 55, 93, 133, 142, 157, 158, 161, 179, 185, 187, 190, 203, 214

Supervisor tools
  active voicing, 151, 152, 171–180
  demands, 19, 152–165
  emotions, 127–135, 221
  praise, 21, 22, 151, 152, 165–171, 221
  questions, 21, 22, 151–165, 221
  recommendations, 22, 152–165
  scaffolding, 151–152
Swedish context, 22, 28, 38n1, 45

T
Transfer of responsibility, 23, 133, 194, 221

Printed in the USA
CPSIA information can be obtained
at www.ICGtesting.com
CBHW050836211024
16148CB00007B/502